STRUCTURES
OF
DESIRE

THE **SUNY** SERIES

CULTURAL STUDIES IN CINEMA/VIDEO

WHEELER WINSTON DIXON | EDITOR

STRUCTURES
OF
DESIRE

British Cinema,
1939–1955

TONY
WILLIAMS

STATE UNIVERSITY OF NEW YORK PRESS

Published by
State University of New York Press, Albany

© 2000 State University of New York

All rights reserved

Printed in the United States of America

For information, address State University of New York Press,
State University Plaza, Albany, N.Y., 12246

Production by Marilyn P. Semerad
Marketing by Patrick Durocher

Library of Congress Cataloging-in-Publication Data

Williams, Tony, 1946 Jan. 11–
    Structures of desire : British cinema, 1939–1955 / Tony Williams.
        p. cm. — (The SUNY series, cultural studies in cinema/video)
    Includes bibliographical references and index.
    ISBN 0-7914-4643-3 (hc. : alk. paper) — ISBN 0-7914-4644-1 (pbk. : alk. paper)
        1. Motion pictures—Great Britain—History. I. Title. II. Series.

PN1993.5.G7 W55 2000
791.43′0941′09044—dc21

                                                                                00-023991

10 9 8 7 6 5 4 3 2 1

CONTENTS

ILLUSTRATIONS

ACKNOWLEDGMENTS

———————— ▦ ————————

I wish to thank the following people: series editor Wheeler Winston Dixon for his encouragement and support; Alan Kibble for access to important and commercially unavailable work; Dr. Victoria Molfese of the Office of Research and Development of Southern Illinois University at Carbondale for support in enabling me to see many of these films; Francis M. Nevins for the fortuitous loan of Nigel Balchin's *Small Back Room*; research assistant Eva White; Bob Bell of Learning Resources, Michael Anderegg, Philip Mosley, the Morris Library, Southern Illinois University for access to PAL VCR players; Professor Vincent Lacey, director of the CAIRL Laboratory Faner Hall; the Humanities Librarians of Morris Library for countless interlibrary loan requests and book acquisitions; the Spring 1998 English 494 class for feedback, questions, and various insights into forties British cinema; and the Department of English, Southern Illinois University for providing a supportive environment toward research and learning. Special thanks to the following SUNY Press staff: acquisitions editor James Peltz, production editor Marilyn Semerad, and marketing manager Patrick Durocher. Stills are supplied courtesy of Jerry Ollinger's Movie Material Store in New York.

CHAPTER ONE

Introduction

The reality of any hegemony in the extended political and cultural sense, is that, while by definition it is always dominant, it is never either total or exclusive.

—Williams, 1977, 113

This book intends to deal with a specific feature of British cinema from 1940 through 1955, namely, representations of desire during a historical period of turbulent change. It was an era that saw Britain's involvement in the Second World War, social changes leading to the landslide victory of the postwar Labour government, succeeding years of hope and disillusionment, the return of the Conservative Party to power in 1951, and (despite certain material advances) a rigid return to status quo patterns of thought. It is a depressingly familiar picture. Both American and British society have equally suffered from decades of right-wing reaction reinforced by opposition parties initially pledged to reverse those trends.

Despite changes in gender relationships over the past fifty years, men and women still find themselves dominated by the *Homo economicus* model sketched by classical Marxism over a century ago. Change has occurred but also regression. Ironically a supposedly anachronistic nineteenth-century model is more relevant today in understanding such dilemmas. We live in an era characterized less by thirties totalitarianism and more by consensual "everyday Fascism" as R. W. Fassbinder once put it. Market values directly responsible for the horrors of the thirties again rule in an indirectly ideologically oppressive manner. Antonio Gramsci's concept of hegemony is now particularly useful for examining relevant cinematic depictions of human relationships indirectly influenced by prevailing social structures.

Structures of Desire concentrates upon certain personal representations within one era of British cinema, an era influenced by hopes for a better world, the manufacturing of a "People's War" ideology, conservative retrenchment, and prevailing consensus politics before the right-wing hegemonic and political victory of Thatcherism in 1979. Although the current era has seen the collapse of the Soviet Union and the discrediting of socialism as practiced in both East and West, this is not "The End of History" despite claims of right-wing apologists. While classical Marxism needs major restructuring toward the different demands of a new century, one aspect of its tradition does not: the legacy of Antonio Gramsci. His concept of hegemony involved a willed, noncoercive consent to a dominant oppressive order which need not be permanent. Since cinema forms an inherent part of a cultural production manufacturing consent, Gramsci's ideas are crucial not only for understanding cultural and emotional realms often ignored by classical Marxism but also for tracing the peculiarities of specific phenomena within the 1940–1955 period of British cinema. These phenomena involve representations of human relations that either struggle against or passively submit to contemporary prevailing ideological norms.

Both *Cahiers du Cinema* and *Movie* damned British cinema as a national institution lacking the dynamic vitality of its American counterpart. While true in certain formal and aesthetic senses, the judgment tended to ignore other aspects worthy of attention such as cultural, ideological, and oppositional alternatives to dominant class and sexual patterns of behavior. Recent anthologies such as *Fires Were Started: British Cinema and Thatcherism* and *Re-Viewing British Cinema, 1900–1992: Essays and Interviews,* edited by Lester Friedman and Wheeler Winston Dixon respectively, and studies such as Antonia Lant's *Blackout: Reinventing Women for British Wartime Cinema,* Andrew Higson's *Waving the Flag,* Sue Harper's *British Costume Melodrama,* and Pam Cook's *Fashioning the Nation* reveal British cinema as containing more complex cultural representations than previously realized. While British cinema may lack the types of artistic innovations common to American, French, and German national cinemas, it does contain significant material on cultural, historical, and political levels. British cinema during 1940–1955 is a revealing object of study when approached in terms of the flexible critical ideas associated with Antonio Gramsci and Raymond Williams rather than reductionist concepts defining the cinema as an ideological tool designed to captivate audiences by the deliberate use of false consciousness. In *British Genres: Cinema and Society, 1930–1960* and her later work, Marcia Landy has already begun this process of interrogation.

British cinema reveals tensions, contradictions, and recuperations as do other national cinemas. It is not to be defined exclusively within rigid terms of class, race, and sexual representations nor under monolithic definitions of realism versus fantasy. The 1940–1955 period is a worthy subject for hegemonic exploration. Wartime era and postwar society experienced a temporary erosion of Britain's rigid class and social structures until recuperation began in the early fifties. This period parallels tensions undergone in Western society after World War I when the fall of the old order seemed to promise new political and cultural movements until coercive and ideologically recuperative powers again gained control. The post–World War II situation was not as dynamic and contradictory as in the aftermath of the "war to end all wars." No major radical political movements or cultural forces emerged to challenge the status quo, but tensions did exist and appear within certain cinematic representations. If we wonder today about what happened to sixties hopes and challenges, the same applies to aspirations common to British wartime society which were later savaged by the right-wing hegemonic victories of Margaret Thatcher in 1979 and Tory Blair in 1997. This phenomenon also affected representations of human relationships in certain films. Active state intervention did not brutally manipulate particular representations. Consensual operations involving the oppressed contributing to their own domination often explain the poverty of desire characterizing certain cinematic depictions of human relationships. Gramsci's philosophy explains such operations.

During his ten-year incarceration in Fascist Italy, Gramsci had plenty of time to consider why totalitarian ideas achieved victory in his country after the brief hopes and radical directions following World War I. The State had won not by direct coercion but by the willing consent of a population unsympathetic to new ideas. In his political and cultural writings, Gramsci moved away from many classical Marxist definitions of state control toward a concept of hegemony including cultural ideas that had never before received explicit recognition. As Carl Boggs points out, Gramsci's work emphasized certain cultural and ideological dimensions of class and political struggle. Some immanent processes exist within capitalism resulting in the majority internalizing dominant ideological and cultural values in a manner conflicting with their actual personal and political values.

> For Gramsci the primary focus was not the objective determinants of crisis but rather the subjective responses to it; not simply a structural analysis of political economy but comprehension of the dynamics of mass consciousness; not the institutional engineering required for the conquest and management of state power, but the ideological-cultural preparation for a new type of society. (x)

This hegemonic operation involving the battle of ideas was not dogmatically monolithic. It dialectically understood specific functions of history and politics in a dynamically vital manner. As Gramsci (1985) noted, "A given socio-historical moment is never homogenous; on the contrary, it is rich in contradictions. It acquires a 'personality' and is a 'moment' of development in that a certain fundamental activity of life prevails over others and represents a historical 'peak': but this presupposes a hierarchy, a contest, a struggle" (93). Robert Bocock also notes the variable nature of a hegemonic process where some historical situations see partial control by the dominant class in some spheres but not in others.

> To suppose otherwise is to fail to distinguish the analytical model of hegemony from the analysis of concrete cases. In other words, the degree of hegemonic leadership which is successfully provided by a ruling group or alliance, can vary from a relatively fully integrated situation, at one end of the continuum, in which all classes and groups give their consent to the leading hegemonic arrangements in the economy and in philosophy and morals, through to a situation in which there is an almost total lack of leadership being provided by the ruling group outside of the upper class. (94)

Hegemony can encompass the realms of popular culture and desire as well as politics and ideology. British cultural theorist Raymond Williams (1977) developed Gramsci's dynamic definition of the hegemonic process when he stated that rather than being seen in terms of manipulation or indoctrination, hegemony is really "a whole body of practices and expectations, over the whole of living: our senses and assignments of energy, our shaping of perceptions of ourselves and our world. It is a lived system of meanings and values—constitutive and constituting—which as they are experienced as practices appear as reciprocally confirming" (110).

Williams lived through a formative period, experiencing the changing nature of British society during the thirties and forties. Born into a working-class family, a member of the Communist Party during his youth, he went to the ivory tower of Cambridge, interrupted his studies during World War II, and worked in adult education before receiving a lectureship in his alma mater. He became one of the most important cultural theorists in Britain, affirming the true values of socialism throughout his life. His suspicions of the British Labour Party have received confirmation with the emergence of Tony Blair's right-wing "New Labour" and its manipulative spindoctors. Williams recognized the crippling dogmatism within certain British and European definitions of Marxism and championed the ideas of Lucien Goldman and Gramsci. His famous 'structures of feeling' concept is a notoriously elusive definition, perhaps deliberately so. It avoids the danger of falling into certain reductive sterile definitions of classical Marxism. But it also champions important humanistic and personal dimensions within Gramsci's cultural and political writings. Deeply affected by his working-class roots as well as contributing to the important field of British adult and extramural education (now gutted under Thatcherism), Williams recognized the crucially intertwined roles of personal feelings and popular culture. His 'structures of feeling' concept is applicable both in defining certain popular levels of desire attracting audiences to cinematic representations as well as leading toward interrogating these very practices.

Cinema is as much a social form of dramatic representation as the theater. If the personal is political, the cultural realm may also reproduce ideological values. Robert S. Dombroski notes the compatibility of Gramsci's early theatrical criticism with his later work as a political journalist and emphasizes his awareness of the operations of the entertainment industry. "He recognizes the power of the stage to manipulate minds by expressing the values of those who control society, but is also mindful of its potential to challenge and subvert those values" (24). Although Gramsci scorned trivial representations in contrast to certain contemporary postmodernist totalizing celebrations of popular culture, he critically aimed toward enlarging the cultural perspectives of his readers "by showing them how dramatic art elicits reflection on their social and human condition" (Dombroski, 35). Rather than distinguishing high from low culture and condemning the latter as false consciousness, Gramsci recognized the importance of understanding the pleasurable operations of popular culture.

> Subaltern social groups experience as satisfying and fulfilling fictions what from another point of view may seem uninspiring, banal, and contradictory. They experience it from the inside, in terms of their own social and material existence, perceiving in the artifact a combination of cultural elements through which they identify themselves, recognize the limitations of their historical existence, and fantasize solutions. (Dombroski, 114)

These insights equally apply to a British cinema whose artistic status has never been officially recognized. They also call into question officially discursive hierarchical divisions separating realism from fantasy and melodrama. Any examination of Gainsborough melodrama productions need not imply championship of their supposedly undiscovered aesthetic values. It rather suggests recognizing the validity of their cultural appeal to particular audiences within a specific social and historical formation. Aimed at working-class, female audiences, the melodramas belong to a Gramscian popular cultural realm that (if not embryonically Marxist) contain features that *may* oppose dominant cultural patterns. By interrogating these and similar works, some films might become "part of that transformational process of which a Marxist praxis is object and model," displaying a potentially subversive arena for cultural politics (Dombroski, 116). Like most representations, films contain contradictory positive and negative features. Some films may contain potentially powerful counterhegemonic elements. Others may simply reinforce the dominant ideology. Audiences may accept or reject certain representations.

This is important in terms of recognizing the role of human agency in producing change as opposed to the prison house of Althusserian and poststructuralist ideas, which see subjects as inmates constituted by structures and discourses over which they have no control. Although theorists such as Ernesto Laclau and Chantal Mouffe suggest returning to Gramsci to counter this monolithic conception, they ignore the very Marxism con-

FIGURE 1. The celebration of sensual desire. Jean Kent as Rosal in *Caravan*.

tained within his works. It was neither dogmatically scientific nor subjectively humanist but involved a philosophy of praxis containing a "'materialism' perfected by the work of speculative philosophy itself and fused with humanism" (Gramsci, 1971, 371). Despite Laclau and Mouffe's poststructuralist objections against a supposedly rigid classical Marxist model influencing the thinker, Gramsci acknowledged that important macrolevels of economics, politics, and culture are never deterministic. Laclau and Mouffe not only deny the relevance of socialism as an agency for human freedom but also fall into a dogmatic position by ignoring the role of economic and ideological factors attempting to condition subjectivity within their privileged minority activist microlevel forces.

Although subjective factors exist in an area Mas'ud Zavarzadeh defines as "ludic postmodernism," they also occupy an important position in Gramsci's particular definition of a Marxism that contradicts later misreadings by Laclau and Mouffe. Noting Gramsci's relevance to later developments in critical theory, Renate Holub recognizes that culture industries such as the cinema both manufacture and negotiate subjectivity within given historical periods. "What also emerges from Gramsci's pages is the notion of a culture industry, of the production and manipulation of needs and desires, of consuming subjects that are unable to define their needs, subjected to the powers that manipulate the public into acceptance of a static status quo" (15). Although the younger Gramsci rejected cinema in his earlier writings, he revised his ideas in 1930 and noted its potential for producing counterhegemonic meanings capable of challenging the status quo. Holub (46) notes Gramsci's affinities to Walter Benjamin and Bertolt Brecht here. Classical Marxism saw literature and art as embodying tensions and contradictions inherent within superstructural areas relating to the material forces of society. But problems lay in defining exactly how culture functioned. Like Georgy Lukacs, Gramsci viewed art as a territory where certain values are promoted and others silenced and marginalized. He investigated the nature of these values whether progressive or regressive (Holub, 46). By taking the popular realm more seriously than his predecessors and contemporaries, Gramsci viewed its adherents (whether majority or minority) as subjected to domination, discrimination, marginalization, and contempt, whenever they consented to their own subjugation. However, as Holub continues:

the popular creative spirit is capable of producing an alternative or counter-cultural consciousness to the predominant or high culture, capable of rupturing the silence which is imposed. The popular creative spirit is the object of desire of hegemony not because it lacks desire, but because it is, as collective and individual, subject of desire itself, human beings that desire something more than they have and are. (55)

This recognition is important. It relates desire to collective operations within social and historical eras rather than confining it to individualist terrains of Freudian analysis. Why do certain cinematic representations occur within particular historical eras that are not entirely the result of individual producers or audiences? Gramsci took popular cultural representations of desire and fantasy seriously and related them to wider issues within society.

Understanding why people overwhelmingly chose to read certain texts, including kitsch, and why they refused to read other texts, even nationally monumental texts . . . meant for him to understand the structure of their fantasies and desires; and addressing that structure with a different, more democratic content, would contribute to changes in consciousness, would contribute to what he called the moral reform. (Holub, 66)

Leaving aside the utopian aspects of this belief, it is important to note that Gramsci avoided any cultural hegemonic traps assiduously guarding boundaries of "good taste" against officially defined "other" and "inferior" representations. By viewing certain films within their wider social and historical contexts, particular representations may possibly reveal complex articulations of a changing national consciousness. This does not mean seeing productions as direct social representations but viewing them in terms of their dynamic embodiment of complex and contradictory hegemonic and counterhegemonic features. As Holub (80) notes in a definition applicable to cinema, "The play or work of art is viewed not so much in terms of its origins as in terms of the social dynamics it elicits and resists, unravels and silences, affirms and denies, reveals and conceals, at the various moments of its reception."

Williams's definitions of dominant, residual, and emergent cultural ideas help in analyzing such contradictions and tensions. The dominant involves hegemonic control of the status quo, which Gramsci never regarded as monolithic. It may be threatened at any time. The residual is a concept applicable to the popularity of Gainsborough melodramas set in imaginary historical worlds. As Williams (1977, 122) points out, any culture has

> available elements of its past, but their place in the contemporary cultural process is profoundly variable. . . . The residual, by definition, has been effectively formed in the past, but it is still active in the cultural process, not only and often not at all as an element of the past, but as an effective element of the present. Thus certain experiences, meanings, and values which cannot be expressed or substantially verified in terms of the dominant culture are nevertheless lived and practiced on the basis of the residue—cultural as well as social—of some previous social and cultural institution or formation.

A dialectical process of fusion and negotiation may occur between dominant and residual meanings. The former's influence on the latter involves "the incorporation of the actively residual—by reinterpretation, dilution, projection, discriminating inclusion and exclusion—that the work of the selective tradition is especially evident" (Williams, 1977, 123). This particularly applies to Gainsborough melodramatic devices. Although they formally compete with British realist cinematic conventions and feature strong heroines, the films often restore ideological closure in their various conclusions. The closing shot of *The Man in Grey* (1943) repeats an earlier camera angle used in a past sequence when Clarissa Rohan comments, "Isn't it a lovely day" before leaving Swinton Rokeby behind on the steps and mounting her horse. The Regency scene involves the dominance of class structures inhibiting their romantic union. But the concluding scene is set in wartime Britain with the descendants of Clarissa and Rokeby in uniform. They leave the Rohan mansion for the last time. Clarissa again repeats the comment of her aristocratic predecessor. However, she and Peter Rokeby now descend the steps. The camera movement follows them, repeating its past trajectory. But it continues the earlier overhead panning shot by swinging to the left and following the lovers as they run to catch a more egalitarian form of transport—a double-decker bus.

This is a typical happy ending. But it is residual in nature. The individual Regency lovers are finally reunited in the bodies of their descendants within a "People's War" conclusion. But certain features are excluded. Neither the marquis of Rohan nor Hester appear in the present. They have left no progeny to contaminate an optimistic brave new post-war world envisaged by the People's War ideology. The attraction of costume appealing to female audiences is also gone. Clarissa and Rokeby wear sober service uniforms. Rokeby's former handsome Regency features are now blurred by a moustache. The past becomes renegotiated within dominant mechanisms of the present. Finally, the union occurs not through some transcendental romantic act of karma but by Rokeby's ancestor returning to his island off the coast of Jamaica and quelling a slave revolt inspired by the French. Rokeby's future return depends on his forefather regaining his inheritance. He and Clarissa can now enjoy future happiness in a pastoral English island in the sun. But Rokeby's original displacement happened due to democratic feelings following the French Revolution. *The Man in Grey* makes no reference to these class and racial factors. It chooses instead to concentrate upon romance, costume, and gender instability. The young black slave Tobey (played by a white juvenile!) frequently refers to Rokeby as "the black-white man" after he sees him performing Othello on stage. When Clarissa later sees Rokeby at a racecourse fair, he plays another role as a fairground barker promoting the physical strength of a black slave (this time played by a real black extra). Although Rokeby performs in a fairground inviting his audiences to compete in a trial of strength, his activities resemble those of a New Orleans slavemaster selling his wares. These features reveal Rokeby as less of an ideal romantic lover and more of a manipulator of a social system he affirms rather than opposes. Despite the film's attempt to separate dashing, handsome Swinton Rokeby from the moody marquis of Rohan, both men bear certain similarities. They not only react in frustration against conformist social patterns but are totally subjected to them. Rokeby and Rohan may not breach certain social codes. Rokeby has to return to his island to become a gentleman again by putting down a revolutionary uprising. His callous slapping of Hester reveals affinities to Rohan's brutal manner. It foreshadows Rohan's later whipping-to-death of Hester concluding the Regency narrative of *The Man in Grey*. The film may contain female pleasure, but it also attempts to eliminate other important contradictions within its textual structure.

These arguments do not necessitate the total rejection of recent research reevaluating Gainsborough melodramas as well as theories noting the importance of costume within filmic discourse by scholars such as Cook (1996) and Harper (1994). But they do involve considering a broader picture. Supposedly progressive traditions within fantastic realms of British cinema may contain similar ideological problems also contaminating their realistic counterparts. The films may contain progressive aspects. But they can also function according to conservatively dominant and residual mechanisms controlling the play of desire. Although the melodramas may validate some female perceptions, they also contain negative representations of class and racial factors that question any progressive readings about the dilemmas of white aristocratic heroines within such melodramatic contexts. Realist and melodramatic traditions emerging from the same era may respond in similar ideological ways despite different stylistic forms.

Williams's definition of the "emergent" may question certain ideas concerning the supposedly progressive and revolutionary meanings existing in these films. New meanings and values occur within any tradition. But Williams (1977, 123) cautions that "it is exceptionally difficult to distinguish between those which are really elements of some new phase of the dominant culture (and in this sense 'species specific') and those which are substantially alternative or oppositional to it: emergent in the strict sense, rather than merely novel." The emergent always faces incorporation. Any text may contain levels of confusion between the residual as a form of resistance and the emergent as an genuinely active oppositional element. Certain films may contain residual levels of expression, but they are often undermined and renegotiated toward conservative closure as a result of certain textual operations.

The Gainsborough melodramas may be regarded as residual, but they also contain repressed emergent elements altered to prevent any form of radical oppositional expression. Rohan and Hester appear as monstrous embodiments needing removal from the text so their acceptable counterparts, Rokeby and Clarissa, can live happily ever after. The excessively masculine Rohan and sensual Hester enter into a romantic relationship containing the potential to rupture class and sexual barriers. Although their relationship is more dynamic than that of their counterparts, the film cannot allow any expression of positive alternative oppositional ideas. Desire becomes dangerous for both partners and leads to a violent climax. Hester dies, and Rohan may face execution for his deed. The future happiness of Clarissa and Rokeby occurs within the ideologically manufactured context of the supposedly egalitarian People's War (see Calder, 1969; 1991). But Charlie's speech in *Millions like Us* (1943) counters its ideological premises. He refuses to entertain false utopian feelings con-

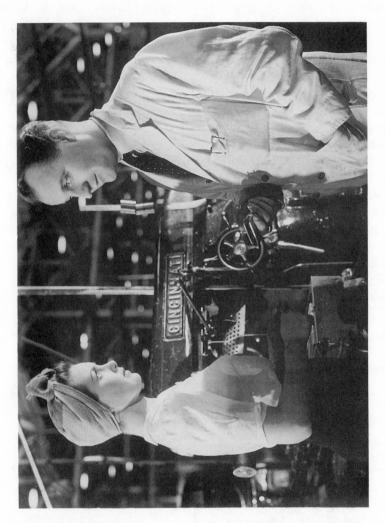

FIGURE 2. The skeptical figure of Charlie (Eric Portman) addresses Celia (Patricia Roc) in *Millions like Us.*

cerning the abolition of prewar class barriers and postpones his engagement to upper-class Jennifer until he is sure that wartime egalitarianism is not a temporary phenomenon. Future circumstances prove him correct.

The emergent is subject to incorporation. But, as Williams notes, its presence is undeniable in certain textual representations. However, any simple definitions involving dominant control or emergent breakthrough must consider the actual texts themselves. Although tensions among dominant, residual, and emergent appear class terms, other factors such as the emotionally textual elements often appear. Williams (126) points out that aspects of social consciousness such as "alternative perceptions of others, in immediate relationships; new perceptions and practices of the material world" (126) may occur in any text whether political, social, or cinematic. But historical circumstances often determine whether these alternatives are radically oppositional. Many films exhibit different alternative levels, yet they often never rise to levels involving radically emergent meanings.

Raymond Williams warned against the tendency of hailing new ideas as emergent, when in reality, they form "a *pre-emergence*, active and pressing but not yet fully articulated, rather than the active emergence which could be more confidently named" (126). Williams defines a mode of interrogation recognizing dialectical operations of formal (structure) and personal (feeling) levels within any text. His version of alternative oppositions to dominant structures represents "a kind of thinking which is indeed social and material, but each is in an embryonic phase before it can become fully articulate and define exchange" (131). He makes an exceptionally complex recognition of a *process* involving various levels of feeling that may move toward positive directions. Williams related any emergent structures of feeling to either the rise of a class or a time when "a formation appears to break away from its class norms, though it retains its substantial affiliation, and the tension is at once lived and articulated in radically new semantic figures" (134–35). Williams obviously owes much to Gramsci, who never isolated structures or feelings into exclusive categories.

Such complex structures of feeling characterize certain representations within British cinema during 1940–1955. But rather than retaining Williams's definition of "structure of feeling," "structures of desire" is more appropriate. It better expresses the nature of emotional negotiations involving contemporary conflicts among dominant, residual, and emergent factors within wartime and postwar British cinema. The emergent probably does not exist in the terms Williams defined it. But certain

British films may embody conflicts between dominant and potentially emergent realms of desire that exist on the pre-emergent level. They occur not as isolated individualized features but in relation to contemporary social and historical structures of meaning influencing levels of desire.

Desire is best understood neither in exclusively Freudian terms nor by the concepts of Michel Foucault but more in terms of the combative philosophy of Mas'ud Zavarzadeh. Arguing for more radical definitions of postmodernism relating local to the global levels, Zavarzadeh (1991, 43–44, 46–47; 1991, 205–6) takes issue with a ludic postmodernism celebrating subjectivity while ignoring the presence of wider social and historical factors conditioning its very existence. Freudian microlevel definitions by critics such as Appiganesi are insufficient if they do not consider relevant external levels of historical and social determination. Precedents for this form of investigation already exist in Gramsci's writing. As Landy (1994) notes, desire is not entirely absent from his writing. "Gramsci's brief comments on sexuality also validate his concern for a complex understanding of social forces, but always in the context of a specific social and historical conjuncture" (94–95). It is a methodology she applies in her analysis of the Gainsborough melodrama *They Were Sisters* (1944), which is set in the present and not the historical past. Cook (1983) also recognizes the importance of examining the Gainsborough women's pictures "in terms of the way they discuss femininity to appeal to a female audience" whether "British and wartime, or immediately postwar" (21).

The expression of desire in fictional texts may be influenced by historical, political, and social factors that producers and readers are unaware of at the time. Such expressions are usually indirect but are never entirely free or individual. Instead they follow particular ideological structures that often become recognizable at a later time. Although film is generally regarded as harmless entertainment, like the romance novel it is never entirely isolated from prevailing cultural forms of expression, no matter how much audiences and individual readers may wish to retreat into what they believe are private fantasies. If fantasy is both public and private, so, also, are manifold expressions of desire. Like political and social life, they are determined by certain historical conventions or structures implicitly controlling the expressions of each particular text. Desire is never entirely spontaneous but is governed by particular ideological structures operating within any historical era. This work studies their various forms of expression within a certain period of a national cinema generally regarded as lacking any coherent expression of both desire and emotion. Such factors exist within cinematic texts but are expressed via ideologically structured forms of expression. In this sense, British cinema manifests specific structures of desire.

Desire involves males as well as females. One gender crisis does not exist in isolation from another. Although popular memories of wartime cinema tend to be clouded by stereotypes such as the "stiff-upper-lip" heroes and "dutiful waiting women" in fifties representations starring Richard Todd, Kenneth More, Veronica Hurst, Ann Todd, and Ursula Jeans, the male order also suffered its form of crisis. Although Jack Hawkins is now associated with the "stiff-upper-lip" leader in films such as *Angels One Five* (1950), *The Malta Story* (1952), and *The Bridge over the River Kwai* (1957), he also exhibited masculine crisis in other films, such as his emotional breakdown in *The Cruel Sea* (1953) and his vulnerable need for friendship in *The Two Headed Spy* (1958) illustrate. After playing Guy Gibson in *The Dam Busters* (1955), Richard Todd became associated with controlled leader figures in *D-Day the Sixth of June* (1956), *Yangtse Incident* (1957), *Danger Within* (1959), *The Longest Day* (1962), and *Operation Crossbow* (1965). But he came to public attention playing the terminally ill, vulnerable Scottish soldier in *The Hasty Heart* (1950). Todd's repressed persona in *The Dam Busters* ideologically contradicts other vulnerable military males in *The Cruel Sea* (1953) and *The Ship That Died of Shame* (1955). But even he expresses desire in a particular manner in *The Dam Busters*. Male representations were by no means one dimensional during this period. Medhurst and Geraghty's (Hurd, 1984) explorations into this neglected area reveal the existence of contradictory features texts attempt to conceal in various ways.

As Landy (1994) urges, knowledge of past traditions

> is essential to any charting and understanding of the uneven development of culture and its relation to technology and capital formations. In the spirit of his [i.e. Gramsci's] insistence on the importance of common sense, an analysis of cultural production must articulate both the persistence of dominant forms from the past and the presence of new elements which can either be considered as further aspects of traditional hegemony or can be identified as counterhegemonic emergent forms. (35)

Films in this study belong to a particular historical context of British cinema. They are not only determined by the past but also anticipate future cinematic movements. The "kitchen sink" films of the early sixties continue class and realist narrative concerns of their wartime predecessors. Hammer horror films also continue the excessive romantic agonies of Gainsborough costume films. James Mason or Stewart Granger could have played Count Dracula had they not migrated to Hollywood. Institutional constraints of censorship and ideological control during the forties and early fifties affected British cinema particularly in terms of gender and political representations. Walter Greenwood's *Love on the Dole* (1933) never reached the screen until 1941. Its diluted images of Salford poverty in the Great Depression functioned as grim reminders of a world that a utopian postwar society would never again accept. But most thirties British films contain regimented images of hierarchical class structures and strictly controlled gender representations.

The Four Feathers and *The Lion Has Wings* (both 1939) embody this dominant British structure of desire. As Harper (1994, 29) notes, *The Four Feathers* appealed to Alexander Korda's fascination with British culture, sexuality, and pleasure. It adapted A. E. W. Mason's imperialist novel about a young aristocrat determined to rebut charges of cowardice made against him. It resembles a conservative structure of meaning narrating the compliance of vulnerable hero Harry Faversham (John Clements) with the demands of the dominant ideology. But other factors also appear that anticipate later British cinematic themes of male crisis. Although Harry resigns his commission, reacting against an oppressive family tradition and wanting to rescue his estate from generations of neglect, he is haunted by accusations of cowardice. His fiancée Ethne (June Duprez) also rejects him. Her dialogue articulates an oppressive ideology dominating the film's major characters. "Some people are born free . . . but you were not born free, nor was I. We were born into a tradition, a code we must obey even if we do not believe it. . . . The pride and happiness of everyone surrounding us depends on our obedience." *The Four Feathers* supports this repressive British ideology, which differs little from its Fascist counterpart. Although Harry proves his heroism by rescuing three friends, he still submits to the system. *The Four Feathers* is an ideologically repressive text enclosing everyone in conservative structures of desire. But even the humorous happy ending contains contradictions. Although Harry proves himself to Ethne by revealing the false nature of a Crimean war story repeated incessantly by General Burroughs (Sir C. Aubrey Smith), the film concludes with the revelation that a pillar of society has lied about his own heroism for most of his life!

The Lion Has Wings is a propaganda film hammering its audiences into submission with British cinematic documentary realist techniques. As well as propaganda images of rural conservatism and social improvements, the film also contains staged fictional sequences with Ralph Richardson, Merle Oberon, June Duprez, and Brian Worth representing dominant upper-middle-class values. The women stand to attention during the national anthem following Britain's declaration of war. Their men stiffly stand to attention until the last bar before they embrace their sweethearts and march off to war. The final sequence concludes with the uniformed Richardson and Oberon reunited again after a hard day's wartime work. Deciding to visit a park (recalling those opening rural English values), they relax in the sunshine. Oberon makes a patriotic speech in close-up, articulating British values. When she turns to Richardson, she finds him asleep, a position humorously paralleling the average audience reaction!

Oberon's climactic image is more positive than Vivian Leigh's Lady Hamilton in Zoltan Korda's *That Hamilton Woman* (1941). Although suffering condemnation for her sexually free life style, Emma ensures that Lord Nelson (Laurence Olivier) constantly does his naval duty despite constant risks to life and limb until the fatal Battle of Trafalgar where Hardy achieves that final kiss. After Nelson's death, Emma has served her wartime purpose. She now faces a death-in-life existence as wino and bag lady. As Short and Draper show, oppressive codes of propaganda and censorship stifle the possibility of any liberatory desires emerging in the film.

Similar rigid class and sexual codes structure *Convoy* (1940) and *Ships with Wings* (1942). Both feature John Clements, an actor associated with status quo values in this era of British cinema. As in *The Four Feathers*, Clements finds himself doing the ideologically "right thing" after falling from social grace. But his sacrifice is much higher as he gives his life to save his former squadron. In *Convoy*, naval lieutenant David Cranford (Clements) wins back the respect of his superior officer Captain Armitage (Clive Brook) not only by his eventual heroic death but also by revealing that the latter's wife had left him rather than the other way around! Similarly, in *Ships with Wings*, court-martialed and cashiered Fleet Air Arm pilot Stacey (Clements) loses Celia (Jane Baxter), daughter of Vice-Admiral Weatherby (Leslie Banks), after a reckless incident. Although Celia marries another officer (dashing Michael Wilding), Stacey refuses the love offered by his devoted Kay (Ann Todd). As a singer her

FIGURE 3. An English gentleman (Leslie Howard) faces the wartime enemy (Eric Portman, John Chandos) in *49th Parallel.*

ideological status resembles the "dance hall girl" of Hollywood Westerns as well as gypsy Rosal in *Caravan* (1946). Like Marlene Dietrich in *Destry Rides Again* (1939), Kay expires from the scene. Stacey recovers his lost honor as an officer and a gentleman by dying for God and Country.

David MacDonald's *This England* (1941) covers several historical episodes in the life of this sceptered isle. Beginning and ending in the contemporary era, it presents rural English life as essentially unchanging despite earlier historical challenges during 1086, 1588, 1804, and 1918. The same actors portray their forebears in these episodes. *This England* opens when an American journalist (Constance Cummings) visits rural Cloverly Downs and meets home guard squire John Rookeby (John Clements) and trusty farmhand Appleyard (Emlyn Williams). After all three feel historical familiarity with each other, the film moves to post–Norman Conquest times. Despite its mundane nature and critical eclipse by another rural film, *A Canterbury Tale* (1944), *This England* has several dark features critics overlook. Like *Went the Day Well?* (1942), it reveals the vicious strains in a British character indelibly committed to dominant status quo values. Although the Saxon Rookeby leads a successful revolt against his Norman master in 1086, he achieves it by brutally breaking the latter's neck after overpowering him in fair combat. The bleakest episode in the film involves the *Armada* period. When free-spirited Miss Fiske (Cummings) wishes to entice Rookeby away from his farm toward the pleasures of the "open road," Appleyard frames her for treason and witchcraft and incites a mob against her. He has already murdered an absentee landlord's steward to protect Rookeby's land. Since Miss Fiske wears a gypsy costume (anticipating later Gainsborough melodrama females) and speaks Spanish, she is a sexual and European threat to English country values like Rosal in *Caravan*. Miss Fiske commits suicide to escape rural British justice. Her 1918 descendant is a Cockney gin-drinking widow who has lost her husband in the Great War. Her mother has decided she is unfit to bring up her own daughter and has sent the child to America where she will grow up and return in 1941. *This England* presents her as an unfit, single parent who will move on to the next city and not contaminate rural values by her presence. But she is also a victim of social forces the film chooses to neglect. Women were abruptly dismissed from the workforce after 1918 and forced back into the ideologically proscribed roles of wives and mothers. Their brief status of economic independence was "for the duration only." Similar events happened after 1945.

As Alberto Cavalcanti (Sussex, 209–210) noted concerning the violent reaction to the invaders in *Went the Day Well?* the tranquility of English rural life often depends on forces of repressed violence ready to emerge against any unwelcome intruder.

> It is devastating to see the cold-blooded revenge they [the villagers] now wreak on the men they had initially entertained as guests in the vicarage, the manor-house and elsewhere according to their station. Sweet young English girls are seizing the guns from German corpses, vying with each other to shoot down as many of the beastly hun as possible. It's not like killing real people. It's a sort of sport. People of the kindest character, such as the people in that small village, as soon as war touches them, become absolutely monsters.

Cavalcanti recognized a revealing trait of the English rural character. In Arthur Conan Doyle's "The Copper Beeches," Sherlock Holmes informs his pastoral-influenced companion of his horror concerning the English countryside. "It is my belief, Watson, that the lowest and vilest alleys in London do not present a more dreadful record of sin than does the smiling and beautiful countryside. . . . Think of the deeds of hellish cruelty, the hidden wickedness which may go on, year in, year out, in such places, and none the wiser" (299). Calder (1991, 234) points out that Aldeburgh native Benjamin Britten, a "pacifist and homosexual, projected village people less than favorably, as persecutors of the non-conformist Grimes" in his opera *Peter Grimes*. These features certainly contradict idealistic visions presented by People's War ideologues such as Humphrey Jennings.

England's mythic and ideological "green and pleasant" depends upon oppression and violence for its survival. In his interesting study of hegemonic discourses associated with interwar Conservative Prime Minister Stanley Baldwin, Bill Schwartz analyzes the latter's attempt at building an organic relationship between past and present in terms of ideological closure. By naturalizing the historical nature of England's past in terms of rural harmonic conservatism, Baldwin's discursive strategies eventually became the property of both Labourite left and Conservative Right. Schwartz concludes by noting that "some of the most radical political positions of the 1940s . . . became compromised—not necessarily by identification with the nation as such, but by the cultural dominance of what has been described here as Baldwinite nationalism. It was the particular strength of Baldwinism that, in adopting and re-working the language of the Englishman's birthright, it was able to displace and neutralize the antagonism between the people and the state" (18). Many cinematic representations unthinkingly reproduce this ideological heritage tradition, which sees "the countryside as the timeless and uncorrupted source of England's moral strength" (Richards, 1984, 176).

The Rookeby character of *This England* also exhibits male crisis during his historical incarnations. In 1918 he is a blinded World War I Victoria Cross veteran warning his celebrating countrymen about over optimism concerning the "war to end all wars" and looking to their future children to continue the struggle. Rookeby's Elizabethan counterpart is nearly tempted away from his rural duty into a life of sexual pleasure. His 1804 descendant resembles a male fop refugee from Gainsborough melodrama. But chance and his growing sense of responsibility toward agricultural workers affected by threatening industrial encroachment turn him into a proper social and masculine role model for 1804 rural values. This change in historical destiny also parallels Rokeby's ideological role in *The Man in Grey*. Pleasures of male freedom and dashing costume become subordinated to a historical destiny of reclaiming property from newly liberated slaves and putting them back in chains. Despite their different generic formats, *The Man in Grey* and *This England* share ideological similarities that warn us against separating realist propaganda films from feminist melodramas. *This England* explicitly recognizes that England's traditional social and sexual rural life relies on repression and violence for its very existence.

Constance Cummings portrays a character free from any traditional patriarchal order in *The Foreman Went to France*. But this is more due to her role symbolizing American allied wartime values than anything else. However, in contrast to the film's title character, traditional Britisher Fred Carrick (Clifford Evans), she is no "ugly American." Unlike Fred, she speaks French fluently and is more politically aware about the dangerous nature of a Fifth Column. Although Fred initially attempts to propose to her in a dangerous moment, the film mercifully eliminates his succeeding lines saving her from incorporation into the British way of life. As American secretary Ann Stanford, Cummings exhibits an intelligence and self-awareness refreshingly different from most contemporary female depictions. But this is more due to wartime politics than any conscious intention on the part of Ealing, a studio notoriously uneasy over female representations as *San Demetrio London* (1943) reveals. Women are mostly absent from the film. Whenever they are seen or mentioned, their roles are subordinate ones. Robert Beatty's "Yank" is a more suitable foreign representative for the film. He is easily incorporated into the community when the seamen discover he has a wife and kids.

Structures of Desire covers various films that exhibit particular hegemonic features. Chapter 2 examines wartime Gainsborough melodramas such as *The Man in Grey* (1943), *Fanny by Gaslight, Madonna of the Seven Moons, Love Story, They Were Sisters* (all 1944); *The Wicked Lady, The Seventh Veil* (1945); and *Caravan* (1946). Chapter 3 examines the wartime films of Powell and Pressburger in terms of gender. Chapter 4 interrogates utopian "People's War" aspirations in wartime films such as *Waterloo Road* (1945). Chapter 5 investigates postwar Gainsborough melodramas such as *Bedelia, The Magic Bow* (both 1946); *The Brothers, Dear Murderer, Jassy, When the Bough Breaks, Good Time Girl* (all 1947); *Broken Journey, Daybreak, Christopher Columbus, Snowbound* (all 1948); *The Bad Lord Byron*, and *So Long at the Fair* (1949). It also notes the presence of male hysteria in films such as *The October Man* (1947), *Obsession* (1949), and *They Made Me a Fugitive* (1947). Chapter 6 analyzes the changing nature of the Archers in terms of productions such as *A Matter of Life and Death* (1946); *Black Narcissus* (1947); *The Red Shoes, The Small Back Room* (both 1948); *Gone to Earth* (1949); and *The Tales of Hoffmann* (1951). Chapter 7 interrogates Ealing Studio films such as *Against the Wind* (1947) and *Saraband for Dead Lovers* (1948), as well as the familiar comedies. The role of women in *Pink String and Sealing Wax* (1945), *It Always Rains on Sunday, The Loves of Joanna Godden* (both 1947), and *Esther Waters* (1948) is also important here. The final chapter examines the complex depictions of desire in fifties films such as *Pool of London* and *Dance Hall* (both 1950) and *The Ship That Died of Shame* and *The Dam Busters* (both 1955).

British cinema may not be as artistic as its other national counterparts, but it does contain particular forms of identity governed by historical mechanisms. These mechanisms arise from factors E. P. Thompson documents that resulted in "the formation of a middle-class 'class consciousness,' more conservative, more wary of the large idealist causes (except, perhaps, those of other nations), more narrowly self-interested than in any other industrialized nation" (820). However, contradictions appear during the formative period between 1940 and 1955 that are not entirely insignificant. They involve particular structures of desire that contemporary British cinema articulates in some highly specific ways.

They may not be entirely utopian or aligned to progressive or revolutionary ideas, but they reveal the existence of competing tensions either doomed to conservative co-option or indicative of pre-emergent means that may fully develop in some future era. The films belong to different genres and display several conflicting ideas still relevant to an ideologically stagnant and conservative society still continuing today.

CHAPTER TWO

⬚

Forever Gainsborough?

During the 1980s Gainsborough melodramas underwent critical reevaluation in terms of their representations of female desire. Sue Aspinall, Pam Cook, Sue Harper, and Robert Murphy championed the work of a studio previously ignored by realist discourses and Ealing comedies. As Mass Observation studies show, Gainsborough melodramas appealed to contemporary female audiences wishing escape into historical pasts that fictionally renegotiated contemporary issues of gender. Harper (1994) notes the studio's emphasis on working-class female audiences. As critics show, Gainsborough costume films never engage in any historically accurate reconstructions. But key differences distinguish the "past" as discourse from history. Following J. H. Plumb's definition in *The Death of the Past* (1969), Patrick Wright (47–48) sees the latter as "an intellectual process—the endeavour to establish the truth of earlier events—which is pitched against the 'past,' conceived as a more mythical complex inherent in the present as a 'created ideology with a purpose.'" Gainsborough films never entirely escape from this ideologically defined 'past.' They may engage in allegorical explorations of contemporary problems but never use history to suggest any oppositionally emergent structures of meaning which may effectively combat ideologically dominant representations of male and female desire.

Although costume melodramas such as *The Man in Grey, The Wicked Lady, Caravan,* and *Jassy* may define studio output during

1943–1947, other melodramatic representations occurred in the present such as *Millions like Us, Love Story,* and *They Were Sisters.* Despite a different emphasis on present concerns by the postwar Box Gainsborough regime, which followed the wartime Ted Black/Maurice Ostrer/R. J. Minney productions, the studio alternated between past and present representations during its entire history. Dividing past from contemporary Gainsborough films is as arbitrary as separating realist from fantasy films in this period. Historical issues affected all types of cinema. Censorship restrictions and ideological issues dominated wartime as well as thirties and postwar films. The People's War ideology promoted by the Ministry of Information represents one relevant example of ideological control. Angus Calder, Harold L. Smith, and others show that the supposedly spontaneous People's War premises were cleverly manufactured by the governing class. They were as illusory as World War I definitions of the "war to end all wars" and "a home fit for heroes." As Phillip Taylor (2–3) cautions, "what was not appreciated fully by contemporaries, or by their offspring, at least until comparatively recently, was the degree to which those attitudes and values were being shaped by a British government whose control over the wartime media was near enough total and the object of admiration from no less a figure than Joseph Goebbels himself." Wartime Nazi cinema also comprised entertainment genres such as comedy, costume adventures, melodramas, and propaganda films. Boundaries between propaganda and entertainment often dissolve in wartime. Gainsborough melodramas illustrate this principle. They contain ideological values characteristic of traditional British cinema revealing that the fantastic realms of female melodrama are not entirely devoid of conservative hegemonic meanings aimed at controlling female pleasure.

Higson shows that realistic and fantastic components mingle in the Gainsborough film *Millions like Us* (1943). Although produced by Black and Ostrer it bears little resemblance to the studio's succeeding work. It resembles a typical People's War film promoting egalitarian efforts to win the war. While noting its realistic ingredients, Higson (1995, 220) also characterizes the film as "a rich and complex melodrama of everyday life about women factory workers during the war, and the family of one of those women." He also notes the manner in which it constructs the nation as a national community. *Millions like Us* does this by negotiating not just private and public spaces but also realist and fantastic discourses. Higson notes certain sequences eroding these boundaries. In the first sequence, Celia (Patricia Roc) awaits an interview in the Labour Exchange concerning her drafting as a "mobile woman." She dreams about various service opportunities available to her. They involve romantic fantasies. Her wish-fulfillment desires collapse when she learns of her posting to a munitions factory. The second sequence involves masochistic fantasies after she believes Fred (Gordon Jackson) has stood her up on a date. Successive images show Fred in a romantic garden liaison with another woman, Celia's expressionistically shot suicide, and a judge scolding Fred in court. Unlike typical British males, Fred bursts into tears. Fred later tells Celia that he missed the date because he was ordered to fly on his first bombing mission. Security reasons prevented him from informing her at the time. Like Celia's rude awakening in the Labour Exchange, Fred's revelation undermines private female fantasy, subjecting it to dominant institutional public concerns. Although the film temporarily allows Celia to experience private female fantasies and melodramatic desires, they are abruptly subordinated to the service of the state. Celia compromises her desires for wartime duty. Although Higson sees *Millions like Us* as validating some female qualities, the film is ambivalent over gender representation. The populist factory community exists within "a respectable, lower-middle-class position which is finally privileged within the social formation of ordinary people, an emphasis which is only achieved at the expense of erasing the visibility of the state and the ruling class" (243). State and class factors are not entirely absent. They invisibly structure the play of desires within the film, allowing for their temporary expression before abruptly terminating them and returning their subjects to the community fold. The process anticipates Ealing comedy mechanisms in films such as *Hue and Cry* and *Passport to Pimlico*.

Waterloo Road (1944) has no fantasy scenes, but it complements Gainsborough's costume melodramas in several ways. The film casts handsome studio star Stewart Granger as Ted, the spiv. But it also ideologically attempts to contain problems concerning disruptive wartime sexuality. Separated from her mundane husband, Jim (John Mills), Tilly Colter (Joy Shelton) engages in a liaison with dashing Ted. But she is finally saved from the consequences of her actions and redeemed into the safe ideological realm of motherhood. The process resembles the treatment of Queenie (Kay Walsh) in David Lean's conservatively nostalgic *This Happy Breed* (1945). Tilly and Queenie are both "good time girls" needing firm thirties masculine control now lacking in wartime England. In *Waterloo Road*, puny Jim finally overpowers the more powerful Ted and returns his wife to domestic subordination. *This Happy Breed* sees upwardly mobile Petty Officer Billy Mitchell (John Mills) travel to France to return "wicked lady" Queenie back to her conservative family so she can bear children for the national good. Ideological concerns dominate the realms of fantasy and desire in these films. Tilly's flirtation with Ted nearly ends in rape. Queenie ends up seduced and abandoned in the land of Britain's traditional enemy in morals and culture—France. These motifs also resemble discourses operating in Gainsborough costume melodrama.

Gainsborough melodramas need further evaluation against a broader cinematic context in order to place them within an appropriate historical and ideological context. *This England* (1941) actually antici-pates the dangerous figure of Lady Eleanor Smith's gypsy female in films such as *The Man in Grey* (1943) and *Caravan* (1946). It also shows how traditional conservative English values treat her. Female costume pleasure and spectatorship are not the only elements operating in Gainsborough films.

The Associated British Picture *The Night Has Eyes* (1942) also con-tains features that reoccur in Gainsborough melodramas. Written and directed by future Gainsborough director Leslie Arliss, the film is a con-temporary wartime melodrama dealing with the adventures of two schoolteachers, Marian (Joyce Howard) and her Canadian friend Doris (Tucker McGuire), in the Yorkshire moors. They encounter the tor-mented Mr. Rochester figure of Spanish Civil War veteran Stephen Dera-mind (James Mason). He appears to suffer from trauma and has a history of violence. Mason's character foreshadows his violent male roles in *The Man in Grey* and *Fanny by Gaslight* (1944). Although Stephen has suf-fered from involvement in a conflict censored from British screens in the thirties, *The Night Has Eyes* cannot adequately depict the significance of these disturbing historical events within its narrative. Stephen remains merely a troubled man with a violent past in the narrative. His "past" obliterates the political significance of his historical background.

As Ellen Draper notes (59), certain melodramatic representations appear "untrammeled by historical fact." They choose to appropriate his-tory for deliberate ahistorical purposes. These films often display tran-scendent moments of improbability diminishing the potentially challeng-ing nature of features within the material. Draper chooses *That Hamilton Woman* to illustrate her thesis, a film Harper (1994, 93–94) sees as antici-pating aspects of Gainsborough melodramatic address to female wartime audiences. But other aspects within these narratives often compromise such addressees by making their presence marginally "resilient" and finally subordinated to conservative mechanisms. Lady Hamilton's ideological purpose is to aid the wartime effort by rallying the nation in past and present before her humiliating disposal after Nelson's death. *The Night Has Eyes* raises the specter of Stephen's involvement in the Spanish Civil War and its relevance to wartime struggle only to submerge it in an inane melodramatic plot involving the conspiracy of working-class characters (played by Mary Clare and Wilfred Lawson) to drive their master insane. Marian wears a Gainsborough-style costume after she falls into a trough to Stephen's amusement. She may appear as a pleasurable object for the cinematic gaze (whether male or female), but she also occupies a subordinate position throughout the film. Female audiences may gain pleasure by looking at Marian's "past" glamorous appearance in an era of wartime rationing, but the pleasure is brief and dominated by other negative plot motifs involving wicked servants driving their rich master mad. Marian's Jane Eyre eventually gains her Mr. Rochester, but she is also a submissive heroine like Clarissa Rohan in *The Man in Grey*. Although Canadian and more assertive than Marian, Doris resembles a female version of Bonar Colleano's archetypal Yank—vulgar, "oversexed and over here." Her role foreshadows those secondary "good time girl" characters Jean Kent plays in Gainsborough melodramas, which represent ideologically unacceptable images of wartime women.

Although justifiably forgotten, *The Night Has Eyes* reveals the importance of seeing Gainsborough films against a broader and relevant historical and cinematic canvas. It anticipates certain melodramatic and ideological features operating within the studio. Melodramas may attempt addressing history. But, as Draper shows, they are also "untrammeled by historical fact" and may choose to emphasize ideological factors placing them within Wright's definition of a conservatively mythic past. Gainsborough melodramas may allegorically address contemporary patterns of female desire, but ideologically dominant structures of feeling also hinder their development into radically emergent structures of desire. As the success of later costume dramas such as *Upstairs, Downstairs* and *Sense and Sensibility* show, audiences may nostalgically desire for past worlds of hierarchical order and glamorous costumes. But the absence of uncomfortable historical factors, such as class oppression and poverty "untrammelled by historical fact," compromise such desires. Audiences thus emotionally identify with upper-class, beautiful people and obedient servants rather than ideologically unacceptable areas of history and politics. Even if characters such as Hester in *The Man in Grey* and Barbara in *The Wicked Lady* articulate challenges to overprivileged hierarchical orders, ideological mechanisms undermine their oppositional potential by depicting them as murderesses in need of patriarchal control.

Contemporary reports show that Gainsborough films appealed to audiences more than "realist" works identified with classic British cinema. But did these films represent indirect images of women's changing role during wartime? Durgnat (1985, 260) cautions that the relationship is problematic. He argues that the films are more "highly (though not absolutely) equivocal through polycausality and dramatic irony" revealing women equally abusing power as well as men. They only deplore past excesses, and their relationship to wartime moods is highly questionable. Female audiences may have become attracted by essentially conservative images of glamour as a release from insecurity and drab utility clothing. In 1953 Vera Brittain commented that "the current conviction that British women owe their advance to war still appears to be not so much a paradox as an illusion" (195). She points out that the actual picture was more ambivalent and contradictory, one confirmed by recent historians such as Penny Summerfield.

> Wartime improvements in the position of women have seldom been due to any new realisation of women's dignity and needs; they originate in the selfishness of States seeking additional workers for temporary and unconstructive ends. The insecurity of the wartime prizes conferred on women became clear from the reversion to old habits and conventions which followed the First War, though they were less easily re-established after the Second. In so far as war changes practices which cannot be restored it brings progress, but the progress is incidental, and springs neither from principle nor from a revolution in values. (196–97)

Although cinema never provides a direct reflection of historical concerns and often displaces, complicates, and disguises class and gender interests, contemporary issues are never entirely absent. Is female desire progressive or apolitically escapist in these films? Durgnat also takes issue with the realism and fantasy divisions dominating critical interpretations. Two decades later aristocratic male bodice rippers become misogynistically inclined working-class "angry young men" within a realist aesthetic. Forties costume sexual excessiveness reappears within Hammer productions.

It's often far better to think of overlaps which enfold oppositions, rather than binary oppositions. . . . The more sophisticated paradigms allow us to see Gainsborough and Ealing as two (of many) intersecting structures within the national psyche, sometimes conflicting, sometimes alternative, sometimes coincident, and allowing wide permutations of unpredictable choice. (261)

The Man in Grey (1943) proved an outstanding success for Gainsborough and led to other costume productions. Unlike the original novel by Lady Eleanor Smith, which begins with a Rebeccalike heroine discovering the history of the Rohan family she has married into, the film version contains a prologue and epilogue influenced by the ideological patterns of the People's War. The past is now a distant landscape, temporarily recoverable by memory but otherwise relegated to an auction room. Uniformed forties descendants of two key players in the historical drama meet in the Rohan London mansion as an auction is in progress. The last male Rohan descendant has died in Dunkirk leaving W.R.E.N. Clarissa (Phyllis Calvert) as the family's sole survivor. She meets R.A.F. officer Peter Rokeby (Stewart Granger) who attempts to bid for one of the family heirlooms. An air raid interrupts the auction. Clarissa and Rokeby look at a box of trinkets that will feature in the historical flashback. As they leave the auction room, the camera slowly tracks into the brochure advertising Miss Patchet's Establishment for Young Ladies. This leads viewers to a journey into the past.

Like most melodramas, *The Man in Grey* contrasts two types of relationships: the ideal love between Clarissa and Swinton Rokeby and the similarly adulterous, but transgressive, affair between Rohan (James Mason) and Hester (Margaret Lockwood). While Clarissa and Swinton parallel the "normal" couple of melodramas such as the Rock Hudson and Lauren Bacall characters in *Written on the Wind* (1956), Rohan and Hester represent their dynamically subversive counterparts. But although this latter relationship could represent a progressive "return of the repressed" undermining traditional ideological normalities, it is uncertain whether this really characterizes themes within *The Man in Grey*. The film presents the excitement of a return to a mythically glamorous, costumed past. But it undermines any attempt to mediate its contradictions on a more coherent historical level. Although Hester may represent a symbolic embodiment of working-class female resentment against an oppressive class status, her activities are viciously perverse in ridding herself of an obstacle preventing her from being the second Lady Rohan. Hester warns Clarissa about the dangers of friendship and states that she is envious of her. Although she complies with Clarissa's demands, she also states that "after school our status will be different." Although Hester may voice independent wartime female reactions against the status quo by telling Rohan, "One day I'll get the things I want without charity," she finally experiences what rising above her status actually involves in a manner she never expected. Like Joe Lampton in Jack Clayton's 1959 film, she desires her "room at the top." But she experiences a more definitive physical and ideological punishment at the climax. Although Rohan is not the socially damaged hero of the original novel, he is seen as a victim of social convention as his pathologically violent defense of family honor and grudging submission to marriage and heirs reveal. Like Hester, his energies are never allowed any form of expression above those of monstrous displays. Hester and Rohan are victims of the same social system. But the film never interrogates a society that makes monsters of two dynamic characters who breach class taboos. They are safely relegated to the domains of a mythic past that the People's War ideology will "never" allow to return again. Neither Rohan nor Hester reappears in the contemporary world of prologue and epilogue. They are problematic characters with which wartime cinema expresses unease.

The Man in Grey moves toward removing class and social barriers, which prevented Clarissa and Rokeby's union in Regency days by reuniting them in the present via their descendants. But like the wartime conditions queried by Charlie in *Millions like Us*, the conditions for their successful consummation are transitory and dependent on the exorcism of unpalatable aspects of the past. The epilogue concludes the film with Clarissa uttering the lines of her ancestor, "Isn't it a lovely day" as she descends the steps. But this time (in contrast to his downwardly mobile Regency ancestor), Rokeby can join her in rushing down the steps of the Rohan mansion to catch a democratic double-decker bus. The Rokeby family has regained its fortune by putting down a French-inspired slave revolt and restoring chains to its idyllic island in the sun. However, although Granger's Rokeby offers a handsome cavalier counterpart to Rohan, he also exhibits disturbing symptoms of male control and violence. He not only viciously (and undeservedly) hits Hester when she returns from her nightly tryst with Rohan but also indirectly causes Clarissa's death by preventing her from sailing with him: "If you're to be my wife, you must learn to obey me." *The Man in Grey* differs from the

FIGURE 4. The Marquis of Rohan (James Mason) about to punish his wicked lady in *The Man in Grey*.

realist wartime aesthetic. But it is still dominated by social codes contradicting attempts to understand it as an uncomplicated text of female independence.

Hester is a lower-class descendant of Livia in Thomas Middleton's *Women Beware Women*, as equally vicious and unredeemable as her aristocratic forebear. The film provides little evidence for sympathizing with Hester as an oppressed, lower-class woman who becomes monstrous due to lack of upward mobility. As Harper (1987, 179) comments, "the affective, spectacular aspects of mise-en-scene are foregrounded, to produce a vision of 'history' as a country where only feelings reside, not socio-political conflicts." Although progressive currents of the melodramatic imagination often produce structured ambivalence between the spectacular and the repressed, the former may operate conservatively by overwhelming traces of residual structures of desire attempting to become radically emergent and oppositional. Like other Gainsborough melodramas, *The Man in Grey* displays ambivalent desires within a conservative framework. The original 1941 novel by Lady Eleanor Smith contains several elements that contrast significantly with the film version. Rohan is a more sympathetic figure who chooses to wear gray rather than flamboyant Regency fashion as a reaction against male excess. Mistreated by an older female lover during his youth, Rohan hides his vulnerable feelings under an aloof manner. In the epilogue, his portrait actually attempts to warn the new Lady Rohan about Hester's malign influence. The novel's Rokeby is little more than a buccaneer gentleman of fortune who sleeps with Clarissa and dies on board ship before he can regain his fortune. The book's Clarissa is less virtuous than her screen counterpart. She accrues gambling debts and becomes pregnant by Rokeby. Eight months after her death, Rohan does marry Hester. However, after she confesses her role in Clarissa's murder, Rohan does not kill her but shuns her. Hester then commits suicide. The novel contains a prologue and epilogue depicting the new Lady Rohan left alone in the family estate after her husband has left to fight (and eventually die) in France. She discovers some hidden documents pertaining to the secret Rohan family history, emotionally identifies herself with Clarissa, and tells her story in the main narrative. Although using classic Gothic conventions, the epilogue asserts Mary Rohan's gradual realization that entering the past brings terror to the present, not any wish-fulfillment mode of pleasurable escapism contained in the Gainsborough film version. The novel states that the past may contain a fascinating spiritual territory, but it is also one with dangers for the present and future. A similar point occurs in the prologue to Magdalen King Hall's *Life and Death of the Wicked Lady Skelton*. In contrast to the film, the original novel actually warns against any journeys into the past and implicitly urges the necessity of remaining securely within the present. The new Lady Rohan does not evoke Clarissa but the murderous spirit of Hester who finally disposes of the Rohan family.

Like *The Man in Grey*, the People's War ideology also operates in *Fanny by Gaslight* but this time more indirectly. The film aims to condemn the repressive aura of Victorian times and emphasize the new classless and egalitarian vision represented by Fanny (Phyllis Calvert) and Harry Somerford (Stewart Granger). As in *The Man in Grey*, the elimination of dangerous obstacles such as evil Lord Manderstoke (James Mason), Alicia Seymour (Margaretta Scott), and "good-time girl" cousin Lucy (Jean Kent) is necessary for this goal.

The film opens in 1870 with young Fanny's discovery of a "knocking shop" situated within the basement of her stepfather's business. Realizing that young Fanny may soon perceive the hypocritical difference between Victorian respectability and its dark underside financially supporting bourgeois home affluence, Hopwood (John Laurie) sends her away to boarding school. Fanny is the love child of cabinet minister Clive Seymour (Stuart Lindsell) and his lower-class lover (Nora Swinburne), whom class barriers have separated. When Fanny returns ten years later, her secure world collapses. Vicious Lord Manderstoke murders her father, a coroner upholds the status quo by blaming Hopwood, and Fanny enters a life of domestic servitude employed by a father who cannot officially recognize her. Fanny's future life appears in danger of following the same socially sanctioned dead end as that of her mother. She finds out that her father's wife, Alicia, is having an affair with Manderstoke. Eventually, social and sexual pressures provoked by Alicia result in Seymour's suicide and Fanny's further descent down the social ladder.

She eventually finds employment at the Jolly Bargee owned by Hopwood's former servant, Chunks (Wilfred Lawson). Her father's private secretary, Harry Somerford, arrives to inform her of the contents of her father's will. Although he initially believes her responsible for Seymour's death, his attitude changes when he learns of the real family relationship. Unlike the other characters, Harry expresses his impatience with a repressive class structure—"It's time people were judged on what they are"— and hopes for a new society a hundred years later. But repressive family values again intervene in the person of Harry's sister Kate (Cathleen Nesbitt) which nearly result in Fanny's decent into prostitution. She then decides to leave the Jolly Bargee. After finding Lucy (now a stage actress), she accidentally encounters Manderstoke again. He now sadistically enjoys making Alicia's life hell. Following Harry's physical encounter with Manderstoke, he and Fanny go to Paris. But destiny intervenes again with Harry forced into a duel with Manderstoke. Although Harry survives, his life hangs in the balance especially when Kate intervenes and attempts to separate him finally from Fanny. Fanny then understands the deadly nature of Kate's possessive attitude and avows her intention of standing by Harry.

Fanny by Gaslight is a heroic family melodrama affirming the enduring and persevering status of a heroine who survives personal and social alienation by finally standing up for her own rights. It contrasts Victorian bourgeois hypocrisy with the new classless world represented by Fanny and Harry who eventually find true happiness in France. Fanny's stepfather confines French culture (signified by naughty Can Can routines) to the basement of his bordello. Rigid class structures ruin Fanny's mother and nearly finish off her daughter's chance of happiness. The film appears to be a positive representation of the People's War ideology in which women gain recognition and class barriers dissolve. However, contradictions exist in the film. It is the upper-middle-class Harry, not Fanny or any working-class character (the latter continuing to remain in prewar stereotypes), who utters the speech about the abolition of class difference. Liberation is the prerogative of the upper class. Although the film emphasizes private school-educated Fanny's dilemma, it also takes a condescending attitude toward lower-class females who belong to subaltern national classes. *Fanny by Gaslight* contains stereotypical representations of Alicia's Welsh, Irish, and Cockney servants. Fanny actually uses violence against two of them in one scene! Her role really resembles a class-oriented version of the suffering mother archetype of the maternal melodrama in more complex representations such as *Stella Dallas*. Fanny only lives for her man. Her closing speech emphasizes her maternal aim in healing Harry—"I'm going to give him life"—rather than moving toward feminist solidarity with women of different classes and nationalities. Like *The Man in Grey*, the heroine's supposedly positive representation occurs at the expense of other marginalized figures. Although depicted as selfish, Alicia at least attempts to assert some form of female independence from the male order, as does Lucy. But the film condemns these alternative and attractive females. Like Googie Withers in Ealing melodramas, Margaretta Scott's Alicia displays an independent female desire with which neither the film nor British cinematic ideology feels comfortable. Jean Kent's Lucy represents the nonacceptable side of the class structure. Like Alicia, she ends up with Manderstoke. As Murphy (1992, 48) points out, Fanny remains the ideologically privileged character, an "average British housewife, turning her hand to any sort of work to survive, slogging her way through death and misfortune and in the face of adversity shedding her reserve and blossoming into a full-blooded woman determined to fight for her share of happiness." But as her final speech makes clear, her happiness involves subordinated self-sacrifice to give Harry life away from the death-oriented world represented by Kate. "You've got to get well, you've got to live." *Fanny by Gaslight's* melodramatic imagination is highly compromised. Due to censorship restrictions, it cannot fully use the original novel's critique of Victorian sexual hypocrisy akin to Steven Marcus's later vision in *The Other Victorians* (1966). Although *Fanny by Gaslight* reveals this world in the opening scenes of Hopwood's basement, it does not employ the entire vision of Michael Sadleir's original novel by revealing how sexual exploitation conditions the entire structure of Victorian society. The film safely transfers this to "other" figures such as Hopwood, Alicia, Lucy, and Lord Manderstoke (who plays a relatively marginal role in the original novel rather than his major scapegoat function in the film version).

Unlike its predecessors, *Love Story* is set in the present. It deals with a wartime, triangular, romantic relationship. Diagnosed as terminally ill, concert pianist Felicity Crossland (modeled on Myra Hess) moves to Cornwall for her final months. While there, Felicity (Margaret Lockwood) meets Kit (Stewart Granger), who conceals the fact that a war injury will result in his eventual blindness. Although Judy (Patricia Roc) looks after him, Felicity discerns that her rival's feelings have possessive overtones. Judy refuses to allow Kit's cure by surgery. Eventually, aided by the benevolent patriarchal guidance of elderly entrepreneur Tom (Tom Walls), *Love Story* ends with the reunification of Felicity and newly uniformed Kit, who has undergone an eye operation. *Love Story* is a wartime romance emphasizing the temporary nature of a fragile present rather than engaging in fascination with the past or promoting utopian hopes for the future. It concludes with Felicity watching Kit's squadron fly off to battle. She is still terminally ill, and Kit's future is also in doubt. As Landy (1991, 222) points out, *Love Story* is a contradictory work juggling together "competing notions of female identity and desire" involving "independence and dependence." But unlike in *The Man in Grey* and *Fanny by Gaslight*, the male figure becomes less the subject of desire and more an object of female combat. Felicity and Judy desire their man. Kit is more of an infantile figure (before his eventual cure) than a self-sufficient Gainsborough male like Rohan, Rokeby, Manderstoke, and Somerford. *Love Story* emphasizes two assertive females whose desiring conflict and antagonisms are more resilient than their counterparts in costume melodramas. At one point in the film, Kit's presence and voice become silenced and subordinated to Felicity and Judy's verbal contest! Women, not men, make the final decision in *Love Story*. In her final scene, Judy exhibits resignation and realizes the futility of any romantic involvement with Kit. Murphy (1992, 48) and Landy note that the transitory nature of wartime romance determines *Love Story's* sexual politics. The conclusion is temporary rather than permanent. Like many wartime couples, Kit and Felicity can only live for the moment. As he tells her, "Happiness such as we can have is worth grasping, even if it is for just a day, an hour . . . we're all living dangerously; there isn't any more certainty. Just today and the possibility for tomorrow." This present uncertainty conditions the resilience Felicity and Judy show in their different expressions of desire. Their world offers no secure grounds for any securities concerning the return of status quo values.

But while *Love Story* appears to contain oppositional elements in a narrative about two strong-willed heroines, these features make no strong impression in the text. They are merely ascribed to emotional conflict resulting from wartime conditions that are not regarded as permanent. Felicity may die, Kit may go down with his squadron, and Judy may find somebody else. These desiring relationships are purely transitory and lack any secure foundations for their development.

Although set in thirties Fascist Italy, the real location of *Madonna of the Seven Moons* is a country of the female mind. Pam Cook (1996, 95) believes the film gives audiences the sense of "being transported into a fictionalized eroticised past." The conflict involves two sides of the protagonist played by Phyllis Calvert: submissive, religious, repressed wife, Maddalena, and her sexually libidinous alter ego, Rosanna. They represent tendencies within wartime females who may either maintain traditional values or take advantage of the brief encounters wartime sexual freedom offers. When Maddalena's daughter, Angela (Patricia Roc), returns home from school in England, her libertarian attitudes provoke a crisis of conscience leading to the return of her mother's repressed gypsy persona, Rosanna. Significantly, both Maddalena and Rosanna control their male partners, Giuseppe Labardi (John Stuart) and Nino (Stewart Granger), whenever they question her disappearances. But only death may resolve this heroine's personal contradictions. Despite her libertarian education, Angela never represents any positive alternative. Although she wishes to solve the enigma of her mother's disappearance, the supposedly independent daughter nearly ends up raped by Nino's brother and only escapes by a fortunate accident. She finally becomes engaged to colorless English diplomat Evelyn Penhurst (Alan Haines), whose insipid personality parallels her father's.

The film concludes with a shot of Giuseppe's cross and Nino's rose on the dead heroine's breast. Shot in artificially high studio lighting accompanied by an emotional melodramatic score, the scene expresses the contradictory nature of the heroine's conflict. But it also denotes the impossibility of ever resolving it in an ideologically satisfactory manner. The film is as split as its heroine's personality. Rosanna certainly articulates female desire for independence. She fiercely affirms, "I live in the present, the past and the future mean nothing to me." When Jimmy Logan (Peter Murray Hill) asks if she is married, Rosanna replies, "No. I belong to nobody but myself." She drives her otherwise tough lover Nino to tears by threatening to "clear out" when he attempts to enquire about her past life. Ironically, Nino's own mother (Nancy Price) counsels him (via the feminine intuition of her own "gypsy mother") to accept Rosanna's word. In these brief scenes, the male order undergoes subversion. But it is only temporary. The film rules out any viable permanent alternatives as the characters of Mrs. Fiske (Hilda Bailey) and Nesta Logan (Dulcie Gray) reveal.

Mrs. Fiske is as silly as her original counterpart in Margery Lawrence's novel. Roland Pertwee's screenplay ascribes her silliness to her divorcee status. Madonna flinches when Mrs. Fiske emphasizes this in the fashion salon. Later, Mrs. Fiske speaks of a recently divorced friend in terms indirectly warning audiences about following Rosanna's path. "She got a divorce and that's always the critical period." Although Rosanna enjoys sexual freedom, fear possesses her whenever she encounters churches or religious processions. Jimmy and Nesta Logan appear as a happily artistic married couple. But the original novel emphasizes that they are happily living in sin since Nesta's cold-blooded rich husband has refused to divorce her. The film does express contradictions, but, unlike the novel, it resolves them by conservative closure. *Madonna of the Seven*

Moons ends with lover and husband mourning at the bedroom shrine of Maddalena/Rosanna. Giuseppe says goodbye and expresses his failure as a husband: "I wish I could have made you happy." Nino bids his lover farewell and tosses a rose on her breast. Both men claim her, but the Madonna of the Seven Moons now belongs to safe, transcendental realms beyond society, history, and life itself.

They Were Sisters (1945) appeared in the final months of the war. Like Margery Lawrence's *Madonna of the Seven Moons*, the action occurs in the 1930s, suggesting that postwar normality is linked with the previous decade rather than any radically challenging future. *They Were Sisters* begins in 1919, introduces us to its main titular characters, and then moves rapidly toward 1937 after the wedding of Charlotte (Dulcie Gray) and Geoffrey (James Mason). The film examines marital relationships and necessary adjustments. Opening with fashion images from a 1919 magazine, the film depicts the balanced Lucy (Phyllis Calvert), opportunistic Vera (Anne Crawford), and masochistically inclined Charlotte. As in *Fanny by Gaslight*, Calvert portrays an organized wartime heroine. She responds to Vera's question, "Why do you take things so seriously?" with, "Well, if I don't, nobody in the house will." The 1919 prologue sees her two sisters rushing into unsatisfactory relationships with no thought of their possible consequences. Charlotte's attraction for ruthless, upwardly mobile Geoffrey fulfills Lucy's comment about her sister having "a passion for stray dogs, and one day she'll be bitten by one." Her marriage results in masochistic subordination to a sadistic husband and her eventual suicide. Vera attaches herself to the dull, but loyal, Brian (Barrie Livesey). He marries her after ignoring her warning that she does not love him. Lucy marries stable William (Peter Murray Hill). Her other sisters have children for whom they are unable to properly care. Lucy and William's child dies in infancy.

While following themes in Dorothy Whipple's original novel, *They Were Sisters* really deals with problems concerning dysfunctional wartime families. Although shot in 1945, the film uses the "past" 1930s era as a background to resolve ideologically turbulent wartime conditions "untrammeled by historical fact." Like *Madonna of the Seven Moons*, the period reveals an ideological desire to return to a securely mythic past rather than face new postwar challenges. While the original novels by Lawrence and Whipple contain disturbing historical references to the thirties, the film adaptations erase them to focus upon solipsistic middle-class countries of the female imagination. Lucy eventually gains all the children of her errant sisters. She reveals Geoffrey's marital brutalities at a coroner's inquest after refusing a bribe involving custody of his two younger children (whom she gains anyway). Vera falls in love with the more masculine Terry (Hugh Sinclair). When Brian decides to move to America, she gains her divorce but loses daughter Sarah (Helen Stephens) to Lucy. Sarah overhears her mother expressing total devotion to her new love. Brian loses his family due to masculine impotence. But Terry insists on Vera accompanying him to start a new life on a South African farm far away from her affluent London existence. As William later notes, exile from country and family represents her appropriate punishment. "You can't act the way she did and not expect a jolt."

They Were Sisters moves toward its ideological conclusion of a British family reunited under the dominance of solid William and caring Lucy. William's final speech refers to this new postwar family as "a very ordinary lot" and being just "millions like you going along but in the main muddling through." He uses language familiar from People's War films such as *Millions like Us* and *The Foreman Went to France*. But his character and words express middle-class values. They undermine the People's War ideology by incorporating it within an affluent family unit neither working class nor egalitarian. As Pam Cook (1983, 26) points out, William's lines stating "God's in his heaven and all's right with the world" denote "a final idyllic scene which is almost conscious of its own utopian fictional quality." Desire is a dangerous thing. It needs repression by acceptable middle-class family values. Charlotte's desires for handsome but dangerous Geoffrey lead to her degradation. Geoffrey has little time for his younger son and daughter and has more than a paternal interest in his adolescent daughter, Margaret (played by Mason's then-wife Pamela Kellino). Vera eventually finds a real man, but he insists she exchange her luxurious city life for South African exile. Only Lucy and William remain. But their marriage exhibits little real desire. *They Were Sisters* clearly sets out to exile desire from the new postwar world.

The Wicked Lady contains subversive representations of female desire and pleasure in the figure of Margaret Lockwood's Lady Barbara Skelton. Female audiences relished the fictional representation of a woman eager to achieve her independence by reacting against a stuffy conformist world. Barbara's cross-dressing as a highwayman and enjoyment of a man's life with Jerry Jackson (James Mason) contrast with the boring world of Sir Ralph (Griffith Jones). But the film also emphasizes that Barbara rushes into a marital relationship with the wrong man just like a real-life wartime romance. She seduces Ralph and then realizes too late that Kit Locksby (Michael Rennie) is her real love. Barbara certainly reacts against the patriarchal order. But, despite close attachment to her dead mother ("the only person I ever really cared for"), Barbara later desires a domestic world of marriage and children she initially despised as her final worlds to Kit reveal. Her intended mate retreats in horror after she reveals her deadly past. Shocked by her wicked deeds, Kit leaves her to die alone as the camera cranes overhead, framing her dying posture through a window.

The Wicked Lady also indirectly refers to the changed world of wartime society. While Barbara enjoys her adulterous relationships, Ralph and Caroline (Patricia Roc) refuse to consummate their love in that manner. Ralph rails against the restrictive divorce laws of 1683 as much as his forties descendants did before the granting of "no fault" divorces two decades later. Eventually, he decides to end his state of "marital misery" by petitioning Parliament for a divorce, so everyone can be happily reunited. By this time, it is too late for Barbara, who accidentally dies at the hands of Kit. *The Wicked Lady* may be read as an allegory of the precarious nature of wartime romances, which often ended unhappily. It also privileges the world of Sir Ralph, who looks after his tenants in a more caring way than do the other country squires, who regard him as a traitor to his class. Sir Ralph responds, "They're just human beings like you and me." With Barbara's demise, Ralph speaks in relief about a "dark shadow lifted." The worlds of 1683 and 1945 can now continue normally after undergoing respective temporary disruptions involving the anarchic wartime nature of female desire.

Caravan appeared in 1946. Pam Cook (1996, 97–103) sees its visual and auditory codes defining it as a complex film, distinguishing it above any reductive themes of Englishness in peril and the desirability of rejecting the exotic realm of Spain. Impoverished English writer Richard (Stewart Granger) travels to Spain, hoping to gain sufficient money to marry debt-ridden aristocratic Oriana (Anne Crawford). While there he temporarily loses his memory and marries glamorous gypsy dancer Rosal (Jean Kent). Eventually he overcomes his worst enemy, Sir Francis (Dennis Price), who has married his sweetheart, and settles down with her in England. Rosal conveniently dies after stopping a bullet meant for Richard. The death of both "aberrant" spouses means that Richard and Oriana live happily ever after.

The previous summary does not do justice to the exotic and alternative nature of *Caravan*. Pam Cook notes the film's treatment of the pre-

FIGURE 5. Margaret Lockwood transgresses class and gender boundaries in *The Wicked Lady*.

carious nature of national identity. Both Spain and England have positive and negative values, but *Caravan* emotionally privileges Spain's sexual and exotic realm. Richard learns a violent version of the manly art of boxing from his early life with the gypsy community. Richard's mother was Spanish, and his return to his homeland results in mixed identity, a "feminization" signified by unmasculine gypsy costume, and his changed position as an agent who can no longer control his destiny. Spain as a maternal realm is more dangerous for the male than the one influencing Barbara in *The Wicked Lady*. For Barbara, her mother's memory represents the desire for control, but for Richard, his mother's geographical territory leads to temporary loss of masculine control. Cook cogently examines *Caravan's* "hybrid" nature as well as its visual celebration of Gainsborough's gypsy spirit. But the film also operates on other levels.

Caravan certainly celebrates the exotic gypsy culture of Spain as well as Jean Kent's sympathetic performance as Rosal. But Richard's initial immersion into Spain resulting from temporary amnesia and loss of identity, complements other wartime cinematic representations dealing with loss of male control. In films such as *I'll Walk Beside You* (1943), *Twilight Hour* (1944) and Hollywood's *Random Harvest* (1942), the hero's return to normality is closely aligned with the restoration of a healed community. In *Twilight Hour*, the amnesiac World War I hero (played by Mervyn Johns) loses his class status and becomes a gardener. A subplot involves the disrupted romance between his daughter and the son of the lady of the manor (played by Marie Lohr), who is devoted to the continuation of traditional values in the family of Earl Chetwood (Basil Radford). The film eventually engages in an astonishing character reversal when formerly disdainful Lady Chetwood eventually accepts her new successor once she realizes she will fit into the status quo. Like Greer Garson in *Random Harvest*, the female partner (played by Lesley Brook) works in the unacceptable world of entertainment and has to prove she has the "right stuff" for admission into a rigidly hierarchical class society. In *I'll Walk beside You*, an amnesiac naval officer (Richard Bird) recovers his memory and becomes masculine and independent so he can marry his devoted sweetheart (played again by Lesley Brook). The same motif also occurs in *Random Harvest*. These films privilege class structures dominating the play of desire in which traditional customs continue by incorporation and co-option. In all these films temporary amnesia occurs as a plot device. Recovery leads to the renewed return of status quo values. Isolating Gainsborough melodramas from other contemporary wartime dramas leads to neglect of significant cultural concerns influencing the studio. These factors call into question the studio's supposedly unique progressive depictions.

Caravan displays similar ideological concerns. These involve class, desire, and sexuality. Although the film presents an ambivalent depiction of the exotic realm, it finally incorporates Richard into the status quo by cleansing his character of aberrant elements and projecting them onto figures such as melodramatically villainous Sir Francis and his gay henchman Wycroft (Robert Helpmann). Although *Caravan* sympathizes with Rosal, she also represents an obstacle to Richard's trajectory into a comfortable English class position and must be removed from the film. Jean Kent's performance contains none of her "good time girl" connotations from *Fanny by Gaslight, House of Two Thousand Women, Madonna of the Seven Moons* (all 1944), and *The Wicked Lady* (1945). But she is culturally unacceptable by virtue of her lower-class and gypsy status. Rosal is a more attractive figure than the ladylike Oriana. During their eventual meeting, a series of alternating close-ups, matched with competitive dialogue concerning Richard, eventually privileges the blackmailing tactics of Oriana. She threatens Rosal unless she informs on her own tribe to clear Richard's name. She says, "I will take him from you." Although Oriana supposedly acts on Richard's behalf, her threatening demeanor reveals hostile class overtones against a lower-class foreigner. While the visual style of the film privileges exotic elements, it resolves desire in an ideologically acceptable manner along traditional class lines. The male achieves a higher status, allowing him to gain a female above his station. This ideological closure also occurs in *The Magic Bow* (1946), in which Stewart Granger's Paganini finally gains not only romantic access to his aristocratic sweetheart, Jeanne (Phyllis Calvert), but also incorporation into the establishment via a knighthood granted by the pope, before whom he performs in the Vatican. Although Cook (108–9) suggests that Paganini's upward mobility is accompanied by costume changes from more formal to feminine attire, the violinist actually wears court livery before the pope—an outfit marking the artist as a mere servant, a costume and status Richard Wagner reacted against in 1848.

Caravan ends with Richard and Oriana happily reunited in a studio-constructed pastoral landscape. Again, the English countryside overpowers those negative representations of the city (Sir Francis, Wycroft), ethnic underclass (the gypsy community), and Spain's dangerous foreign landscape. The film symbolically utilizes motifs of wartime cinema. It

FIGURE 6. Paganini (Stewart Granger) seeks his room at the top with Jeanne (Phyllis Calvert) in *The Magic Bow.*

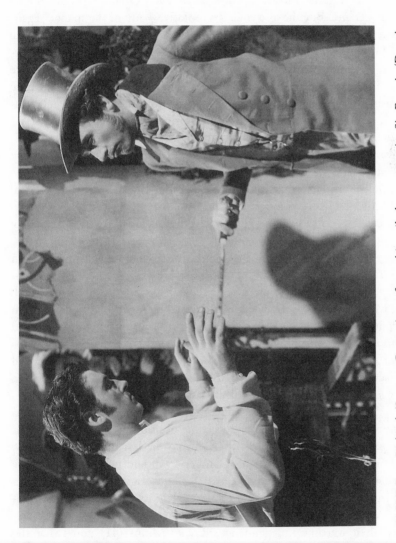

FIGURE 7. Richard (Stewart Granger) confronts his evil class antagonist Sir Francis (Dennis Price) in *Caravan.*

echoes the People's War egalitarian ideology by allowing the writer Richard, son of "a country doctor who spent more on his patients than he got from them" access into a privileged class world. While Sir Francis represents the negative image of prewar aristocracy, Oriana experiences economic decline. But she also makes a tentative "lady of the manor" egalitarian gesture toward "ladies of the night" Sir Francis sends to humiliate her. Bertha (Enid Stamp Taylor) and her entourage recognize "true" aristocratic values when they see them. Richard's loss of Oriana, his dalliance with Rosal, and his eventual return to the status quo parallel wartime British social dislocations. After an insecure world of wartime relationships, promiscuity, and marital breakups, stability finally returns. As William states in the concluding scene of *They Were Sisters*, "God's in his heaven, and all's right with the world." *Caravan* thus hegemonically resolves desire according to dominant values. But Lady Eleanor Smith's original novel contains a much darker vision. Richard loses both Rosal and Oriana. He dies a lonely and anachronistic figure lost within a late-nineteenth-century technological world that regards his vision as merely quaint and sensational.

Although not specifically a Gainsborough film due to its production by Ortus Films, *The Seventh Veil* (1945) echoes many studio concerns as Murphy (1992, 108) notes. After antagonism between J. Arthur Rank and Maurice Ostrer, Sydney and Muriel Box took over the studio. Studio output had declined with only three films released in the postwar period (*Caravan, The Magic Bow*, and *The Root of All Evil*) and one in development (*Jassy*). Sydney Box acted as producer while Muriel Box supervised the script department. Although they preferred modern subject matter, they initially continued with projects associated with the previous regime.

The Seventh Veil complements motifs in *Brief Encounter* as well as fictionally renegotiating women's wartime position within melodrama. It also parallels *They Were Sisters*. Shot during the last months of the war, *The Seventh Veil* was released in October 1945 and became a box-office success. It eventually gained an Oscar for best original screenplay. Parallels with the prevailing national mood explain its success. As contemporary evidence and recent historical scholarship shows, not all women relished their wartime independence. Raynes Minns (41) noted that the 1945 Control of Employment Act led to demobilized women taking second place at the Labour Exchange, "despite the fact that many of them wanted to continue to work and retain their hard-won independence." But, in 1943, Margaret Goldsmith (Harold Smith, 225) commented that "a number of wives to whom I have talked are so homesick for their pre-war way of life that they seem to have created in their imagination a glowing fantasy of what this life was like." Raynes Minns (200) comments that far-sighted contemporary works such as *Living Together Again* (1946) recognized "the possible implications of forcing unwilling women back into the home." Cinema participated in this ideological process. *The Seventh Veil* illustrates contemporary hegemonic negotiation of contradictory desires involving the return to dominant patterns of thirties ideology.

Laurence Olivier's *Hamlet* (1948) opens with the sound bite, "This is the story of a man who could not make up his mind." *The Seventh Veil* narrative relates this indecisiveness to problems affecting traumatically disturbed Francesca Cunningham (Ann Todd). Adopted by the equally tormented Rochesterlike figure of Nicholas (James Mason) at the age of fourteen, Francesca undergoes spiritual isolation from her female peer group (her only school friend is depicted as being as superficial as divorcee Mrs. Fiske in *Madonna of the Seven Moons*) and subordination to Nicholas, who wishes to mold her into a concert pianist. His manipulation of the female character evokes Maxim de Winter's designs on the anonymous narrator of *Rebecca*. Traumatically disturbed since the age of twelve by his mother's abandonment, Nicholas seeks refuge in his bachelor existence and indulges in misogynistic behavior. His mother's portrait dominates the mantelpiece in *The Seventh Veil* like those domineering parental images in Hitchcock films such as *Suspicion* (1941), *The Paradine Case* (1947), and *The Birds* (1963). Nicholas is as disturbed as Francesca. He breaks up her affair with affable musician Peter Gay (Hugh McDermott) and sadistically raps his cane over Francesca's knuckles as she plays the piano after announcing her intention of living with artist Max (Albert Lieven). After a car crash injures her hands, Francesca undergoes a traumatic collapse. Psychiatrist Dr. Larsen (Herbert Lom) then attempts to heal her soul.

Although Larsen recognizes Nicholas's psychological sickness, he ignores this clear evidence of male hysteria. He chooses instead to restore Francesca to sanity and male control. Larsen resembles patriarchal psychologists in forties Hollywood cinema who aim at restoring the female to her appropriate role in society. He succeeds. *The Seventh Veil's* climactic scenes depict Francesca rushing past her more caring lovers into the arms of psychologically disturbed Nicholas. Although he later reveals his tender feelings for her, the film concludes with no secure assurances as to whether Francesca will again experience either his dark moods or his cane.

The Seventh Veil is a classic cinematic text of male sadism and female masochism. It is also a contemporary allegory about the necessity of returning wartime women to male control. Although the film never mentions the war, it acts as an important "structured absence" throughout the narrative. Francesca is a vulnerable single women needing an authoritarian male to guide her into artistic and romantic fulfillment. Her girls' school and only friend Susan (Yvonne Owen) give her no female solidarity. Like Stephen in *The Night Has Eyes*, Nicholas is psychologically disturbed. But the film chooses to emphasize Francesca's condition rather than his! The role of Nicholas really symbolizes returning postwar males needing nurturance and reassurance like those real-life psychologically disturbed ex-soldiers documented in contemporary manuals such as *Living Together Again* (see Raynes Minns, 187–200). Minns (164, 175) also notes that wartime conditions caused disturbing cases of marital stress and breakdown. Such features influence the depictions of Peter and Max as "unworthy partners" for Francesca in *The Seventh Veil.*

When Francesca returns to Peter after the seven-year absence resulting from Nicholas's possessiveness, she finds that her lover has married and not waited for her. Peter's action symbolizes the "Dear John" syndrome affecting wartime relationships. Although a music student, he works his way through college by playing in a band at night—a very un-British thing to do! Francesca eventually finds him leading his own band, but it is in a nightclub where half the customers are black. Although the scene presents a rare instance of contemporary interracial mixing, it is a taboo mise-en-scene element for *The Seventh Veil.* The upset Francesca later tells Larsen, "I hate love. I hate being in love. I'd rather be dead." Francesca really appreciates her privileged status involving class and affluence as her cold attitude to working-class servant James (John Slater) shows when he attempts to rise above his social role by becoming too friendly! Toward the end of the film, Peter reveals that he is divorced: "She just walked out on me." Although Max appears to care for Francesca, he initially offers her an affair and not marriage. When he removes her from Larsen's care over concern for her health, the psychiatrist criticizes his motives and not those of Nicholas. He urges her return to the hospital. Max later decides to marry her, but by then it is too late. The cured and glowing Francesca rushes down the stairs into the arms of her former oppressor, ironically described by Larsen as "the one she is in love with, cannot be happy without, or the one she trusts."

FIGURE 8. Francesca (Ann Todd) desires return to a brutal masculine world in *The Seventh Veil.*

The Seventh Veil succeeds in its aim of restoring English roses to the arms of a returning, psychologically disturbed veteran while rejecting "un-British" alternatives of affairs, brief encounters, and divorces marking wartime society. The two actors playing Francesca's lovers represent North American and European threats to the British female. Although never approaching the brash vulgarity of Bonar Colleano, Hugh McDermott specialized in playing American roles throughout his career in British cinema and television. He undoubtedly embodies British xenophobic attitudes toward Yanks, "overpaid, oversexed, and over here." *The Seventh Veil* reveals conservative hegemonic values aiming to structure desire in accordance with postwar definitions of normality. However, other alternative voices also appear during this period.

CHAPTER THREE

The Wartime Archers

The collaborative work of Michael Powell and Emeric Pressburger is now fully associated with British cinema as Ealing comedies were previously. Due to critical work by Ian Christie and others as well as Martin Scorsese's enthusiastic championship, the place of the Archers in British cinema is now assured. But such positioning contains limitations. It may isolate their work within certain critical categories while ignoring its broader aspects. The work of the Archers is certainly not realist, but neither does it belong exclusively to fantastic realms. Many of their films reveal hybrid associations. For example, although Powell (1987, 389) "decided on complete naturalism" for *One of Our Aircraft Is Missing* (1942) in contrast to his usual preferences, the film displays a complex mixture of various styles. Formally, it is a realist British wartime film. But it also deliberately avoids the classical realist linear style of narration. It begins in the middle, jumps backward in time, and moves abruptly forward in its climax. When the empty plane crashes, the Archers depict this by using the then-outmoded iris technique of silent cinema. Toward the end of their collaboration, Powell and Pressburger worked on two films belonging to the dominant fifties war movie genre, *The Battle of the River Plate* (1956) and *Ill Met by Moonlight* (1957). Although both films are lesser achievements, they still exhibit faint traces of those "discordant" elements characterizing their major works. In *The Battle of the River Plate* (a.k.a. *Pursuit of the Graf Spee*), the Archers film the declining hours of the Graf Spee using light-

ing techniques reminiscent of a Wagnerian *Twilight of the Gods.* In the latter film, Dirk Bogarde's Major Leigh-Fermor first appears wearing a
highly feminized (to British eyes) Greek national dress exhibiting transna-
tional and transgender characteristics, supposedly the exclusive prerogative of Gainsborough melodramas.

The previous examples are admittedly marginal aspects of disappointing films. But they do reveal certain major characteristics of the
filmic style of the Archers—fluidity and heterogeneity. Their films are
neither entirely realist nor fantastic. Furthermore, despite groundbreaking
critical work undertaken over the past few decades, the films of Powell
and Pressburger should not be divorced from their cultural and historical
contexts no matter how rich and strange they may initially appear to be.
Both director and scenarist were certainly influenced by their respective
cultural contexts, but they achieved their major successes in the forties
and fifties, decades that experienced significant changes within British
society. Although the excessive romantic agony of films such as *The Red
Shoes* and *The Tales of Hoffmann* appear worlds apart from traditional
British cinematic representations, they also display structures of desire
echoing those within contemporary films. The Archers' films exhibit
dynamic male and female representations involving oscillating gender and
performative roles. In *The Red Shoes,* Lermontov and Vicky symbiotically
resist and feed off each other's desires. Dominator and dominated frequently change roles. This characterizes not only the fantasy films of the
Archers but also their other works associated with an earlier period of
wartime cinema.

Powell and Pressburger first collaborated on *The Spy in Black*
(1939), a Korda production written specially for Conrad Veidt and
Valerie Hobson. Although filmed before the declaration of war, it became
a smash hit when it opened in Leicester Square the week of Neville
Chamberlain's fateful announcement. *The Spy in Black* is an early work
often neglected like the commercial follow-up *Contraband* (1940). However, in *A Life in Movies* (335–36), Powell recognizes amusing contrasts
between the film and its reception: "It didn't matter that the hero was a
heroic German. It didn't matter that all the values and sympathies of the
story were in direct contradiction to the current course of events. It was a
war picture, all about submarines and spies, full of action and suspense,
looking authentic. The British Navy triumphs in the end and it was all
lovely!" Powell hints at the fact that there is much more than meets the
eye in the film.

FIGURE 9. An international triangle of desire. Conrad Veidt, Valerie Hobson, and Sebastian Shaw in *The Spy in Black*.

The Spy in Black may certainly be categorized as a World War I film anticipating another future conflict. In 1917, U-boat Captain Hardt (Conrad Veidt) finds himself reluctantly employed in John Buchan's "great game" on a mission to destroy the British fleet anchored off Scapa Flow. He makes contact with German agent Fraulein Thiele (Valerie Hobson), who masquerades as kidnapped schoolteacher Anne Burnett (June Duprez). Hardt finds his new "commander" in league with British naval traitor Lieutenant Ashington (Sebastian Shaw) politically and sexually. However, Hardt eventually discovers himself the victim of a trap set by British naval intelligence. Fraulein Thiele is actually Joan Blacklock, the wife of Commander Blacklock, who performs the role of Lieutenant Ashington. Although *The Spy in Black* stylistically belongs to espionage and war movie genres, it thematically exhibits many traits within the more fantastic works of Powell and Pressburger, particularly those involving desire and frustration.

When Hardt leaves his submarine, he finds his natural male authority subordinated to a female from whom he must take orders. Although Hardt finds himself in a destabilizing role-reversal situation, he refuses to masquerade as a spy by wearing his own tweed suit fitted with British labels by his German intelligence. Hardt prefers his own uniform. When Joan sees this, she counters Hardt's comments concerning his military gender privilege, "If I am to be shot, it is as an officer, not as a spy," with her knowledge of a vulnerable feminine status, "Being a civilian, I have no defenses." However, she gives orders and locks Hardt in his room every night like a little boy. Despite temporary gender and national reversals, both characters begin to form a deep romantic attraction to each other, which calls into question their respective missions and wartime allegiances. Since Anne/Joan is married to Ashington/Blacklock, her brief embrace and kiss with Hardt threatens to elevate desire above her British national identity. This does not happen. Duty reigns. Hardt escapes arrest by the overbearing Blacklock, and the film's sympathies are clearly on his side. The film ends with Hardt "going down" with his ship to join his men in the depths and Joan reunited with her husband.

The Spy in Black is less a generic product and more one anticipating the Archers' later interest in the blurring of national and sexual boundaries. Despite different missions and nationalities, Hardt and Joan feel powerful desires toward each other that threaten to blur divisive national identities and cinematic traditions. Hardt wishes to take Joan back to Germany and eroticize her into being "the only woman wearing silk stockings." But ideologically repressive forces and conservative narrative resolution oppose this. When Hardt overhears Blacklock and Joan plotting his arrest, he is filmed back to camera in a shadowy, crucified position emphasizing feelings of national and sexual betrayal. At certain moments in the film, barriers between the participants threaten to collapse, especially those involving cosmopolitan internationalism (personified by the Veidt of Weimar Republic cinema) and insular Britishness (Hobson's typical national female roles). But the free play of desire never occurs. When Joan later realizes her actions turn Hardt into a suicidal warrior on board the captured ferry, her words reveal awareness of sexual betrayal rather than any care for the passengers. "We are at the mercy of a man who cares not for his life or ours. And it is all my fault. I forgot the war kills every fine, decent feeling." She blames herself for expressing desire under the circumstances. *The Spy in Black* differs from other contemporary British films by revealing the presence of an emergent "structure of desire" striving for expression as well as expressing explicit regret for its nonrealization.

Contraband contains no development of the significant insights contained within *The Spy in Black*. However, *One of Our Aircraft is Missing* does develop new expressions of ideas suggested by the earlier film. Like Captain Hardt, the six-man crew of B for Bertie find themselves isolated in a strange environment. To reach the Dutch coast and escape to England, the crew members have to divest themselves of nationality and uniform and place themselves under the command of strong, independent women such as schoolteacher Els Meertens (Pamela Brown) and landowner Jo de Vries (Googie Withers). Jo engages in a masquerade similar to that of Joan in *The Spy in Black*. She performs the role of an Anglophobic quisling to aid the Dutch resistance. While Jo acknowledges German propaganda listing her husband as killed in a phony British air raid, she knows he is in Britain broadcasting for Dutch Free Radio. Although Jo appears a positive figure by aiding the flyers in the film, her masquerade contains darker overtones threatening the stability of traditional submissive female images in contemporary British cinema.

In her first appearance Jo wears trousers as she guides the airmen to safety. Her guise anticipates the male attire worn by Margaret Lockwood in *The Wicked Lady* three years later. Like Els, she is strong and assertive. When the airmen first meet Els, they do not know whether she will betray or help them. The male group's encounter with a different type of female places them in subordinate positions. Although Yorkshireman Tom Earn-shaw (Eric Portman) later acclaims the qualities of Dutch resistance females, asserting that British women "would do the same if they had half a chance," his comments are double-edged. With the exception of Jet van Dieren (Joyce Redman), it is doubtful if the airmen would really welcome an England populated by strong females presenting challenging images of attraction, desire, and danger. Although Jo later relaxes in evening gown with the airmen and states, "It's nice to be a women again, even for half an hour," she uses female masquerade devices to overpower three German soldiers like a *film noir* femme fatale. *One of Our Aircraft Is Missing*'s enemy territory is occupied not only by Germans but also by powerful, alluring foreign women contradicting traditional images of British femininity.

The masquerade is a dangerous game for all. Like Richard in *Caravan*, the airmen change costume, enter dangerous territory, and encounter exotic females before they finally return to an all-male world of safety represented by naval officer Roland Culver. Former actor Frank Shelley (Hugh Williams) makes the most transgressive costume change. He dresses as a Dutch female. Temporarily missing wireless operator Bob Ashley (Emrys Jones) later reappears in his former prewar role of football player. Despite the rationale for Frank's own form of masquerade (as a former actor he enjoys playing roles), his particular choice involves class, gender, and national transgression. While other airmen don working-class Dutch clothes, Frank wears female attire. This not only places Frank in a dangerously transgressive boundary role paralleling Jo's first appearance but also aligns him with the taboo category represented by quisling De Jong (Robert Helpmann). De Jong is not just a traitor to his nation. His very manner of fussy, effeminate dress and behavior reveals him as an embodiment of the logical conclusions of transgressive behavior. Helpmann's role also parallels his similarly constructed character of Wycroft in *Caravan*, where he performs a gay parody of Stewart Granger's masculine hero, Richard. De Jong also has certain associations with Frank and Jo. He is a music lover as seen by the records he mistakenly gives to the Germans. When Frank's wife sings on the radio one evening, he performs the role of musical tutor, guiding her recital from afar. Jo's unseen husband also performs on Dutch Free Radio. When Frank first meets Jo, he enacts an un-British, unmasculine performative gesture by kissing her hand, an action he repeats on their parting. These three characters have connections with transgressive realms. But once Frank reaches safety, he changes back into his Air Force uniform, becoming once again a masculine team player. The Holland of *One of Our Aircraft Is Missing* is a world of dangerous, transgressive desire in more senses than one.

Strictly speaking, *The Silver Fleet* (1943) is not a Powell and Pressburger film. It was co-directed by Vernon Sewell and Gordon Wellesley, who display joint credit in the manner of the Archers. Although Powell and Pressburger agreed to make another Dutch Resistance movie only as producers, it is still an Archers film originating from their production base. Powell and Pressburger were filming *The Life and Death of Colonel Blimp* at the time and not actively involved with the film. Powell (400) states that although Pressburger was to supervise the writing of *The Silver Fleet*'s script, "he would not be directly involved except as co-producer." But Powell also (413) mentions that *The Silver Fleet* was "very much Emeric's production." According to Kevin MacDonald (200), Sewell altered Pressburger's screenplay, eliminating theatrical references to Nazi brutality and racism, thus "dulling the impact of the story." However, the film has fascinating links with other themes in the Archers.

Like *One of Our Aircraft Is Missing*, the film opens by revealing an enigmatic situation. After the dedication to the Royal Netherlands government, "I know death hath ten thousand doors for men to take the exits," the first image displays a sunken German U-boat. The camera tracks in to the U-boat and then uses an iris-out to reveal the dead crew within. The next shot is a midclose-up of Jaap van Leyden (Ralph Richardson). A dissolve reveals the following image of a written message: "Goodbye my dear wife." Another dissolve follows, showing Helene (Googie Withers) reading this text. The camera then tracks out as it shows her sitting at Jaap's desk and reading the letter.

The Silver Fleet superficially resembles a wartime patriotic film, but, like the opening of *One of Our Aircraft Is Missing*, romantic images influence the film. However, rather than encountering another deserted Marie Celeste empty bomber, viewers enter a world of romantic agony in which the hero has died not for art, like Vicky in *The Red Shoes*, but for love of country. However, patriotism and desire are not inseparable. Shipbuilder Jaap decides to adopt the past historical theatrical role of seventeenth-century Dutch patriot Piet Hein to defeat another occupying force. He performs a quisling role before his devoted wife and fellow countryman to accomplish the mission of destroying the U-boat and major figures of the German occupation force. For Jaap, it is a solitary performance. His acclaim will be posthumous.

Jaap dies a lonely man. Before he leaves on his last mission, Helene allows her political doubts to overcome her romantic feelings and condemns her husband as a quisling. Although he knocks on her bedroom door, pleading in vain, "If you love me, open the door," his efforts are useless. His physical position in the frame, his back to the camera, resembles Captain Hardt's in the betrayal scene of *The Spy in Black* as well as that of Vicky's lover in *The Ballet of the Red Shoes*. Like Hardt, Jaap leaves his normal everyday life due to circumstances beyond his control and moves into a world of national and romantic isolation. As he listens outside the window to the schoolmistress (Kathleen Byron) reciting the story of Piet Hein to her class, he feels a sense both of calling and of isolation. The schoolmistress appears in midclose-up, emphasizing Jaap's realization of his call to national glory. But window bars separate him from those inside, foreshadowing his future emotional isolation. Jaap's wife eventually condemns him as a traitor and denies him any romantic consolation during his last hours of freedom. Like Hardt, Jaap dies a lonely death beneath the sea, the sacrificial victim of a national cause paradoxically frustrating the realization of romantic desire. The patriotic text of *The Silver Fleet* forms an ironic counterpoint to darker structures of desire existing within the Archers' work and contemporary British cinema. It suggests that wartime issues of duty, service, and patriotism are sometimes damaging to human relationships. This theme later occurs in Ealing Studios' *Against the Wind* (1948).

Jaap begins his last journal entry with, "I never thought that the last hours would be so difficult." He finishes his farewell message by sublimating his romantic feelings for Helene to the good of his nation, which needs his sacrifice to ensure continuity: "A nation will always live when it has people ready to die." Wartime patriotic themes are certainly present in *The Silver Fleet*, as well as those romantic agonies of love, death, and separation peculiar to other Archers films. Jaap is another tragic hero like Hardt, Lermontov, Hoffmann, Langsdorff, and Mark Lewis, sacrificed on the altar of some unobtainable goal whether Art, Love, or Patriotism. Although Powell's memoirs suggest his reluctance toward undertaking this project, *The Silver Fleet* does contain recognizable links to other Archers productions.

The climax of *The Silver Fleet* resembles a film that influenced Powell throughout his career: Rex Ingram's *Mare Nostrum* (1926). When writing about the doomed Captain Langsdorff (Peter Finch) of *The Battle of the River Plate* (1956), Powell (1987, 65) recalls "the very first film I ever worked on involved another doomed man who died at sea." In addition to *Mare Nostrum*, other Ingram films, such as *The Four Horsemen of the*

Apocalypse (1921), *The Prisoner of Zenda* (1922), and *The Garden of Allah* (1927), contain significant themes of desire, frustration, and separation influencing Powell throughout his career. Although set in Holland and not a direct Archers collaboration, *The Silver Fleet* is another example of the team's fascination with those peculiarly British psychic romantic agonies involving desire and frustration.

The Life and Death of Colonel Blimp remains one of the team's most enduring achievements both in artistry and in national character depiction. Although various studies analyze the film's emphasis upon the change from an old to a new order (as well as the possible continuity between both), desire has received little attention. The film's Blimp, Lieutenant-Colonel Clive Wynne-Candy (Roger Livesey), undergoes a physical metamorphosis from a reckless young soldier to a venerable lovable version of David Low's *Evening Standard* cartoon character during selected scenes in a forty-year narrative. But Candy remains constant in one particular aspect: the realm of desire. As Powell wrote in his letter to Wendy Hiller (Christie, 17), not only is Candy caught within the mold of the typical English gentleman but he puts a female on a pedestal "quite against her will or inclination." He constantly recreates her with new object choices. *The Life and Death of Colonel Blimp* is a touching story in many ways. But the most poignant feature involves the image of an awkward and self-absorbed man who loses his one chance of romantic happiness in his youth and stubbornly recreates it throughout his entire life. As Candy solidifies in both girth and attitude during his later years, so does his quest for the eternal woman. Ironically, although all three women (Edith, Barbara, and Angela, played by Deborah Kerr) resemble each other, they also represent the changing social attitudes of their particular eras. While Candy develops into a traditional icon and only slowly realizes the need for change, the women in *Colonel Blimp* all represent new personalities and potentials British males are slow to recognize. The published screenplay emphasizes this point. Powell and Pressburger (Christie, 111–12) describe Edith as a "New Woman" who "intended to live her own life and know her own mind." In the Cafe Hohenzollern scene, she reacts with "delicate scorn" (125) to Candy's suggestion of an "appropriate" career. Barbara chooses to work as a nurse during World War I while Angela is a forties woman in uniform acting as Candy's driver. All these women represent different female role models during various historical eras. But for Clive Candy, they are one and the same. Darker overtones complement the sentimental elements within this film. They suggest the existence of enduring psychopathological British character traits stubbornly stressing continuity and tradition as a means of controlling any new social changes, especially those affecting females.

The Life and Death of Colonel Blimp analyzes an England caught between a now-stagnant tradition and unforeseen future. But it is also a tragedy dealing with the thwarted expression of desire significantly occurring during periods of wartime: the Boer War, World War I, and World War II. The film opens in 1902 against a background of colorful genteel Edwardian tradition. But the nostalgic, bright colors already represent a lost world fondly recreated by carefully chosen evocative set designs. World War I sequences reveal a world of khaki and darkness. The film's contemporary scenes mix these color designs together in an undefinable manner, suggesting resolution and uncertainty over what a future postwar period will have in store for its characters.

The film originated from a discarded scene in *One of Our Aircraft Is Missing*, where Sir George (Godfrey Tearle) recognizes his youthful side in another airman, pointing out that the younger man would be like him many years in the future. This continuity theme led to the genesis of *The Life and Death of Colonel Blimp*, but the film also echoes other features of wartime cinema. Livesey's Blimp represents a satirical view of the Englishman "muddling through" from one disaster to another as recognized by Ann in *The Foreman Went to France*. We first meet young Candy as a decorated Victoria Cross recipient near the end of the Boer War. Despite her 1902 setting, Edith is both a "New Woman" and a representative forties wartime female. Belonging to a once-prosperous family, she has experienced downward mobility and moved to Berlin to work as a governess to learn German. She teaches English in Germany, so she can eventually return home and teach the German language to English students. Edith indirectly calls Candy's attention to negative propaganda spread by Kaunitz, which the War Office chooses to ignore. She and Candy never develop any romantic involvement, but the potential exists. However, it becomes thwarted as one scene in the hospital shows when young Candy fails to read Edith's expression of interest before Theo enters the room to join them in a game of cards. From that moment on (as Powell himself notes in the Criterion laserdisc audio commentary), Candy has lost. When Theo announces his love for Edith, Candy plays the English gentleman role to perfection and congratulates them. He only feels his loss on the journey home.

At this point of the film Candy still realizes the difference between image and reality. He recognizes his mistake in taking Edith's sister out on his first night home. Clive then settles down to live in the den of his aunt's home, filling the wall with trophies from his various expeditions. The film then moves from another wartime narrative to another.

Candy's World War I discovery of Barbara and his subsequent loss have parallels with Hitchcock's *Vertigo* (1958). Although the mood and narrative of both films differ, they equally involve quests by obsessive males to recreate lost love objects in another woman. Despite *Blimp's* warmer tones and Candy's more attractive persona, the film foreshadows *Vertigo's* romantic agony but presents it in a more subtle manner. Candy accidentally discovers Barbara in the virginal confines of a nunnery. She is among a group of British nurses temporarily billeted there. To his surprise, Candy finds his perfect woman revirginalized, unmarried, and waiting for him to engage in another version of a pursuit he bungled long ago. The lyrically fond depiction of this brief encounter contains perverse undertones. Ironically, the English gentleman Candy displays more dark romantic characteristics than his Germanic counterpart, Theo (Anton Walbrook), by indulging in a highly questionable repetitive, compulsive mode of behavior. His search for the ideal object foreshadows the dark pursuit of Mark Lewis for the perfect image in *Peeping Tom* (1960).

The Life and Death of Colonel Blimp contains several structures of desire characteristic of British wartime cinema. Powell and Pressburger's females are dynamic, assertive, and independently attractive figures. But they are still liable to recuperation and containment within restrictively ideological controlling realms of wartime and postwar society. But however dark the Archers' British romantic agonies may appear, they never echo dominantly conservative resolutions of contemporary British films by attempting to reaffirm conclusively status quo ideas. Powell and Pressburger's films often depict a sense of tragic loss for both male and female victims as diverse characters such as Thomas Colpepper of *A Canterbury Tale*, Vicky in *The Red Shoes*, and Hazel in *Gone to Earth* all illustrate.

Candy's romantic pursuit pathologically foreshadows the perverse world of *Peeping Tom*. It suggests the presence of dark, repressed passions existing within the soul of an English gentleman. He may not kill his victims in searching for the perfect image like Mark Lewis, but he still wishes to possess them. Candy loses Edith but rediscovers her in the figure of Barbara Wynne (whose surname more than coincidentally corresponds with his name, Clive Wynne-Candy!). Candy finds Barbara in the aptly named "Crown of Thorns" Convent. The editing sequence unites the perspectives of Candy and the audience by using shot-reverse imagery. It complicity links both in a British masculine cinematic gaze. Candy later pursues and successfully woos Barbara, achieving a brief period of domestic happiness until her premature death. Although the film presents three female objects of Candy's desire, the screenplay also mentions that there were many others. After the chance meeting between Candy and Barbara in the convent, Candy's batman, Murdoch (John Laurie), suggests that neither Edith nor Barbara is the sole object of his master's peculiarly British male national pursuit. "There was that girl in the film, sir. You remember, you went nine times. And there was that girl in the group out of the Bystander. We lost it in the big Push" (Christie, 210).

Barbara is the most enigmatic of Candy's females. She appears to have little personality like Edith and Angela and abruptly disappears from the film. But her character is significant. Why does Barbara die suddenly? Certain sequences revealing her perceptions provide the answer. When Barbara and Candy visit the internment camp for the latter's abortive meeting with Theo, she shares the skepticism of camp commandant Major Davies (Harry Welchman) about the German character. Both implicitly recognize Candy's naivete about Theo at this point of the film. Barbara represents a potential obstacle for the homosocial bond linking Candy and Theo. Furthermore, as Powell (411) recognizes, Barbara and Candy's last scene together represents something "which scandalized Emeric—the anti-feminist" when she takes the sexual initiative following her husband's lines, "But what will I do if I don't hum?" Since she expresses the independent sexuality of a "wicked lady" and breaks Clive's female pedestal image, she suffers punishment for her transgression. She significantly interrupts Clive's humming of "Mignon" in this scene, the musical link between him and Theo. Ironically, the last image of Barbara in the film is of her portrait hanging prominently in Candy's trophy room. Theo does not share in his friend's desire. He never recognizes Clive's fascination with Barbara's resemblance to his deceased wife and comments, "It's a strange place to hang such a lovely picture."

Although Angela represents the contemporary wartime female in uniform performing a man's job, her choice by Candy has ominous overtones. It foreshadows one theme in *Peeping Tom*. When driving Theo home in the blackout, Angela tells him she worked before the war as a photographic model! After light penetrates the car's interior, Theo then notes the resemblance to Edith and recognizes the nature of Candy's attraction to her. But the dark figures of Thomas Colpepper and Mark Lewis also lurk beneath the deceptively benevolent nature of Clive Candy's personality.

Eventually, Candy realizes how his "Blimp" characteristics hinder appropriate understanding of a new world of total war. But whether he finally understands the nature of his perverse desires is another matter. Pressburger regarded the film as providing a particular national insight into "the brute power of sexuality to shape our lives" (MacDonald, 265). However, the same pathological set of behavioral patterns may continue into the future. Spud (James McKechnie) and Angela represent the new generation in the film. But they may soon resemble their predecessors by falling into traditional patterns of British behavior. Ironically, in 1943 David Low published an ingenious autobiographical satire in the January 15 *Evening Standard*. It anticipated Thatcherism and New Labour by several decades. "Blimp" launched broadsides against subjects such as the Welfare State, which "will rot the stamina of the nation." Capitalism contained better knowledge of "what is good for the country than members of Parliament, because private people are inspired by the Profit Motive which is the spirit of service" (Christie 1994 (6), 307). Ironically, a 1990s *Sunday Times* opinion column later commended the Blimps for foreseeing the dangerous nature of the British Welfare State. *The Life and Death of Colonel Blimp* engaged in an admittedly gentle attack against the outmoded attitudes that hindered the war effort. But it also revealed dangerous psychological mechanisms of perverse desire threatening female independence and crippling British male development.

A Canterbury Tale (1944) belongs among the Archers' most significant achievements. As Powell (437) commented, "we were explaining to the Americans, and to our own people, the spiritual values and the traditions we were fighting for." Powell and Pressburger delivered a deep, sincere commitment and artistic conviction into this film. This appears in the closing thirty minutes where three pilgrims receive their respective blessings while another character undergoes penance. But, as with most Archers productions, darker elements lie beneath the surface.

The film begins with a prologue set in Chaucer's day. It then rapidly cuts from the falcon sent by the Knight (Esmond Knight) to a Spitfire before returning to a soldier (also played by Esmond Knight). This sequence stresses the spatial and temporal continuity of Britain's present and historical past. The film proper begins by showing three travelers on a train journey to Canterbury. They arrive in a nearby station during the blackout. According to Pressburger's original synopsis, they represent "one who came seven thousand miles, one who came three hundred miles, and one, the furthest traveller of all, who came from the great city of London, fifty miles away" (MacDonald, 236). They are, respectively, American Sergeant Bob Johnson (Sergeant John Sweet), ATS girl Alison Smith (Sheila Sim), and Sergeant Peter Gibbs (Dennis Price). All have suffered disillusionment in their personal lives as well as experienced dislocating effects of wartime existence.

The three join in a search for a mysterious Glue Man who terrorizes any females who wander out late at night. They soon discover that the likely suspect is local Justice of the Peace Thomas Colpepper (Eric Portman). Since the film leads toward the blessings three modern pilgrims eventually receive, the Glue Man episode appears to be a distraction. Many contemporary reviewers experienced problems with Colpepper's character in relation to the film. On a spiritual level, Colpepper's role achieves resolution at the climax when he undergoes penance in Canterbury Cathedral for his punitive nightly expeditions against errant females. However, Colpepper's character has crucial connections to the film's structure of desire and manner of resolution.

Colpepper's attack on Alison performs several functions in the narrative. It delays the journey of the three pilgrims and allows them to achieve their various desires within Canterbury Cathedral. Bob eventually meets his army buddy, who bears letters from a girlfriend he has not heard from for several weeks. Alison discovers her sweetheart is alive. His formerly rigid class-conscious father welcomes her into the family. Peter eventually fulfills his artistic desire by playing a real church organ prior to his other role in a D-Day pilgrimage from which he may never return. But although the three main pilgrims eventually understand the English countryside's role of tradition and continuity, narrative resolution occurs by the same type of violent activity characterizing films such as *This England* and *Went the Day Well?* Colpepper explains the Glue Man's motives on the final train journey to Canterbury.

> "He didn't think what he did was a crime . . . some parents have to force their children to go to school. Is that a crime?"
>
> "You're not going to defend pouring glue on to people?"
>
> "Certainly not. But I am going to defend pouring knowledge into people's heads, by force if necessary."
>
> "What knowledge?"
>
> "Knowledge of our country." (MacDonald, 237)

As self-styled heavenly messenger, Colpepper's aim is laudable. But he achieves it only by inflicting a reign of terror on his village and enforcing patriarchal prewar codes against girls wanting a "good time." Although Colpepper appeals to the three modern pilgrims by stating his intention to protect the interests of husbands and sweethearts serving abroad, his real motivation lies in getting soldiers to attend his lantern slide lectures. But, despite his sincerity and enthusiasm, his male audiences are not interested, as one sequence clearly shows. They are there because they have nothing better to do. One soldier (John Slater) even reads a book during the presentation and uses the light from Colpepper's projector to aid him! The victims Alison interviews in her search for the Glue Man's identity are clearly not "good time girls" of the Jean Kent variety. They are ordinary women who enjoy the independence working in the formerly male-defined occupations wartime offers them. Alison travels to the village to work on Colpepper's farm. When Colpepper finds out that his requested worker is female, he refuses to allow her to work in his domain. Despite Powell's later protestations against comparisons critics later noted between *A Canterbury Tale, The Red Shoes,* and *Peeping Tom* (MacDonald, 381), several associations do exist.

Colpepper's role anticipates the perversely aggressive characters of Boris Lermontov and Mark Lewis. They are all celibate males who devote themselves exclusively to their artistic goals by dominating others. Colpepper devotes himself to disseminating his love of the English pastoral tradition. But despite his laudable goal, the methods he uses to achieve it are as questionable as those used by Mark Lewis in *Peeping Tom.* Colpepper is a bachelor living at home with his mother. He exhibits aberrant behavior symptomatic of extreme sexual repression. His pathological devotion to his art has sexual overtones that attract others. Like Vicky in *The Red Shoes,* Alison begins to fall under his spell. A platonic romantic attachment begins until she receives news about her lost lover and forgets Colpepper.

Immediately following Colpepper's attack, the three pilgrims enter a misty village landscape shot in somber expressionist lighting. They encounter a particular realm of dark desire dominated by a gargoyle prominently featured outside Colpepper's office, which foreshadows those seen outside Lermontov's Nice office in *The Red Shoes.* When Alison reports the Glue Man's attack to Colpepper, he significantly points to "an old ducking stool very sensibly used to silence talkative women." Later, his misogynistic attitude begins to weaken when he sees that Alison is the only member of a uniformed audience interested in his lantern slide lecture. Powell links Alison and Colpepper by significantly lit close-ups articulating their initial attraction to each other. It is almost as if Colpepper performs the role of a magician enchanting a lady into his deep love for the English countryside, a love that contains the potential either to change his attitudes toward women or to submit them to his domination. Later, Alison hears the sounds of the original Canterbury pilgrims on the old road overlooking the cathedral. She sits with Colpepper on the grass, where they are featured on opposite sides of the frame in typical romantic imagery. Alison becomes the one modern pilgrim sympathetic to Colpepper. When she discovers the now moth-eaten caravan, the scene of her past love affair, confined to a small garage and bereft of its tires due to wartime requisition, she becomes upset. Colpepper then comforts her, as if they have now become symbiotically attuned to each other. He criticizes the "impermanent nature" of a caravan, which has to be "moving some time or another." The scene appears to suggest a romantic union between them. But like Lermontov's thwarted approach to Vicky in *The Red Shoes*, destiny intervenes. Before Alison falls completely under his spell, she receives news of her sweetheart's survival and experiences the "miracle" of which Colpepper spoke earlier. "I believe in miracles for everyone. Shopgirls have more need of miracles than a millionaire." Her sweetheart's formerly hostile upper-class father welcomes her into his family, exemplifying the egalitarian nature of the People's War ideology. Colpepper suddenly vanishes from the scene. During his final appearance in *A Canterbury Tale*, he watches Alison pass him in the cathedral on her way to the service. Accompanied by her future father-in-law, she is oblivious to his presence. Colpepper displays a look of sadness on his face. He is nearly as anguished as Lermontov when he loses Vicky in the climax of *The Red Shoes* and as knowledgeable about lost opportunities and desires as Mark in *Peeping Tom*. Colpepper becomes the first in Powell's artistic trajectory of tragically creative masculine monsters. Like the Frankenstein monster of Mary Shelley's novel, they lack personal and social alternatives offering them other positive channels for creativity and desire. Colpepper's overpowering love for the English countryside proves as fatal for him as ballet does for Lermontov and photography for Mark Lewis.

Unlike Vicky, Alison does not "die for art." She experiences temptation by temporarily falling under Colpepper's spell. Alison becomes overwhelmed by a powerful form of desire projected onto her by a controlling male figure. But she is saved from submission by a "miracle," allowing her prewar northern, working-class identity access into a higher class system. Like Eric Portman's later role in the Rodney Ackland-Pressburger scripted *Wanted for Murder* (1948), Colpepper may have wished "salvation" from a redeeming female, but it would be exclusively on his own terms. Ironically, Colpepper's individualistic coercive efforts at his own form of heritage industry anticipates later developments begun in the Thatcher era. As Corner and Harvey show, the eighties and nineties saw a growth industry of refurbished artifacts from Britain's industrial revolution displaying ideologically manufactured images of past glory for the tourist trade "untrammelled by historical fact." These displays never reveal the coercive dark underside of historical violence and exploitation. Colpepper's contemporary championship of the Kent heritage depends on violence and female oppression for its very existence. During the train journey to Canterbury, he tells the three modern pilgrims, "If harm has been done I shall have to pay. . . . There are higher courts than the bench of local magistrates," His listeners eventually receive their blessings while he undergoes penance for his male hubris. When Colpepper replies negatively to Alison's question about inviting women to his lectures, her final comment, "Pity," and the accompanying shot, revealing his recognition of a deliberately conceived structured absence in his artistic world, speaks volumes.

A *Canterbury Tale* thus presents a complex and contradictory view of the English mentality offering no easy resolution. Both Bob and Alison achieve their personal blessings, which will eventually lead to sexual fulfillment. Alison's prewar, illicit relationship with her lover receives legitimation within a higher class structure, but it is doubtful whether it will ever parallel the potential excitement of the unknown romantic relationship offered to her by Colpepper. Peter achieves the highest form of his artistic desire by playing the organ in Canterbury Cathedral, an act he will probably never surpass even if he survives World War II. Colpepper remains in Canterbury to undergo his penance. The film leaves open the question of his possible future recidivism. However, *A Canterbury Tale* uniquely reveals the dangerous nature of repressed British desire in a film defying any convenient generic classification.

Although *I Know Where I'm Going* (1945) complements *A Canterbury Tale*'s quest for spiritual postwar values, its mood is completely different. Like the previous film, it adopts a style akin to Latin American "magical realism" but lacks problematically coercive aspects associated with Colpepper's role as a messenger in the earlier work. The film deals with the desire of Joan Webster (Wendy Hiller) to rise above her class status and marry a rich man. As the credit sequence reveals, Joan knows where she is going from babyhood onward. At eighteen she prefers dining at the best hotel to attending movies. By twenty-five she has successfully enticed a rich chemical manufacturer into marriage. Despite rationing and other wartime restrictions, Joan's future husband, Sir Robert Bellingham (known cannily to the islanders as "the rich man of Kiloran") plans an expensive wedding on the Hebridean island of Kiloran. Joan intends to travel there and marry her rich catch. On the train she dreams of a future life of postwar affluence and indulgence.

Despite her ambitions and the meticulous transport schedule plotted for her by Bellingham's corporation, Joan finds herself stranded on the Isle of Mull due to a severe storm preventing her crossing. While she waits for the weather to change, she becomes fascinated by the virtues of Scottish highland life and the attractive persona of the real "laird of Kiloran," Torquil MacNeil (Roger Livesey). She also meets Catriona (Pamela Brown), an old sweetheart of Torquil, who enjoys her nonaffluent lifestyle on the island. Despite her marriage to an Englishman named Potts (who is on service overseas), Catriona is a free, independent spirit living in harmony with her environment. Eventually, Joan decides to give up her materialistic desires and enter into marriage with Torquil.

As Kevin MacDonald (244) states, the film's values "hardly seem to differ from those of the standard Hollywood romantic-comedy: love conquers all, and money isn't everything." But as well as recognizing the passionate, almost self-destructive nature of a romantic agony at odds with most British cinematic representations, MacDonald notes the historical relevance of the film's anti-materialism. He quotes from Cyril Connolly's (149) verdict on the 1945 General Election as a reaction against Tory prewar foreign policy as well as "a vote against the religion of money" and "the millionaire hoodlums." This contemporary aspect also appears on the notes of the British videocassette release of *I Know Where I'm Going*. Many scenes in the film reinforce this message. Torquil tells Joan that being poor does not necessarily mean having no money but "something quite different." Catriona later supports this in her conversation with Joan following her unsuccessful attempt to reach Kiloran. When Joan suggests that she and the dignified, nonaffluent Rebecca Crozier (Nancy Price) could sell their property and live elsewhere, Catriona replies, "Yes. But money isn't everything." The exchange also complements the critique of Joan's selfish materialistic nature made by Bridie (Margot Fitzsimmons) when she learns about Joan's bribe to Kenny (Murdo Morrison) over undertaking the dangerous journey to Kiloran. When Joan visits Bellingham's friends, the Robinsons (Valentine Dyall and Catherine Lacey), she sees them existing in sterile isolation from the local community, preferring to play bridge rather than attend the Ceilidh held in honor of their gardener's diamond wedding. Their daughter (Petula Clark) exhibits the same perverse attraction, preferring to read rather than experience things. She resembles her counterpart in Hitchcock's *Shadow of a Doubt*. But Joan finds her defenses breaking down and sees her fascination with Torquil hindering her progress toward materialistic goals.

I Know Where I'm Going is certainly romantic in tone, paying homage to a Scottish ideal already disappearing at the time it was made. But the film is no sentimental escapist Brigadoon. Despite its escape from reality, it is really one of the most progressive Powell and Pressburger films dealing with a particular representation of desire. It suggests that an equal relationship between the sexes can occur only in a foreign land away from the contaminating class materialism of the English landscape. Before parting from Torquil for her ostensible journey to Kiloran, Joan takes the initiative and *asks him* to him to kiss her. Torquil immediately responds, and both embrace passionately. He makes one request, asking her to request pipers to play "The Nutbrown Maiden" at the wedding. Joan leaves, and Torquil watches her walk away. He then decides to enter the MacNeil castle and face the family curse without fear. Many generations before, the male Kiloran heirs were cursed by a woman punished by her husband for violating the restrictions of their unhappy marriage. Although Torquil heard of this curse since childhood from his nursemaid, he decides to enter. He undoubtedly wishes to embrace the curse and break family tradition as a means of possibly gaining Joan. Interestingly enough, Torquil decides to ignore a patriarchal system that condemned a female to death many years before in order to submit himself to a curse emanating from a realm usually regarded as accursed and other. The actual curse reads, "Never shall he leave this Castle a free man. He shall be chained to a woman until the end of his days and he shall die in his chains." Torquil's action turns the curse into his own personal blessing. As a reward for breaching family tradition, he hears pipes playing "The Nutbrown Maiden" and sees Joan walking behind the three pipers stranded on Mull during the storm who played during the Ceilidh celebration. They both walk away together.

The climax has a particular significance. Both Joan and Torquil decide to give up something that characterized their personal lives up to that point. Joan relinquishes her goal of an affluent, but loveless, marriage with Robert Bellingham. Torquil breaches a family tradition that he knows will result in his "entrapment." He makes the decision fully aware of the consequences. Both partners lose something, but they gain much more in the process. They have to make separate, independent decisions on the basis of equality rather than allow themselves to be dominated by higher patriarchal authorities whether Glue Man or ballet director. *I Know Where I'm Going* is romantic, idealistic, and hopelessly utopian. But by resolving desire outside the restrictive barriers of English culture, it suggests another avenue toward the positive realization of aspirations denied satisfactory fulfillment in other areas of British cinema. The film thus moves toward a more affirmative conclusion rather than the one facing Captain Hardt and Joan in *The Spy in Black*. Like *A Matter of Life and Death* and *The Small Back Room*, it offers an alternative to those deadly and frustrating stalemate situations seen in *A Canterbury Tale* and *The Red Shoes*.

CHAPTER FOUR

Utopian Desires

During wartime, the Ministry of Information formulated the concept of the People's War. As Calder notes, this ideological mechanism aimed at denying interwar divisions to ensure necessary solidarity to fight the enemy. Although manufactured from above, it played a significant role in certain wartime cinematic representations influencing personal and political hegemonic consensus. The People's War ideology also stimulated the Labour Party's electoral landslide of 1945. If Britain cynically experienced an illusionary "homes fit for heroes" ideology after World War I, a prevailing feeling now existed that conditions would change definitively after the conflict. Despite the success of pathologically conservative films such as *In Which We Serve* (1942) reinforcing monolithic class systems of gentlemen officers and forelock-tugging lower orders, others appeared expressing faint hopes for a better life in the future.

In many cases these films were little better than wish-fulfillment fantasies infected by dominant ideological structures. However, several attempted to express openly residual ideas competing against rigid structures dominating individual freedom and desire. The first group encompasses films by John Baxter, such as *Love on the Dole, The Common Touch* (both 1941), and *The Shipbuilders* (1944), as well as *The Halfway House, Waterloo Road* (both 1944), *This Happy Breed* and *Brief Encounter* (both 1945). But *They Came to a City* (1944) and *Perfect Strangers* (1945) differed from the above in significantly expressing important desires for a brave new world following the cessation of hostilities.

73

These films all feature traces of realism and fantasy in their composition. Although *The Common Touch* is ostensibly a realist narrative, it exhibits wish-fulfillment desires of a fantastic nature. Ealing Studios' *Halfway House* displays tensions involving fantasy and realism, which erupt into full expression in *Dead of Night* (1945). *They Came to a City* is Ealing's version of J. B. Priestley's theatrical fantasy displaying utopian aspirations shared by many hoping for a postwar Labour victory. Like Korda's Hollywood-influenced production *Perfect Strangers*, it emphasizes the collaborative nature of mutual sexual desire and the necessity of moving away from the past. As Murphy (1992, 40) points out, late wartime cinema contained a diverse mixture of realism and fantasy. However, despite optimistic hopes in these films, hesitation, failure of nerve, and poverty of desire (Barr, 17) as well as wish-fulfillment fantasies and overtly sentimental hopes characterized the immediate postwar world. Two 1945 films, *Dead of Night* and *The Agitator* contain pessimistic feelings contradicting optimistic hopes for a better tomorrow.

During the prewar period, any film version of Walter Greenwood's devastating attack on the misery of social deprivation and unemployment was taboo. However, eight years after its literary appearance, *Love on the Dole* reached the screen in an era more open to allowing some of the harsh realities of thirties British life to reach a wider audience. Greenwood's original novel focused upon the Salford Hardcastle family, especially young Harry, who moves from the shabby, genteel occupation of a pawnshop clerk to the dead-end nature of a shipbuilding apprenticeship in the depression era. After losing her Labour Party sweetheart, Larry Meath, Harry's sister, Sally, decides to prostitute herself not only to save her family from social deprivation but also to compensate herself for lost opportunities resulting from Larry's death. Ironically, had Larry lived, they would have fallen into the same squalid existence as her parents. Sally's only option in a depressed society dominated by social deprivation and hypocritical working class morality is to become the mistress of greasy bookie Sam Grundy. In her defiant outburst against her unforgiving father, Sally emphasizes that she has made an arrangement with Grundy on her own terms. She also condemns patriarchal oppression conditioning female existence in British society. Her father eventually excuses her and blames himself after realizing the impotence of his own situation. "What had he done for his children? Out of his despair rose a counter question which he clutched as a drowning man might a straw: What had he been *able* to do other than what had been done? The responsibility wasn't his. He'd worked all his life; he had given all he had to give" (Greenwood, 247).

The novel ends bleakly: "The melancholy hoot of a ship's siren sounded from the Salford Docks" (Greenwood, 256). But the film concludes on a more hopeful note, wishing for future change. In 1940, John Baxter's British National version of *Love on the Dole* opened to critical and popular acclaim. But as Peter Stead (1989, 72) notes, "there never was to be any serious attempt to build on the foundations laid by it," and Baxter's "subsequent work was never to be quite as satisfactory and it certainly received far less critical attention." However, serious flaws characterize the film. Despite Baxter's sympathy for the British version of the "lower depths," his films often exhibit excessive sentimentality and debilitatingly political visions that never move beyond George Orwell's apolitically vague definitions of commonsense "decency." Baxter's autobiographical notes emphasize that he regarded the film as a counterpoint to "the policy of laughter" he projected in his other work designed to relieve temporarily working-class misery. He also comments, "I felt the successful outcome of the war depended in no small measure on the loyalty and hard work of, for want of a better term, 'the working man'" (Brown & Aldgate, 78). Baxter's remarks not only display People's War ideological mechanisms but also parallel comments by Herbert Wilcox concerning British people's unquestioning natural patriotism in his autobiography, *Twenty Thousand Sunsets*. Although Brown and Aldgate (13) acknowledge censorship constraints affecting Baxter's films and applaud his attempts "to present the feelings and problems of people at the bottom of society's ladder at a time when many feature directors were still dazzled by the top rungs," his films often reveal debilitating images of political and personal desire.

British National acquired the rights to Ronald Gow's stage version of *Love on the Dole* in May 1940. Before reassignment to *This England*, David MacDonald was to direct with Greenwood as scriptwriter. Greenwood continued to work on the film as principal scenarist with additional contributions by Barbara K. Emary and Rollo Gamble. Most of Greenwood's plot remains in the film. But even wartime cinema could not allow the radical political implications of Greenwood's novel to reach the screen. Baxter honestly depicts the debilitating conditions of thirties unemployment. But he chooses particular narrative structures diluting any radically emergent expressions of politics and desire. Although Larry (Clifford Evans) still remains the dedicated, down-at-heel Labour Party activist discarded by local council colleagues when he becomes unemployed, the film blames his death indirectly on the dangerous machinations of an obviously evil and violent Communist Party agitator (John Slater). Certain scenes emphasize Larry's passivity within the original novel. Two sequences reinforce the impotent nature of relationships between naive and youthful Harry (Geoffrey Hibbert) and Helen (Joyce Howard) and their more mature counterparts, Sally (Deborah Kerr) and Larry. Harry and Helen's touching meeting on the unpolluted hillside overlooking Hankey Park precedes the sequence of Sally and Larry on a countryside ramble. Both pairs of lovers retreat briefly to an environment real-life circumstances will never allow them to enter. Their pastoral retreat is illusory and hopelessly escapist. Second, when Harry throws away a ticket he has kept from his brief Blackpool holiday with Helen, the camera follows its progress along a gutter in the Salford slums before it stops at the feet of Sally and Larry. Both couples are doomed by forces beyond their control. Although Sally usurps the traditional pattern of courtship by proposing to Larry and overcoming reservations about living on a low income, she recognizes his demasculinized social impotence after discovering that his redundancy will postpone their marriage. Despite her anger at his attitude, she wisely decides not to attack his passivity in an aggressive manner and contribute to his feelings of male insecurity. As in the novel, the possibility of their relationship surviving the depressing environment of Hankey Park is negative.

Baxter often depicts the forces conditioning relationships and social deprivation affecting Hankey Park's inhabitants by using transcendentally representational devices that deny significant historical and material conditions. Obviously influenced by his Christian Science beliefs, Baxter privileges religious dimensions structuring lives and desires. The film begins with a heavenly landscape of clouds. After a logo stressing desires that "the clouds of depression will one day be lifted," the camera tracks down to the material world of Hankey Park, presenting its inhabitants impotently existing under the domain of forces over which they have no control. "Decent" Orwellian aspirations represent the only hope for a better future. The hillside meeting between Harry and Helen concludes with a dissolve to this cloudy heavenly realm after Harry wishfully states, "If only everybody would lend a hand." Larry's serious injuries during the Salford demonstration result less from the brutal activities of a mounted policeman and more from the heavenly world's protest against a socialist-motivated demonstration against unemployment. Chaos erupts. The image cuts to thunder and lightning on the screen rather than showing the broken body of sacrificial victim Larry Meath. Larry dies like a religious martyr rather than as a victim of class brutality and the politics of betrayal practiced by the Labour Party. Baxter displays ideologically motivated devices in this sequence evoking the evasive nature of twentieth-century British Labour political thought. Larry's rational "commonsense" moderation fails to control supposedly irrational forces of left-wing agitation.

Sally eventually prostitutes herself to save her family from destitution. In the closing scenes, she returns home to collect her personal belongings, including Larry's books. Her poignant situation represents a waste of personal potential as well as the victory of deterministic forces preventing any oppositional meanings emerging from her union with Larry. She finally performs an act of heroic sacrificial martyrdom. Despite censorship requirements necessitating Grundy's voice-over offering marriage rather than economic recompense, Sally is still a "fallen woman" in the eyes of family and community. Although worldly wise Mrs. Bull (Marjorie Rhodes) recognizes the lack of choices facing Sally—"Your daughter has a settlement made on her and you wonder what is to become of her. Why don't you wonder what is to become of us?"—Sally becomes the ideological scapegoat for psychologically oppressive forces dominating the lives of Hankey Park residents that they will never overcome. The film ends on Baxter's hopes for a better world ironically dependent on wartime circumstances when "one day we'll all be wanted." As browbeaten, prematurely aged Mrs. Hardcastle (Mary Merrall) speaks of a world in which "one day, there'll be no Hanky Park no more," the scene dissolves to the camera tracking up into the clouds to privilege a heavenly realm, which the film believes is the only force capable of effecting personal and social change. Baxter's visual strategies and solutions privilege human passivity rather than personal and political struggle.

Both *Love on the Dole* and Baxter's earlier films such as *Say It with Flowers* (1934) hope for communal benevolent activities in which things may be "put right" by socially conscious people motivated by charitable altruism. But Baxter's solutions are transcendentally sentimental in nature. Good feelings, community service, and benevolent feelings toward the less well-off in society are shaky foundations for personal and political growth as the reactionary victories of Thatcherism and New Labour show.

The Common Touch is another version of Baxter's cinematic sentimentalism. In 1943, he stated British National's aim "of pictures with a promise of the better times that are to come, pictures that will show them just what we are fighting for, pictures with a glimpse of the better world we all envisage after these sacrifices and hardships are through" (quoted by Murphy, 1988, 38). Despite Baxter's sincere feelings for working class unfortunates, *The Common Touch* becomes compromised by conservative ideological mechanisms and stereotypical characterization.

Beginning with Baxter's dedication to "the humble people of our great cities whose courage and endurance has become the basis of national survival," the film opens with a scene of a public school cricket match. This is certainly not the working-class environment viewers may have expected from the opening caption. Introductory scenes show the film's nominal hero, young Peter Henderson (Geoffrey Hibbert) on his last day at the wicket before departing to take over his deceased father's business. After forelock-tugging comments by humble waiter Perkins (Bernard Miles) about life being the "hardest game of all," young Peter leaves on the train for London. A voice-over commentary recounts lines from Kipling's imperialist poem "If," particularly emphasizing "the common touch." Eventually, young Peter dons a working-class disguise like Jack London in *The People of the Abyss* and George Orwell in *Down and Out in London and Paris* to enter the heavenly realm of Charlie's doss house in Plover Street. Doomed for demolition by Peter's scheming manager, Cartwright (Raymond Lovell), Charlie's represents a sentimentalized male utopian proletarian realm anticipating a postwar world envisaged by the words of saintly tramp Ben (Bransby Williams). "Fashions will change again and people will turn to simple and beautiful things." His tray contains various toys. The most popular items are ironically war toys rather than the simple designs he wishes people would buy.

Peter and his working-class allies finally thwart Cartwright's schemes and rescue upper-class socially conscious Mary Weatherby (Joyce Howard) from a fate worse than death. The film closes with Peter's speech to his board of directors condemning the machinations of Cartwright and associates who "missed a golden opportunity of using it [power] to benefit the whole community." It then cuts to his letter read by inmates of Charlie's in which he promises the new work of "rebuilding." Tich (Edward Rigby) queries "this talk about better fings." But Ben reassures him, "I think they really mean it this time." Tich replies, "Blimey! It'll be like 'eaven on earf!" The camera then tracks into a close-up of Ben's saintly countenance, "An' whoi not?"

This dialogue parallels several moments in *Love on the Dole* where characters often look to heavenly realms for a salvation they cannot achieve in real life. The film concludes positively. But Charlie's is saved by the "young master" on high rather than by the communal participation of those attempting to achieve their liberation from below. Young Peter Henderson experiences the "common touch" and becomes one of J. B. Priestley's "good companions."

Both Baxter's British National films and later Ealing comedies contain similar ideological mechanisms. These mechanisms involve wish-fulfillment blendings of fantasy and realism designed to evoke escapist feelings. Barr's observations equally apply to Baxter's earlier wartime films. "Within this framework, Ealing can play out at leisure the day-dream of a benevolent community and can partly evade, partly confront in a more manageable form, those awkward 'postwar' issues, social and personal, with which it has hitherto been somewhat glumly trying to deal" (Barr, 81).

The Common Touch never resorts to glumness since it exhibits an assurance of benevolent attitudes among decent members of different classes populating Baxter's cinema. However, like Garland in *Passport to Pimlico* (1949), Cartwright and his capitalist acquisitiveness is too easily expelled from the text as a result of Baxter's hope of better days to come. Like contemporary British wartime films such as *The Prime Minister* (1941) and *Young Mr. Pitt* (1942), *The Common Touch* supports traditional ruling-class values while condemning those who abuse stewardship of the British realm. The vision is paternalistic. Neither class nor sexual barriers are envisaged as fundamentally in need of change. While Charlie's occupants hope for "'eaven on earf," resulting from Peter's benevolence, female characters such as Mary and Sylvia (Greta Gynt) are damsels in distress rescued from respective fates worse than death in the last act. As Stead (1988, 73) notes, "The Cockney types give the film some real ballast, but we are back in the world of Dickens and Victorian music hall rather than in the East end during the blitz." Stead also sees a Dickensian idiom within the world of *The Common Touch*, echoing those conservative ideological mechanisms S. M. Eisenstein (233) saw in D. W. Griffith's "slightly sentimental humanism of the good old gentleman and sweet old ladies of Victorian England, just as Dickens loved to picture them." Such mechanisms severely compromise Baxter's utopian views on the sexual and political levels. He regards female independence as little better than a distracting disturbance needing strong paternal guidance to keep it under control. However, this is not always possible.

The Shipbuilders (1943) is a loose sequel to *Love on the Dole*. It fictionally documents the waste of human potential during the depression years while containing a happy postscript reflecting a contemporary world where people are "wanted" again. The film depicts the changing fortunes of Clydeside shipbuilder boss Leslie Pagan (Clive Brook) and riveter Danny Shields (Morland Graham) from the beginning of the depression to early wartime. Pagan and Danny represent traditional British archetypal symbols of boss and worker who exist in a hierarchically symbiotic relationship to each other politically and personally. Pagan operates as a Greimas "actant" in the narrative, while Danny is the passive recipient of historical and family misfortune. During 1931, the beginning of the depression forces Pagan to close down his shipyard, causing Danny and others to be unemployed. While Pagan acts by joining Churchill's prewar cause and condemning capitalists dealing with future Axis powers, Danny suffers various melodramatic family problems. Like Mr. Hardcastle in *Love on the Dole*, he has to cope with the loss of his breadwinner status. But unlike Sally, he does not prostitute his values when a spiv friend of his wife attempts to seduce him into unpatriotic activities. His son, Peter (Geoffrey Hibbert), falls into bad company, the "Sing Sing Boys"—a term signifying British discursive fears of the bad effects of American culture and movies! He faces a murder charge. But once he is cleared, Pagan arranges for him to leave the bad influences engendered by unemployment and Hollywood movies to become a sailor. Despite her lively manner, Peter's girlfriend, Rita (Moira Lister), represents a threat to male dominance. She cheekily treats the master as an equal by calling him "big boy," a term she has obviously learned from corrupting Hollywood movies. Such negative connotations echo traditional British intellectual fears of Hollywood's retrograde influence, a feature marring J. B. Priestley's Joe Dinmore in the theatrical version of *They Came to a City* (1942) "who assumes a rather rough tough manner, which shows American influence" (Priestley, 163). Although Danny's wife eventually leaves him, both she and Rita return once German bombers attack Glasgow. Mrs. Shields (Nell Ballantyne) exhibits a spirited character very much like that of Sally Hardcastle. But despite her valid reasons for criticizing Danny's servility in hard times, the film chooses to privilege Danny as the injured party. Female grievances are irrelevant in this cinematic version of the national cause.

Like Baxter's other films, *The Shipbuilders* presumes the existence of an order no one may question. Whether good times or bad, everything is for the best. One worker who sneers at Danny's belief in his master as a "shipbuilder first, boss second" appears as an ugly figure. Good deeds from those above (Churchill, Pagan) return the unemployed to work. Despite its grim depiction of the depression years, the film still exhibits the cloying sentimentality and political naiveté of Baxter's other films. As Edgar Anstey noted in his 17 March 1944 *Spectator* review, "the economic issues were simplified down to a point at which one is left feeling that every feat of economic and sociological organisation can be achieved by kindness" (Stead, 1989, 73).

Set in June 1943, *The Halfway House* is a film of containment like *The Shipbuilders*. As Wheeler Winston Dixon shows (1997), it deals with redirection of British national energies that have lost their way toward the expected final victory. Blending realism and fantasy, the film brings together a group of disparate travelers who all suffer from insecurities related to wartime experiences. Dying conductor David Davies (Esmond Knight) wishes to spend his last months in peace rather than undertake a British Council–sponsored tour in the neutral territories of Lisbon and Madrid. Squadron Leader Richard French (Richard Bird) and his wife, Jill (Valerie French), bicker over their *decree nisi* divorce settlement while their daughter Joanna (Sally Ann Howes) wishes them to remain together. Family solicitor (C. V. French) urges the battling parents to arrive at "some sort of truce." Newly released disgraced prisoner Captain Fortescue (Guy Middleton) refuses to rejoin his old regiment as a private to aid the wartime effort. Exiled Frenchwoman Alice Meadows (Francoise Rosay) grieves over her dead son, while her husband, Captain Meadows (Tom Walls), drowns his sorrows in drink. Black marketeer Oakley (Alfred Drayton) dismisses an associate for being "too honest." Margaret (Philippa Hiatt) refuses to marry her Irish diplomat fiancee, Terence (Pat McGrath), if he accepts an appointment in Berlin.

Political and personal problems related to a stressful wartime society affect these characters. As ghostly proprietor Rhys (Mervyn Johns) states, "quite a lot of people who don't know where they're going arrive here." Magically transplanted a year back to the fall of Tobruk—an event that changed the tide for the Allies in North Africa—the guests all overcome their personal problems and resolve to make a common, united effort for Allied victory. The personal becomes political, but only within conservative structures of desire. Davies will eventually die in the service of British propaganda, bringing the best of British culture to neutral nations. Strafed by a German fighter, Terence decides to join up, to Margaret's delight. Fortescue decides to rejoin his old regiment. Potential collaborator Oakley decides to take his medicine and face five years in prison. Captain Meadows decides to return to sea and deny charges of cowardice made against him during a convoy accident. He and his wife come to terms with the death of their son. Unlike many actual wartime and postwar couples, Richard and Jill decide to remain together. In the final scenes, both reappear in uniforms they wore in their introductory scenes. Both are now ready for revitalized family and military roles to aid the wartime effort. They will not divorce and follow any independent desires.

The Halfway House presents a utopian vision for wartime solidarity. However, it is strongly conditioned by past values set within a *Brigadoon*-like enclosure featuring Welsh national caricatures. Rhys (Mervyn Johns) and his daughter, Gwyneth (Glynis Johns), display ethnic patriarchal stereotypes. Earlier in the film, a Welsh lady on a train offers fellow passengers Welsh cakes as a generous communal offering from a relative who used her whole ration on baking. Welsh passengers then break out into hymns, rendering them comic stereotypes. Despite documented evidence provided by historians such as Calder (1991, 71–75), Wales appears as a territory subscribing to People's War ideology. Rhys tells Terence, "I wouldn't put the betterment of Wales before the betterment of humanity." Barr astutely (185–86) recognizes that the film operates as a rallying cry to fictional characters and cinema spectators. As Rhys's final words stress, "But you have *been* here, and your lives will prove the reality of the faded dream. The world is what you make it, for your lives make up the world—and it is a good world." However, the unity achieved is clearly temporary and conditioned by manufactured ideologies governing wartime solidarity. Black marketeering, marital breakdowns, disgruntled former servicemen, disturbing national issues, and dying for art reoccur more problematically in postwar cinema. Like the solicitor, *The Halfway House* calls for a truce, but it will be merely temporary.

Waterloo Road also deals with wartime problems and their resolution. As in *The Halfway House*, the battleground is military and sexual. Although no off-screen narrator such as Leslie Howard in *The Gentle Sex* (1943), Alastair Sim's Dr. Montgomery employs the earlier film's conservative male discourse dominating narrative representation. While *The Gentle Sex* reluctantly attempts to come to terms with female military mobilization, *Waterloo Road* looks forward to the end of disruptive female wartime behavior and restoration of prewar status quo values. Before Dr. Montgomery visits the Colters' male baby, his voice-over introduces a

flashback to 1940–1941 wartime conditions affecting marital relationships and the beginnings of a "spiv," culture which would extend into the
postwar era. Montgomery remembers "working in a battlefield" during a
time when "little people like Jim and Tilly Colter waged their own campaign and won it." Like *Millions like Us*, *Waterloo Road* acknowledges
wartime conditions affecting female relationships. But it also assures
viewers that eventual victory will restore conservative values. Throughout
the film, Dr. Montgomery acts as Jim Colter's ally against the sexually
contaminating influence of glamour boy Ted Purvis. He identifies Jim as
representing those "making sacrifices" on the battlefield who will return
home, rid the community of corrupting influences, and restore traditional morality.

The film offers two British stars as antagonists who symbolize culturally opposed gender roles. As Jim Colter, John Mills represents the traditional British realistic aesthetic of films such as *In Which We Serve, We
Dive at Dawn* (1943), and *This Happy Breed* (1945). Stewart Granger's
artificial "spiv," Ted Purvis, exhibits the flamboyant Gainsborough male
performance despised by mainstream critics. *Waterloo Road* also may
reflect the ongoing battle between the more realistically inclined Gainsborough producer Ted Black and his opposite number, Maurice Ostrer
(see Geoff Brown, 111). But despite Jim's Davidlike victory over his experienced boxer Goliath opponent, *Waterloo Road* intermingles realism and
fantasy like *Millions like Us*.

Waterloo Road desperately attempts to impose a "normalcy" solution
upon past and present events in the manner of a wish-fulfillment fantasy.
Like contemporary British films such as *Madonna of the Seven Moons*,
They Were Sisters, *This Happy Breed*, and *Brief Encounter*, *Waterloo Road*
raises the specter of sexual desire only to expel it from the narrative.
Waterloo Road is another example of a contemporary wartime cinema
unable to envisage radically emergent structures of desire involving a
break with the past. It can only suggest a return to the conservative world
of thirties British society.

Formally, *Waterloo Road* differs from most British cinematic representations. It contains a flashback within a flashback. Appearing within
Dr. Montgomery's own flashback, Tilly (Joy Shelton) gazes at her wedding photograph. The image changes to her honeymoon departure when
she and Jim discuss a supposedly assured future of new home and children during 1939. When the flashback concludes, Tilly walks along the
street listening to extra diegetic voice-overs from the recent past evoking

Jim's vehement arguments against beginning a family in the early years of the war. Jim's reluctance acts as catalyst for Tilly's fascination with sexually and materially mobile Ted Purvis. Ted embodies not only a dangerous seductive fascination but also forbidden affluence within a period of wartime rationing. As Murphy (1992, 148) notes, his stylish clothes designate him as "British cinema's first spiv." Ted also engages in successful business enterprises, such as owning a pinball arcade, a ladies hairdresser shop, and taxis. These activities foreshadow later cinematic materialist threats to community values embodied by Jackie Farnish in *The Root of All Evil* (1947) and Garland in *Passport to Pimlico* (1949).

Tilly's desires for sexual and material flirtation are natural reactions to wartime conditions. She represents many females who engaged in ideologically taboo activities during this period. However, *Waterloo Road* disavows the nature of her desires not just by imposing a fantastic fight scene between "good" and "bad" males but also by guaranteeing Tilly's desires within patriarchal discourse. Spotting Tilly and Ted together, family lodger Tom Mason (George Carney) appears to sympathize with a wartime dilemma affecting both partners. "If you ask me, the youngsters are having the toughest time in this war." But after commenting "La donna mobile" (and implicitly relating it to female mobilization), he then "puts the blame on Mame" by concluding, "Females are a problem all round. Blooming crossroad puzzle. Give me pigeons everytime. Not so blinking whimsical." As Lant (88–89) recognizes, his statement reinforces parallels between homing pigeons and females whose "natural" instincts are in abeyance.

Both Tom and Dr. Montgomery disavow the dangerous nature of wartime circumstances that may lead to new forms of female independence. They yearn for the return of a male dominance lost at the beginning of the war. Like Tom's pigeons, Jim returns home and departs on the Waterloo Road train after accomplishing his family wartime mission. He has done his duty on the marital battleground. Dr. Montgomery stresses the female's natural "domestic" nature. He tells Jim that once women's homemaking instincts are denied, "their repressed and rebellious nature runs amok in a big way." *Waterloo Road* concludes in the present with Dr. Montgomery visiting a now-domesticated Tilly and presenting Jim Jr. with a toy railway engine, symbolizing his father's successful home journey. Montgomery looks to the future.

"He'll be a good citizen *if you bring him up as I tell you*" (italics mine). We'll need good citizens when this is over, millions of them, the more the merrier. I wonder what they'll think of their mums and dads. They'll have to admit that, taking it all in all, they didn't come through so badly."

Gilliat's *Waterloo Road* concludes with a new conception of the wartime female subject who will produce "millions of them" defined by a male baby in the final shot of the film. Normality is restored in the same way *This Happy Breed* reaffirms the stability of a British patriarchal family life questioned by *Waterloo Road*. Although Higson (1993, 250) notes that Lean's conservative melodrama recognizes that its interwar vision of family solidarity is only a fond memory, both films attempt imposing a fabricated national character on their respective narratives structured upon fictional "inter-war domestic arrangements and family life." Like Queenie of *This Happy Breed*, Tilly also escapes "from the private claustrophobic insularity of the family into the exotic, glamorous—and now eroticized—public arena" (Higson, 250) of Ted's world of pubs, dance halls, and Lucky Star pinball machines. In both films, John Mills comes to the rescue of damsels in distress who engage in irresponsible pleasures after leaving safe and secure homes.

The same conservative ideology appears in *Brief Encounter*. As Lant (17) notices, this middle-class narrative is set "entirely just before September 1939," making it a film allegorically exploring the temptations of wartime adultery. It also operates via a flashback technique similar to *Waterloo Road*, evoking the turbulent nature of a sexual and historical past now safely behind the main characters. Like *In Which We Serve*, the stifling and repressive nature of British class values prevents breaching of socially acceptable codes. Laura Jesson (Celia Johnson) eventually refuses the lures of sexual desire and returns to the safe prewar confines of her middle-class home. As in *They Were Sisters*, a supposedly idyllic thirties landscape provides the ideological remedy for female wartime discontent. Operating on lower-class levels, *Waterloo Road*'s solution is an arbitrarily imposed conservative one paralleling Raymond Williams's definition of a dominant hegemonic answer to dislocating social factors. However, the specter of female mobility will still haunt British postwar cinema.

They Came to a City and *Perfect Strangers* reveal different images. Although Barr (52) still retains his original critique of the former as "arid, abstract, statuesquely posed and declaimed," the film's vision is one of the most outstanding achievements in British cinema. Committed socialist and union activist Sidney Cole brought Priestley's 1942 play to Ealing Studios and acted as adaptor and associate producer. As in the original theatrical production, nine people representing different British class types magically encounter a utopian city symbolizing progressive desires for a better postwar world. The working-class representatives are disillusioned seaman Joe Dinsmore (John Clements), oppressed waitress Alice Foster (Googie Withers), and elderly charlady Mrs. Batley (Ada Reeve). Malcolm Stritton (Raymond Huntley) and his repressed wife, Dorothy (Renee Gadd), symbolize the lower middle class, while Cudworth (Norman Shelley) represents the upwardly mobile businessman antithetical to Ealing community values. Sir George Gedney (A. E. Matthews) embodies the idle-rich leisure class. Lady Loxfield (Mabel Terry Lewis) and her daughter, Philippa (Frances Rowe), represent a once-affluent, downwardly mobile aristocratic family. All visit the city and experience an egalitarian world of social justice and harmony. Gedney, Cudworth, Lady Loxfield, and Dorothy Stritton bluntly reject alternatives to their sterile, blinkered, class-ridden values. Dorothy succeeds in using emotional blackmail to turn her husband away from the harmonious society in which he wishes to participate. Mrs. Batley and Philippa choose to remain, while Alice and Joe (the one couple whom the audience would expect to embrace this new utopian world) decide to return and fight for a nonsentimental "heaven on earth" symbolized by the words of Walt Whitman: "I dreamt in a dream I saw a city invincible to the attacks of the whole earth, I dreamt that was the new city of friends."

Although critics might sneer at this now rarely-screened film, it is far more realistic and less sentimental than the other-worldly utopian visions of John Baxter. Framed by a realistic countryside prologue and epilogue where the author encounters a serviceman (Ralph Michael) and his uniformed girlfriend (Brenda Bruce) debating whether things will really change after the war, the film employs the theatrical formula Priestley found useful in dramatically expressing "the hopes and fears and sharp differences of opinion about the postwar world of various sections of the British people" (vi–vii). The countryside location is an interesting choice. It is not filmed in a studio like similar countryside scenes in *Love on the Dole* and *Millions like Us*, where the artificial nature of the sets suggests hopeless yearnings for a better life or pessimism about the future. Despite the National Film Archive's categorization of *They Came to a City* "as an unusual film which represented the first attempt to carry out socialist propaganda in the British feature film" (Barr, 195), the film is less didactic and more personal than this demeaning comment suggests. It is a rare work attempting to unite the personal and political at a

particular historical moment by eschewing both traditional British cinematic realistic aesthetics and escapist devices of fantasy and melodrama.
The film attempts to unite cinematic and theatrical worlds in a progressively allegorical manner. As Priestley commented in his introduction to
the published script, "I was fortunate in this play in finding a dramatic
formula that enabled me to express, in dramatic form, the hopes and
fears and sharp differences of opinion about the postwar world of various sections of the British people. This made it a topical play that nevertheless was not a war play" (Barr, 51).

They Came to a City ruthlessly exposes negative features in the
British national character contributing to hegemonic exploitation in both
past, present, and future. Joe initially exhibits a cynical demeanor due to
his experiences as an oppressed worker throughout his life. He has given
up any revolutionary hopes he once possessed. Alice quits her job of waitress servitude fully conscious of sexual, social, and political oppression—
"Half the time they think they're buying you with baked beans on toast!"
The Strittons live a sterile death-in-life marital existence. When they
arrive outside the city, Mrs. Stritton comments in repressed wish-fulfillment tones, "We've always been together; we've always been together. Perhaps we're dead." Repulsed by the city's democratic public sphere, her
selfish, possessive, private desires for husband, garden, and children reveal
a culturally induced Freudian death instinct. Joe recognizes this. Mrs.
Stritton also shares this quality with Sir George Gedney who states, "I
can't stand people." When Joe notes Malcolm submitting to his wife's
emotional blackmail, he urges him to remain true to what he has seen in
the city: "Don't go dead and cold on it. Keep it alive inside you." He also
condemns acquisitive businessman Cudney as "a typical specimen of the
boss class. Grab! Grab! Grab!" Like Mrs. Stritton, Cudworth exhibits a
malignant form of British middle-class sexual repressiveness devoid of
personal and emotional feelings. Exclusively committed to the business
world, Cudworth avoids female company, an arena he significantly terms
"messy." Although Cudworth answers Alice's astute recognition, "Messy!
What d'you mean *messy?*" by stating his own definition—"How many
times have they got you into trouble—you know—spent your money,
taken your job, taken your mind off your work, landed you into quarrels,
cost you your job—eh?"—the very evasiveness of his dialogue suggests
repressed connections between sexuality and disorder akin to the Freiko-
rps proto-Fascist mentality catalogued by Klaus Theweleit in *Male Fantasies*. *They Came to a City* clearly equates hegemonic British tendencies

emphasizing class divisions and wealth over libertarian emotional desires with Fassbinder's definition of "Everyday Fascism."

Despite Alice's desire to return to the city, Joe decides to remain outside and take the message back to British society. Their relationship parallels the nonsentimental, proletarian commitment exhibited by John Garfield and Ida Lupino in Robert Rossen's screenplay of the 1941 Warner Brothers version of *The Sea Wolf.* Both characters have experienced misfortunes in life and retreat behind cynical armors of personal detachment. But they meet as equals, quarrel as equals, and decide to form a relationship based not on class or gender subordination but as committed partners in a common personal and political cause. Joe persuades Alice of the necessity of sharing their vision with others and beginning the hard task of transforming society. Despite the theatrical overtones of Joe's final speech, the film uses visually romantic cinematic imagery to champion the personal and political nature of the struggle they both face. Joe understands the mission before them. They face a world where people do not want things to be different. "Some of 'em, poor creatures, are so twisted and tormented inside themselves that they envy and hate other people's happiness. And we'll have to talk to plenty of them." Joe also recognizes the corrupting influence of ideological Victorian values. "They will tell us that we can't change human nature. That's one of the oldest excuses in the world. And it isn't true. We've been changing human nature for thousands of years. But what you can't change in it is . . . man's eternal desire and vision and hope of making this world a better place to live in."

The film returns to the countryside of the prologue. Priestley convinces the initially reluctant serviceman to accept the more positive perspective of his girlfriend. The couple function as realistic equivalents of the pair presented within the film's theatrical structure. The theatrical and cinematic formulas are complementary. Priestley comments, "Some like it, some won't, and some are ready to go out and fight for it." He then leaves the couple and the audience to ponder their future.

Unfortunately, Priestley's utopian hopes remained just a dream. His vision of a socialist paradise proved impossible both in reality and in cinema. But *They Came to a City* remains a unique work in contemporary British cinema, which usually reinforced or vainly struggled against the dominant status quo. Several postwar films sought to discredit this socialist vision as either impossible to realize or flawed by the personalities of its adherents.

Like Michael Redgrave's Hamer of *Fame is the Spur* (1947), William Hartnell's socialist Peter Pettinger in *The Agitator* (1945) appears as an arrogant upstart despised both by bosses and by working men. Accusing factory owner Mark Overend of cheating his father, Peter ignores the advice of Letty (Mary Morris) about speaking words without depth. She warns him that "putting forward a personal grievance is a cheap way of furthering a cause." Fueled by selfish individualism, Peter later finds himself in charge of the factory. But, despite socialist dreams of works councils, profit sharing, and bonuses, he finds his aspirations futile and based on lies. Peter eventually relinquishes control of the factory to his servile workmates and leaves the narrative. He moves away from the camera as a black screen falls behind him, resembling a factory shutter cutting off any alternative light from the audience.

The Agitator is a stereotypical film and as dangerously unprogressive as Bernard Miles's *Chance of a Lifetime* (1950). Like *The Agitator*, *Chance of a Lifetime* showed that the very people Priestley set his hopes on prove inadequate and incapable of realizing the challenge of following new radical directions in their everyday lives. Offered the "chance of a lifetime" of running their own factory, the workers prove to be incompetent. They finally ask their old boss (Basil Radford) (who generously helps them in the final scenes) to return to his old position. However, despite Pettinger's portrayal, *The Agitator* does suggest the potential of a working relationship between equals such as Peter and Letty. Although Mary Morris's performance lacks working-class credibility, her Letty is a strong, independent woman resembling Alice in *They Came to a City*. Peter recognizes that she is "different from the ordinary sort of girl. She reads a lot, books about socialism and economics, and things like that." But Letty becomes impatient with Peter's arrogance. She recognizes his insecurities and suggests personal change, but she never manipulates Peter for her own advantage and departs when his class status changes. Unlike Joe and Alice in *They Came to a City*, possibilities for any positive personal and political partnership between Peter and Letty never materialize in *The Agitator*. However, Mary Morris's performance remains in the mind. She was one of those rare actresses in British cinema exhibiting independent and nonsubmissive qualities. But, as with Googie Withers, Margaretta Scott, and Joan Greenwood, British cinema never recognized her potential.

Alexander Korda's 1945 MGM/London Films production, *Perfect Strangers*, presents a more glamorized, but nonetheless highly significant, representation of wartime marital problems than the more "realistic"

Waterloo Road. Criticized during its original release for its utilization of non-British, Hollywood codes of representation, *Perfect Strangers* deals with issues most contemporary films avoided—the sexualization of a couple during wartime and the nonescapist nature of challenges facing them after the cessation of hostilities. The film begins with the ritually sterile nature of George (Robert Donat) and Cathy's (Deborah Kerr) existence prior to his wartime naval service. Beginning on 4 April 1940 the mousy couple sit through a routine breakfast before George begins his final day of work. Although he has worked for eight years as a browbeaten clerk, the meek George allows his boss to refuse him a long-awaited raise on spurious grounds. He then leaves for naval service after refusing to hear of Cathy taking a job. Cathy joins the WRENS. Both couples experience a sense of independence in the wartime community apart from each other and become sexualized in the process. As Lant (117–27) points out, the film moves from despecularizing the couple to specularizing them in terms of Hollywood romantic imagery. Both couples are now "perfect strangers" who achieve personal fulfillment away from each other as opposed to their prewar existence when they were "lacking in star quality," as George states. After considering divorce, they find themselves together again in their old apartment possibly on the way to reconciliation. There is one major difference. The confining wall that blocked their view of the city landscape has now fallen. *Perfect Strangers* ends with a view of the unconfined city landscape, suggesting a world of possibilities awaiting George and Cathy.

The film is certainly romantic and escapist in terms of its imagery. But it is a mistake to condemn *Perfect Strangers* for its use of Hollywood lighting as British critics have done. Both Richard Dyer and British independent director Terence Davies have significantly recognized the importance of Hollywood cinema for its representations of entertainment as utopia. While Davies fled from his unhappy childhood into the realms of Hollywood cinema, it was by no means entirely escapist. *The Long Day Closes* (1992) contains a blend of Hollywood fantasy and British realist discourse echoing the earlier mixture of *Perfect Strangers.* Rather than rejecting the Hollywood influence as antithetical to British cultural values as traditional British intellectuals did, it is more significant to understand this device as a means of articulating utopian desires inherent within the British character. Both realms need not be antithetical. *Perfect Strangers* is one of the few films to deal with sexual dislocation within wartime society and present it in a potentially exciting, nonthreatening manner. Cathy learns feminine glamour from her fellow WREN Dizzy (Glynis Johns). Geoffrey has a brief encounter with his nurse (Ann Todd). Dizzy and the nurse have experienced loss during the war. The nature of their postwar existence is left open. Similarly, although George and Cathy are together the next morning due to the exigencies of the blackout and the difficulty of finding accommodation, there is no suggestion that their relationship will continue. Everything is tentative in terms of the future. As George and Cathy view the damaged landscape of London, the final lines also symbolize the task awaiting them in peacetime. Cathy says, "We've got to build it up again." George replies, "What does it matter. We're young." Both are rejuvenated and have a second chance. They reject the repressive nature of the thirties era. The camera tracks away from their embrace and chooses to close on a ruined city landscape, suggesting hard tasks of reconstruction on both personal and political levels.

Dead of Night (1945) allegorically reveals the personal and ideological hurdles facing those hoping for a better world. As Peter Hutchings (26) astutely notes that *Dead of Night* has specific connections to its social and historical context in being "an intense and obsessive meditation on issues arising from the transition from a wartime to a postwar society." By using a fantastic structure, the film indirectly attempts to negotiate the disruptive patterns of wartime desire and independence toward established norms of prewar existence. But *Dead of Night* reveals the impossibility of doing so. The repressed returns with a vengeance. Viewers encounter a circular narrative, revealing that problems of the recent past will not so easily vanish.

Hutchings pertinently notes the gender crisis occurring throughout the film. It affects those denying private fears and insecurities dominating each particular narrative. The main character, Walter Craig (played by that most down-to-earth character actor in British cinema, Mervyn Johns), is an architect summoned to Pilgrim's Farm to work on reconstructing an old farmhouse and adding two new bedrooms to it. Bedrooms function significantly in all four narratives, containing dangerous overtones of violence and sexuality. Craig's pilgrim's progress will not lead to Priestley's new heavenly city of postwar utopian desires but a hellish vision affecting himself and the viewer. *Dead of Night* opens and concludes with Craig's visit to the English countryside, that bastion of traditional conservative values. The film depicts supernatural episodes within a traditional realistic style before finally collapsing into discordant realms of an expressionist nightmare usually regarded as foreign to British cinema. *Dead of Night* depicts contemporary gender crises involving "strong" women and "weak males" as Hutchings notes. But it also emphasizes that peacetime will not be easy unless past social, personal, and historical nightmares become recognized and renegotiated. The film's climax reveals a community failure of nerve to do this.

The five narratives depict this in different ways. Throughout the linking segments, Dr. van Straaten (Frederick Valk) blandly ignores the implications of each narrator's tale by emphasizing an irritatingly supercilious rationality and commonsense approach. His foreign status represents a convenient displacement for the blinkered British values he upholds. Like Neville Chamberlain, he wants "peace in our time," ignores the danger signals, and dies for his folly.

The first storyteller, Hugh (Antony Baird), functions as a surrogate for the British wartime hero injured in battle. But unlike his later cinematic counterpart, Douglas Bader (Kenneth More) in *Reach for the Sky* (1956), he does not pull himself together. Hugh suffers from posttraumatic stress. Waking up in the hospital, he mistakes nurse Joyce (Judy Kelly) for absent girlfriend Peggy. Peggy never appears in this episode. Presumably, she has rejected him after the crash like Bader's first sweetheart in *Reach for the Sky*. Hugh suffers from feelings of wartime impotence signified by a crooner's song emanating from a radio prior to his fantasy. The lyrics are revealing, "How can you treat me so when you know what you're doing to me." Although Hugh survives his fantasy, we later discover that he has married Joyce as if needing a reassuring maternal nurse figure rather than an independent mobile woman.

Sally O'Hara (Sally Ann Howes) finds herself in the 1860 bedroom of a sobbing boy, Francis Kent, whose stepsister strangled him and cut his throat. Although played by the most demure of adolescent English actresses with an impeccable upper-class accent, Sally's role has historical as well as gender associations. As Hutchings (31) notes, the castrating act of her dark alter ego in the past complements her violent rejection of young Jimmy's advances in the present. However, the emphasis is not just on Sally's role as a potentially castrating female but also on her nationality. Despite her accent, Sally is Irish. Her role indirectly signifies British wartime resentment of her country's neutral status during that period. *The Halfway House* deals with a similar question but solves it by Terence's commitment to the Allied cause. But adolescent, single Sally is a different category. She represents contemporary cinematic fears of the potentially dangerous Irish female represented by Deborah Kerr in *I See a Dark*

Stranger (1946) and Siobahn McKenna in *Daughter of Darkness* (1948). Significantly, despite his promise not to do so, Craig hits Sally in his final fantasy. He thus avenges both Jimmy's humiliation and British anger for Irish neutrality during World War II.

As critics note, "The Haunted Mirror" episode features themes found in Gainsborough melodrama and Hammer horror. Hutchings (14) comments that like the former genre, "British horror does not merely reveal what is unsaid or repressed elsewhere in British cinema but is also capable of offering different ideas and a new way of saying." Hamer's episode parallels the opening story with allegorical associations. Peter (Ralph Michael) represents the returning war hero who finds difficulty adjusting to civilian life with a female partner exhibiting many of the independent characteristics associated with wartime females. Similar domestic problems occur both in contemporary American (*Since You Went Away* [1944], *The Best Years of Our Lives* [1946]) and in British cinema (*The Years Between* [1946]). Played by an actress representing rare qualities of female initiative and independence in British cinema, Joan (Googie Withers) presents Peter with a nineteenth-century mirror as if to diminish his insecurities and repressed jealousy about her former boyfriend, Guy. However, Peter's male crisis results in a murderous, narcissistic gaze in which he sees the bedroom of violent nineteenth-century country squire Francis Everton along with his own reflection. Disabled after a hunting accident and suffering "even more than a man of his mind can endure," Everton strangled his young bride and cut his throat before the mirror. His murderous activities parallel those of young Francis Kent's stepsister in Sally's narrative. Both narratives emphasize male impotence and insecurity. In Peter's case, male insecurities result not just from paranoid jealousy concerning Joan's relationship with Guy but also from suspicions concerning his wife's feelings about his own masculinity. Joan buys Peter the mirror as a birthday present, wittingly commenting, "I thought you'd like to look at yourself."

Learning the mirror's history from an antique dealer, Rutherford (played by Esme Percy, an actor associated with his murderous gay role in Hitchcock's 1930 film *Murder*), Joan rushes back to Peter. Now identified with his crippled predecessor, he accuses her of engaging in an affair resembling a wartime "brief encounter." "You were having a pleasant weekend with Guy, but he was called away, so you came back to me." Peter's accusation parallels insecurities of returning servicemen suspicious about their wives' independent lifestyles during the war. However, Joan promptly acts to save her life as well as Peter's by destroying the mirror. Peter never appears in the framing story. This suggests he never really recovers from his trauma. His character also parallels those disturbed psychological figures undergoing particular forms of masculine crisis played by Eric Portman in *Great Day* (1945) and later postwar films.

As critics note, the "golfing story" is the weakest of all five narratives. But, far from being light relief sandwiched between *Dead of Night's* most menacing stories, it contains humorous, repressed implications concerning the homosocial bonding between Basil Radford and Naunton Wayne. As Charters and Caldicott in thirties and forties British cinema, they first appeared as obsessive cricket-loving English gentlemen who share a bed in Hitchcock's *The Lady Vanishes* (1938). Their two characters of Parratt and Potter fight over a woman, but their real love is golf. Mary (Peggy Bryan) is also an object of surrogate exchange between two males whose real desire is for each other. The theme foreshadows Basil Dearden's later films, such as *Pool of London* (1950) and *The Ship That Died of Shame* (1955). However, their real desires remain unsatisfied. Like other characters in *Dead of Night*, Parratt and Potter cannot negotiate contradictions within their own characters and historical situation.

As Hutchings (33) recognizes, Cavalcanti's celebrated ventriloquist's dummy episode "can be read as representing on a barely submerged level a homosexual love triangle" between American and British ventriloquists Sylvester (Hartley Power) and Maxwell (Michael Redgrave). Dummy Hugo is the object of their desires. But as in *Obsession* (1949), contemporary fears concerning national relationships structure representations of desire in this particular narrative. The homosexual subtext in this episode of *Dead of Night* is depicted in a stereotypical manner and ideologically regarded as a threat to British masculinity. As in *Obsession*, the episode allegorizes British fears of impotence and insecurity toward America after the cessation of hostilities.

Maxwell Frere fears losing his voice/authority to American influence. Sylvester's voice-over narrative introduces a liberated Paris enjoying American entertainment provided by black female Beulah (Elizabeth Welch). Maxwell resents his brash, self-assured American rival. Jealous of losing Hugo, he injures Sylvester in a murderous rage until he eventually destroys Hugo and becomes impotent. This episode is a revealing national allegory. It depicts British fears of their more economically powerful rival. *Dead of Night's* nightmare vision also anticipates certain themes in *Pool of London, The Cruel Sea* (1953), and *The Ship That Died of Shame.* Monja

FIGURE 10. Maxwell (Michael Redgrave) exhibits traumatic desire for Hugo in *Dead of Night.*

Danischewsky (139) humorously records an Ealing figure's reaction to a poem by a Greek homosexual recited at Penrose Tennyson's funeral by John Clements, *"We don't want anything to do with fellows like that at Ealing Studios."* But "Mr. Balcon's Academy for Young Gentlemen" could not entirely banish such feelings from *Dead of Night.*

CHAPTER FIVE

Postwar Representations

Despite the illusionary nature of the People's War ideology, social tensions were by no means absent after wartime. Following the massive election victory of the Labour government, Britain faced exhaustion and rapid change in the immediate postwar years when it became clear that the imperialist days of colonies supplying its economy were now over. The 1945–1951 era is commonly known as the "Age of Austerity" when British society confronted a reduced economic situation paralleling its diminished status in the world. Although rationing remained in force until the early 1950s, the pleasures of cinemagoing still continued as a staple emotional diet for the majority of the population. Several films of this period reveal a complex array of tensions and dislocations.

Cinematic representations never reflect social problems directly. They rather focus indirectly on contemporary issues. Various British contemporary genres such as costume melodrama, *film noir*, social melodrama, and crime thriller echoed the uneasy situation of a society in which things were felt to be changing. Unease and uncertainty occurred over what exactly would happen and whether it would be positive.

Such uncertainty characterizes Kenneth Annakin's *Broken Journey* (1947). This Gainsborough film anticipates later Hollywood disaster movies by bringing together a diverse group of people who personify social contradictions and gloomily speculate on the future. *Broken Journey* does not fall into typical Gainsborough patterns. It belongs neither to the costume category nor to contemporary social melodrama like *Good Time Girl* (1948). *Broken Journey* symbolically examines social dilemmas in a narrative dealing with a plane crash in the Swiss Alps and the ordeal facing the survivors. The celebrities traveling on a private airline owned and run by former R.A.F pilot Fox (Guy Rolfe) are less interesting than other passengers he describes as "quite normal," especially those affected by wartime trauma. Air hostess Mary Johnstone (Phyllis Calvert) eventually comes to terms with her self-deceptive idealization of her deceased R.A.F. boyfriend. She learns the necessity of living in the present with former Battle of Britain pilot Bill Haverton (James Donald). Two years after hostilities, romantic wartime relationships are seen as not always idyllic. Polio-stricken (or war wounded) John (Grey Blake), sacrifices himself for the survivors, while his grief-stricken girlfriend, Anne (Sonia Holm), commits suicide by walking away into the icy wastes. Other passengers such as fading movie star Joanne (Margot Grahame), selfish opera singer Perami (Francis L. Sullivan), and workaholic businessman Edward (Raymond Huntley) become more sympathetic to group values during their ordeal. *Broken Journey* ends with Fox commenting that the survivors will soon forget their experiences and lapse back into previous behavioral patterns. When Richard (Derek Bond) expresses wartime optimism by wanting to "do something for someone else" and telling Fox, "Some of us will remember," the latter answers, "Do you think so?" Despite its minor nature, *Broken Journey* contains several insights into ideological currents dominating postwar history.

Other Gainsborough characters also face an uncertain world. *Snowbound* (1947) begins by showing two former wartime heroes respectively working as director and extra on a Gainsborough studio set shooting a trivial costume melodrama. They then undertake an espionage mission, which ends in complete disaster. In *Christopher Columbus* (1949), Frederic March's plight parallels that of former heroes suffering misunderstanding and neglect in a society that has benefitted from their wartime sacrifice. Although this film differs from other Gainsborough films as a Rank-promoted, expensive production aimed at the American market, it also echoes contemporary postwar dilemmas involving a hero who becomes redundant in a different social world. Frederic March's Columbus is a postwar male crisis figure paralleling Eric Portman's contemporary counterparts.

Several contemporary films feature both male and female dilemmas. The former usually involve allegorical treatments of males who traumatically suffer not only from wartime but also from changes on the home front. Female dilemmas occur in films such as *Bedelia* (1946), *Jassy, When the Bough Breaks, The Root of All Evil, The Brothers* (all 1947); *Good Time Girl* (1948); and *So Long at the Fair* (1950). They complement a relatively unexplored contemporary British cinematic "male hysteria" syndrome in films such as *Wanted for Murder* (1946); *The October Man, They Made Me a Fugitive, Dear Murderer* (all 1947); *Daybreak, Corridor of Mirrors* (all 1948); and *The Bad Lord Byron* (1949). All these films involve the search for desire and fulfillment in a postwar society.

Some films shot in Gainsborough studios are technically non-Gainsborough films. *Good Time Girl, The Bad Lord Byron*, and *The Brothers* are Sydney Box Productions, while others such as *Bedelia* were filmed elsewhere. Although this diffusion hinders rigid ideas of classification, it also reveals that concepts associated with Gainsborough were shared by other studios. *Bedelia* illustrates this. Although it features Margaret Lockwood of "wicked lady" infamy pursuing an equally murderous trajectory of female desire, the film was made by independent producer John Corfield at Ealing and directed by non-Gainsborough director Lance Comfort. Although featuring supporting Gainsborough actress Anne Crawford, *Bedelia* is a composite production, as its credit title reveals—*Vera Caspary's Bedelia*. As Hitchcock later appropriated Robert Bloch's novel *Psycho* as *Alfred Hitchcock's Psycho*, Cornfield associates his film with an American novelist famous for adaptations of melodramas, such as *Laura* (1944) and *Leave Her to Heaven* (1945). The book first appeared in 1945 and was immediately snatched up as a "hot property" by a producer aiming to appeal to the American market. However, *Bedelia's* pre–World War I location moved from America to a post–World War II Britain dealing with problematic gender relationships.

Obviously indebted to Fritz Lang's *Woman in the Window* (1944), the film begins with a track-in to Bedelia's portrait displayed in a window. Ben Cheyney's (Barry K. Barnes) voice-over narration compares Bedelia to a *film noir* "spider woman." "This was Bedelia. She radiated a curious innocence to those she attracted like a poisonous fluid." Unlike Lang's professor, the male is obviously in control of the past narrative he articulates for the viewer. The scene changes to Monte Carlo in fall 1938. Cheyney appears as an artist interested in Bedelia's image as a potential model for his canvas as well as being curious about her current identity as a former widow of a rich husband. She is now married to a man she loves. As Cheyney gazes at her, several scenes show Bedelia framed through a window which evoke the film's opening image. They emphasize Cheyney's male desire to *frame* Bedelia for the audience as in his opening voice-over. Since *Bedelia* reproduces visual and thematic patterns of Hollywood melodrama as well as paralleling the film version of Caspary's *Leave Her to Heaven* (1945), the narration symptomatically depicts pathological postwar male desires to control the independent wartime female. Margaret Lockwood's casting in the title role supports this interpretation.

However, *Bedelia* also criticizes this ideological reading. The film is neither "dull" nor indulgent toward the dilemmas of a "spoilt child" as Murphy (1992, 107) believes. Bedelia is as much a victim of oppressive patriarchal desires as are her counterparts in *Laura* and *Leave Her to Heaven.* She is, of course, a "wicked lady" but one constructed by social circumstances. Anticipating later themes in Laura Mulvey's "Visual Pleasure and Narrative Cinema" essay, the film depicts Bedelia as fearful of a camera associated with the male gaze. "Something happens to me when I look into a camera. I'd rather face a dentist than a photographer." She also takes pleasure in buying dolls and sees them signifying her position as a commodity in patriarchal society. But, as Cheyney remarks to her present husband, the childlike Charlie Carrington (Ian Hunter), she "is not an easy subject" for either the artistic or the detective eye. Although we later learn that Cheyney is a police officer trailing a murderous merry widow, Bedelia is by no means totally evil. When Cheyney pressures Charlie into allowing him to paint her portrait, Bedelia finally agrees but cautions her husband, "All the same I won't let him charge you an outrageous fee." Bedelia wishes to remain anonymous but also cares for Charlie's economic well-being. Immediately recognizing Cheyney's hidden motives, she affirmatively speaks to him about her present husband. "He likes people. He's not like most men who are not as sincere as he is."

The film eventually reveals that Bedelia has murdered at least two husbands but has decided to remain with one she has fallen in love with. As in *The Cat People* (1942), sympathy remains with a woman who is more sinned against than sinning. Cheyney's pursuit of his quarry parallels that of Dr. Judd in *The Cat People,* while Charlie's eventual abandonment of his distraught spouse mirrors Oliver Reed's callous attitude toward Irena in the same film. Charlie finally condemns Bedelia: "You're mad. You're absolutely mad. I loved a woman who doesn't exist." His leaving poison at her bedside table reveals a damning male narcissism and sadistic attitudes existing within his moral persona of an English gentleman. Bedelia misreads Charlie just as much as he misreads her.

Before she dies, Bedelia tells Charlie of her early impoverished and lonely existence, which led to her first marriage to a misogynistic middle-aged Scotsman who used her as cheap labor. Her second marriage to a Manchester businessman was equally miserable. However, after her out-burst, "I hate men. They're rotten beasts. I wish that all the men in the world were dead," Bedelia adds significant information about her previous husbands. "I didn't choose them. They just came along. They wanted me." Although Bedelia's hopes that her new, affluent union with gentle Charlie will change her life for the better, neither salvation nor positive desire is possible in Britain's patriarchal society. Bedelia hysterically condemns the artificial hypocrisy of an upper-class world depicted in the earlier Christmas party sequence in terms reminiscent of Hester's criticism of Regency aristocratic society in *The Man in Grey*. "You! Your world! It's all so nice, so sweet. Jam and sweets everyday. Presents at Christmas. The gardens. So divine when the roses are in bloom. *Divine! Divine! Divine!*" This femme fatale also significantly criticizes England's ideological pastoral world.

Although *Bedelia* attempts to condemn the wartime "wicked lady" aspects of Margaret Lockwood's contemporary star status, it is unsuccessful. Before returning to the opening shot, the film concludes by showing Bedelia's doll on the floor as she commits suicide. Bedelia's demise allows Charlie and Ellen (Anne Crawford) to live happily every after and Cheyney to close his case file. However, like the doll imagery associated with Susan Alexander in her parting scene in *Citizen Kane* (1941), it iron-ically symbolizes that the only role postwar society envisages for the inde-pendent woman is one of subordination. This message also appears in the otherwise silly (but ideologically revealing) film *The Perfect Woman* (1949), where Patricia Roc's character becomes an object of decorative exchange, whether human or robot. Cheyney's voice-over returns for the final time, but it articulates male uncertainty over Bedelia rather than giv-ing definitive answers to the enigma she presents to the audience. "There was no doubt about her motives. She killed for money. But there was the enigma of the soul of a human being who could commit murder. In that mixture of good and evil lies the deepest of human mysteries. The prob-lem no detective or psychologist has ever solved." However, other answers exist beyond the level of deliberate mystification within a male narration that cannot entirely disavow social and historical changes in gender roles motivating its ideological construction.

Despite production problems and script compromises (Murphy, 1992, 129), *Jassy* is by no means a drama of upper-class family rejuvenation "through the efforts of a lower-class female" (Landy, 311) along the lines of *The Courtneys of Curzon Street* (1947). It opposes the dangerous imagery of Margaret Lockwood's wicked lady persona by showing how female independence becomes victimized by hostile social forces. Despite various obstacles, Jassy (Margaret Lockwood) finally regains freedom, property, and downwardly mobile upper-class lover Barney (Dermot Walsh). Their future relationship is one of mutual trust rather than one bound by legal documentation.

Jassy begins by showing the downfall of a rich family headed by dissolute Christopher Hatton (Dennis Price) and its replacement by a more materialistically upwardly mobile unit headed by Nick Helmar (Basil Sydney). Unlike Hatton, Helmar is not a gentleman, nor does he exhibit positive qualities of *noblesse oblige* to his new tenant farmers. Helmar allegorizes feared, ruthless postwar materialism embodied by figures such as Jackie Farnish in *The Root of All Evil* (1947) and Garland in *Passport to Pimlico* (1949) who demolish the utopian premises of Labour's mild revolution. When Hatton realizes that loss of his ancestral home will result in his tenants not getting their roofs repaired during the year—Helmar caustically replies, "Let their roofs rot. It helps their crops to grow" a feeling contrasting with Sir Ralph Skelton of *The Wicked Lady*. He later raises rents and refuses to talk to Jassy's father before murdering him: "You are an ordinary worker. I have no time for you."

Jassy reworks Lockwood's persona in *The Man in Grey* and *The Wicked Lady* into more positive directions. Clarissa Rohan's counterpart, Dilys Hatton (Patricia Roc), now becomes as devious as Hester and Barbara in the earlier films. But this time, negative features become associated with upper-class characters rather than with upwardly mobile lower-class figures such as Hester. Although Jassy is less radical in her methods than Hester and Barbara, she learns how to infiltrate successfully the ranks of the upper classes by cunning and stealth. If Jassy exhibits less "female pleasure" (Landy, 1991, 313) in this film, she manages to achieve her objectives in a more permanent manner than her predecessors in *The Man in Grey* and *The Wicked Lady*. She will, undoubtedly, achieve Landy's idea of "female pleasure" after the final credits. Jassy does not oscillate between being an "unscrupulous schemer" like Hester and Barbara. Nor is she a brave, resourceful, virtuous woman like Fanny and Oriana (Murphy, 1992, 129–30). Lockwood's new character knows the rules of the social game and plays her cards accordingly. When she encounters the man who murdered her father, she responds in an unemotional man-

FIGURE 11. Jassy (Margaret Lockwood) confronts her class enemy Helmar (Basil Sydney) in *Jassy*.

ner ("You are thinking of my father. You shot him dead outside that door.") and uses Helmar's own gambling strategies against him to gain his property and imprison him in a castrating celibate marriage. Both Hester and Barbara lose the game in the long term due to desiring immediate emotional gratification or "female pleasure." Jassy learns from the mistakes of her Gainsborough predecessors. After Helmar suffers an injury in a riding accident, placing him in the same position as Francis Overton in *Dead of Night*, he dies from poison administered by mute servant Lindy (Esma Cannon).

Despite the unconvincing *deus ex machina* solution saving Jassy from the gallows, the film does move toward positively resolving male and female desire. Barney has suffered downward mobility and betrayal by his former sweetheart Dilys (a magnificent change of casting for Patricia Roc). He attempts in vain to save Jassy from execution before the revelation of her innocence. Jassy later relinquishes ownership of the Helmar estate to Barney and refuses his offer of marriage. She understands the unequal nature of the future class relationship that will exist between them when property again falls under male control. However, Barney performs an action parallel to Torquil's sacrificial act in *I Know Where I'm Going*. He tears up the document, violating ideological male rights controlling property and women. If Lockwood's earlier heroines violate convention in their quest for pleasure as Landy notes (1991, 312), Barney also violates patriarchal convention by placing himself in a position of male subordination to gain future egalitarian pleasure with Jassy. After regaining his property and former class position, he decides to earn Jassy's trust by returning to the downwardly mobile status he has occupied throughout most of the film. The resolution appears awkward, but the utopian achievement of equality of desire between the characters deserves commendation.

Lawrence Huntington's *When the Bough Breaks* presents a conservative reaction to *Jassy's* progressive climax. It reveals the postwar bankruptcy of People's War ideals. Seduced and abandoned by a bigamist, working-class mother Lily Bates (Patricia Roc) finds herself unable to care for her baby and offers him for unofficial adoption to upper-middle-class foster mother Frances Norman (Rosamund John), who is unable to bear children of her own. The film clearly recognizes new postwar barriers between women who once united in wartime Britain. They now find themselves separated by traditional prewar class and economic divisions. When Lily marries a suitable class partner, grocer Bill (Bill Owen) she selfishly (in the film's terms) desires the return of her son, Jimmy. Bill offers Lily, "Me, a little security, and a lot of love." Although Lily symbolizes those single women responsible for increased illegitimate births during wartime society, she is no "good-time girl" like Gwen Rawlings. Although confused by her blind refusal to recognize the reality of a class system in which Jimmy's interests now lie with his adoptive parents, the film presents her maternal desires as selfish and destructive. Influenced by Bill, she returns Jimmy from a confining prison of her working-class backyard to his former country garden home. The wartime consensus has now changed. Lily must face new class and economic realities. But the film ends with the ideological reward of her own baby. The final two sequences of the film reveal that rigid class lines now structure individual desires. While the Normans celebrate Jimmy's birthday in their affluent country residence, Lilly and Bill enjoy their baby's first birthday in their working-class home. *When the Bough Breaks* never questions conservative ideological mechanisms influencing its climax. Any wartime utopian relationships between men and women of different classes depicted in *Millions like Us* are now impossible as Charlie shrewdly anticipated.

The Root of All Evil also examines economically divisive postwar themes. Dealing with upwardly mobile, materialistic Jacky Farnish (Phyllis Calvert), the film unconsciously anticipates later developments in British society. It is a Thatcherite Gainsborough melodrama. Farmer's daughter Jackie believes herself engaged to Albert Grice (Hubert Gregg), son of a ruthless, upwardly mobile businessman. The opening sequence occurs in a studio-recreated idyllic countryside, revealing Jackie as hopelessly narcissistic in dreaming about unrealizable artificial romantic goals. As she confesses her love to Albert, the camera tracks down from her face to reflect it in a lily pond. Jackie's desires combine foolish romantic dreams with yearnings for class mobility. However, the film reveals not only the futility of her desires but also dangerous repressed forces within a traditional English Rose who moves toward being a premature Thatcherite wicked lady.

When Jackie's father (Brefni O'Rourke) plunges their farm into debt, her prospective father-in-law George Grice (Edward Young) not only breaks off her engagement to Albert but also refuses to loan her money "to keep you and your family out of the workhouse." Jackie's family loses their farm and become downwardly mobile. Refusing the attentions of devoted farm foreman Joe (John McCallum), Jackie not only substitutes economic desires for her former romanticism but also symbolically and economically castrates George Grice by putting him out of business. Her father and sister, Rushie (Hazel Court), warn Jackie that "money has an unusual habit of tempering our character." But, while Rushie willingly accepts a traditional domestic family life, Jackie relishes playing the male role by taking a ruthless revenge on her former business rival who even humiliates himself further by proposing to her. Jackie refuses the offer, repeating Grice's earlier comments against her: "I don't hold with failures. They're bad luck. They're like weeds, best out of the way." Grice's later death from a heart attack in a pub parallels the masculine humiliation of Waggett in *Whisky Galore* (1949). Both are accompanied by castrating female laughter. Barmaid Pam's (Diana Decker) humiliating mockery parallels Mrs. Waggett's (Catherine Lacey) in the Ealing film.

Pam Cook (1983, 27) sees the film as attempting to negotiate an impossible contradiction between "the mobilization and validation of female desire and the need to channel it in the right direction," as well as mounting a "criticism of materialism, speculation and consumerism." Although Murphy (1992, 109) notes stylistic problems militating against such "an excessively generous assessment," like *Broken Journey*, the film's artistic deficiencies do not undermine its significant ideological message.

The Root of All Evil deals with postwar problems of affluence affecting community values from a female perspective rather than Garland's marginalized position in *Passport to Pimlico*. Like her Hollywood melodrama counterparts, Jackie is a threat to the male order and she embodies Thatcher's vicious future dehumanized revolution. The film uncompromisingly depicts her ruthless economic ambitions and criticizes the weak male alternatives of Joe and her father. Jackie substitutes business for romance. She succeeds in her aims and economically castrates weak males throughout the film. She cunningly fools patriarchal farmer Scholes (Moore Marriot) into selling his oil-rich property cheaply and later economically threatens her affluent lover, Charles (Michael Rennie), when he reacts against her naive desires for marriage. Eventually, Jackie sees the error of her ways. She falls into Joe's arms, affirming the community values she formerly rejected. "I can't live without you. I've tried, Joe. People like us. We belong together." The climax is naturally unconvincing.

Jackie's ruthless independent aggressiveness dominates the film. Her female robber baron capitalism overpowers romantic and communal desires. The film regards such attributes as weak and anachronistic in a changing postwar world. Throughout most of the film, Jackie's single-minded ruthlessness succeeds where Garland and the black marketeers in *Passport to Pimlico* fail. Despite its climax, *The Root of All Evil* does not dismiss as irrelevant the disastrous effects of capitalist exploitation on postwar society.

David MacDonald's *Brothers* (1947) also presents the female as a problem for a patriarchal Isle of Skye community. Although set at the beginning of the century, the film allegorically depicts tensions between the independent wartime female and a traditional community whose rituals rely on repressive violence. Unlike *I Know Where I'm Going*, it is a darkly nihilistic pastoral Scottish film. Cinematographer Stephen Dade's beautiful landscapes parallel English country garden images in *Went the Day Well? This England*, and *The Root of All Evil*, where violence eagerly lurks to destroy any threat to traditional values.

The Brothers opens with convent-bred Glasgow orphan Mary Lawson (Patricia Roc) arriving at Skye. A sexually repressive priest educates her into her new status as servant of the male MacCrae household. While the more cosmopolitan retired Captain McGrath (Will Fyffe) ominously views Mary as "beautiful like a daffodil growing on a dunghill," the priest warns widowed Hector MacCrae (Finlay Currie) of Mary being "a temptation to your sons, if not to you."

Mary symbolizes wartime independent females returning to a postwar society that wishes the return of repressive traditions. She becomes a problem less because of her personality and more due to unresolved tensions within the male psyche. Mary becomes attracted to handsome Fergus MacCrae (Maxwell Reed), who releases his repressions in drunken behavior and lacks the ability to respond to her desires. He finally becomes the agent of her destruction. Mary also refuses the attentions of his equally repressed, but psychotic, puritanical elder brother, John (Duncan Macrae), who wishes to marry her. Ignored by Fergus, alienated by John's dark desires, Mary eventually succumbs to the charms of rival clan antagonist Willie McFarish (Andrew Crawford), who uses her for his own ends. Although condemned by Hector for her "bad blood," she is really a victim of a ruthless male society. Hector's brutal destruction of Willie's harmless present to her foreshadows her violent destruction.

Patricia Roc's assured performance outweighs any attempts by the film to categorize her merely as a destructive *femme fatale*. Tensions within *The Brothers* embody highly complex meanings operating in a seemingly straightforward narrative. Desires clash in an irresolvable manner. As Jeffrey Richards (1985, 289) notes, the film resembles "a British equivalent of a Hollywood Western emphasizing masculine tensions as well as a *film noir* misogynistic tract, a warning of the dangers of unrestrained sexuality." The classical Hollywood Western, evoked by Richards, often comments upon contemporary tensions influencing the period of production rather than attempting any accurate historical recreation. But Mary is no *film noir* destructive heroine. Although her presence results in Hector's death and the compromise of family honor, these problems result from the nature of a society that only allows negative outlets for desire and passion. Dominated by destructive superstitions maniputively evoked by the Isle's repressive spokesman Dugald McLeod (John Laurie), futile clan violence, monetary greed, and grotesque ritual executions represent the only avenues of expression.

Richards cites Pam Cook's (1983, 17) feminist explorations of Gainsborough melodramas, which provide alternative interpretations for Mary's dilemma: "In order to appeal to a female spectator, melodrama must first posit the possibility of female desire and a female point of view, thus making problems for itself which it can scarcely contain." Mary thus becomes a victim of patriarchy rather than a perpetuator of male downfall. Richards's comments on Roc's performance astutely recognize the nature of tensions contained within *The Brothers*. "Patricia Roc's blank inexpressiveness makes Mary a tabula rasa upon which either reading of the film may be inclined according to the inclinations of the spectator."

Mary is trapped within a social structure, frustrating any positive realization of her desires. She turns to Willie McFarnish to alleviate her loneliness. But Willie is not interested in her. He uses her to score points against a rival clan. John lies to his brother about Hector's deathbed wish for Fergus and Mary to marry. Fergus attempts repressing his feelings before falling for her and then brutally ignores her. He later becomes a reluctant partner in his brother's plans to murder Mary, who "has brought nothing but evil on this place." The more cosmopolitan Captain McGrath represents the only alternative to the harsh Skye existence. But his brief reunion of Fergus and Mary results in further alienation and tragedy when Fergus becomes injured in an accident in the rocks. Despite the accidental nature of an injury caused by Fergus's male desire to show off to Mary, Mary bears the blame for this incident. Although no "good time girl," Mary becomes a problem for a patriarchal society unwilling to confront female desire. Trapped within a tragic scenario dominated by repressive forces, *The Brothers* can only end in a violent resolution affecting all participants. However, since the film fails to develop a logical cri-

FIGURE 12. Patricia Roc as Mary in *The Brothers*.

tique of a pathological male society and vacillates between confusing depictions of Mary as *femme fatale* and Mary as victim, it becomes confused. But the very nature of this confusion reflects the problematic nature of postwar female representation in a society attempting to return to prewar normality.

Pam Cook (1985, 290) sees David MacDonald's *Good Time Girl* as a film "trying to negotiate conflicting ideological and institutional pressures at a time of transition." It attempts to contrast society's failed authoritarian way dealing with Gwen Rawlings (Jean Kent) with a "softer, liberal paternalism" so Lyla Lawrence (Diana Dors) avoids the harsh fate of her predecessor. Gwen's character is based on the infamous 1944 Cleft-Chin Killer's girlfriend, Elizabeth Jones, later depicted in *Chicago Joe and The Showgirl* (1990). As Muriel Box pointed out in the *Gainsborough Melodrama* interview (Cook, 1983, 65), *Good Time Girl* suffered from censorship problems affecting the depiction of young girls in approved schools. The difference between Gwen's treatment and that facing unrepentant Lyla is not all that great. As Box commented, "The censor didn't want the British public to know or be frightened by the facts, in case it took exception to them. I thought it smacked of blatant hypocrisy to try and suppress the facts. I was very upset when we were forced finally to alter the film."

Like *The Brothers*, *Good Time Girl* deals with the problematic nature of postwar female sexuality and features an actress known for her "tart" roles in forties cinema paralleling Claire Trevor's "bad girl" image in forties American films. The film focuses on postwar problems of female juvenile delinquency. As Murphy (1992, 90) points out, sexually active good-time girls "were supposedly a leftover from the sexual licence which flourished during the war." However, despite censorship restrictions, the film makes some indirect critiques of disastrous and hypocritically repressive contemporary social attitudes.

Good Time Girl opens in a juvenile court at night. A kindly police sergeant (George Merritt), foreshadowing co-scenarist Ted Willis's Dixon of Dock Green, brings teenage runaway Lyla Lawrence before the juvenile court chairwoman, Miss Thorpe (Flora Robson). He wishes Miss Thorpe "to talk some sense to" Lyla to avoid "another Gwen Rawlings." Although the sergeant describes Lyla's home as "pretty bad," comprising a "family of six, drunken father, mother copped it in the Blitz," Miss Thorpe tells Lyla about Gwen's fate to make her return to these sordid circumstances and prevent any expression of independent desires. Lyla's only "crime" at this point is "hanging around the streets at all hours" and wanting to "live on her own." Miss Thorpe quashes any ideas of female independence: "Gwen Rawlings had the same idea."

The film then moves into flashback ideologically depicting the "decline and fall" of Gwen Rawlings. It initially views Gwen as an innocent female desiring a harmless good time. But such desires are viewed negatively by a repressive society. Like Mary in *The Brothers*, she is a social victim. When Gwen borrows some earrings to wear at a dance, she refuses the sexual bargain her pawnbroker employer offers her in exchange for not informing her father and the police. Later that evening her drunken father (George Carney) brutally assaults her. Gwen leaves home the next day and finds work as a cloakroom girl through the agency of slimy Jimmy Rosso (Peter Glenville). Although club owner Maxie (Herbert Lom) knows she is underage, he decides to employ her. Gwen's dangerous new underworld nightclub environment (with ominous American one-armed bandit near the entrance) eventually leads to her downfall.

Although *Good Time Girl* adopts a moralistic tone concerning the dangers facing girls like Gwen Rawlings, it also suggests that her fate is not entirely deterministic. Other alternatives exist in her life that criminal and legal forces destroy. While Jimmy Rosso sets her up as a criminal accomplice, middle-aged musician Red Farrell (Dennis Price) adopts a caring, paternalistic attitude toward her, which society immediately condemns. Red allows her to stay in his apartment overnight and never takes sexual advantage of her. Touched by a kindness she never experienced from her actual father, Gwen misinterprets his paternal attitude and falls in love with him. Recognizing her adolescent "crush," Red never reciprocates her feelings. But the juvenile court looks on Gwen's relationship with an older man (who has positively changed her life) as abhorrent. It sentences her to three years incarceration at an approved school. Committing her to an environment where "they will look after you and teach you self-control," the harsh sentence condemns Gwen's supposed promiscuity rather than her accidental criminal activity. As Murphy (1992, 91) notes, Miss Thorpe clearly knows the truth about Gwen's circumstances. The sentence embodies her puritanical attitude toward adolescent female sexuality rather than judicial impartiality.

Incarcerated in an environment denying her Red's fatherly letters and influenced by the criminal behavior of "good conduct girl" Roberta (Jill Balcon), Gwen soon becomes corrupted. Despite censorship restrictions, the film does reveal how hypocritical social attitudes contribute to

Gwen's downfall. One sequence contrasts a moralistic middle-class social worker speaking of the institutional "salvation of youngsters from bad company, bad companions, and bad luck" with Gwen's complicity in the torture of an inmate! *Good Time Girl* then rapidly reveals Gwen's descent by depicting her sexual initiation by brutal spiv Danny Martin (Griffith Jones), her guilty role as a homicidal drunken driver, and her final status as criminal accomplice to two American deserters (Bonar Colleano and Hugh McDermott).

Good Time Girl returns to the present after Gwen witnesses Red's murder by one deserter. Sentenced to fifteen years as an accomplice, her fate becomes a moral lesson to her potential successor, Lyla. Lyla decides to return home to the drunken father and squalid circumstances that prompted her to seek an independent life in the first place. But, despite recognizing the social forces that have criminalized Gwen, *Good Time Girl* views female independence as a sexually explosive minefield leading to criminal activity. After escaping from the approved school's contaminating environment, Gwen descends into a British underworld represented by American *film noir* visual techniques and becomes involved with the demonic counterparts of wartime American G.I.s. Formerly, "overpaid, oversexed, and over here," these Americans typify George Orwell's (128) definition of "the false values of the American film" that negatively influenced British good-time girls and the Cleft Chin murderers. As the Bonnie and Clyde of their generation, Karl Hulten and Elizabeth Jones embodied unacceptable forces denied within the official People's War ideology and the succeeding brave new world of the postwar Labour government. *The Krays* (1990) later suggests the negative effect of wartime conditions on the future criminal activities of its title characters. Both Orwell's writings and *Good Time Girl* indicate certain revealing attitudes concerning the repressive nature of contemporary postwar attitudes toward individual desires. Gwen escapes Mary's fate in *The Brothers*. But, as Miss Thorpe points out to Lyla, she has "to wait fifteen years for her second chance"!

Fisher and Darborough's *So Long at the Fair* (1950) confirms observations of David Pirie (53–55) and Murphy (1992, 145) concerning links between Hammer horror and Gainsborough melodrama. It also supports Harper's (1992) thesis about the studio's diminishing lack of interest in feminist sensibility during this period. Although she believes that "Gainsborough's output shifted from libidinous freewheelers to downtrodden conformists with Rank's appointment of Sydney Box" (228) as studio head, many representations were not entirely one-dimensional. Both *Christopher Columbus* and *The Bad Lord Byron* reveal this fact. However, *So Long at the Fair* is a regressive film treating conservatively the theme of a single woman trapped in a dangerous foreign landscape. It sounds a warning to female audiences fascinated by forties Gainsborough depictions of romance and foreign exoticism. *So Long at the Fair* appeared a year before the 1951 Festival of Britain. The 1889 Paris Exhibition in the film allegorizes those repressed symptoms of insularity and xenophobia later influencing its British counterpart in 1951.

Victoria Barton (Jean Simmons) falls in love with Paris and persuades her stuffy brother, Johnny (David Tomlinson), to enjoy the excitement of the 1889 Exhibition. She exclaims romantically, "I've decided to have my honeymoon here!" But Johnny mysteriously disappears. Sinister hotel owner Madame Herve (Cathleen Nesbitt) denies any knowledge of his existence. Victoria then finds herself a misunderstood damsel in distress surrounded by dark forces in an environment she once found charming. Aided by handsome George Hathaway (Dirk Bogarde), she later participates in a less romantic version of her honeymoon romance when she disguises herself as George's mistress for an evening liaison. Victoria finally discovers that Paris's exotic charms cover disease and treachery. Johnny has contracted the plague, and the Parisians wish to conceal this during the tourist season. Although another authoritative English male, Dr. Hart (André Morell), finally tells Victoria that Johnny has a "slight chance" of survival, she clearly learns her lesson about romanticizing foreign shores. Nice young ladies in the 1950s will now become stay-at-home English Roses.

Problems of postwar adjustment also affected males. Although *Dancing with Crime* (1946) and *They Made Me a Fugitive* made links between crime and wartime experiences, most contemporary films denied this. But not all veterans resembled those later images of Richard Todd in *The Dam Busters* (1955) and Kenneth More in *Reach for the Sky* (1956). Several postwar films featured Eric Portman embodying a British male psycho persona influenced as much by actual cases of wartime trauma as postwar murderers such as Neville Heath, John George Haigh, and Donald Hume. Heath and Hume used dubious wartime heroic identities for their murderous activities. Murphy (1992, 168–73, 186) notes the sporadic appearance of this dangerous figure in British cinema. He suggests that Eric Portman's murderous persona in *Wanted for Murder, Dear Murderer, Daybreak,* and *The Mark of Cain* (1948) may derive from Colpepper in *A Canterbury Tale*. But it is more likely that actual cases of disturbed war heroes, as well as Portman's traumatic performance in *Great Day*, influenced these representations. Like World War I "shell shock," male hysteria and trauma were defined as "un-British." Males who found it difficult to function in wartime and postwar society were marginalized and deliberately forgotten.

Co-scripted by Rodney Ackland and Emeric Pressburger, Lawrence Huntington's *Wanted for Murder* (1946) suggests that hereditary insanity motivates Victor Colebrooke's (Portman) serial killer attacks on single females. As the son of a celebrated Victorian hangman, Victor shares his father's pleasure in his murderous activities. The police authorities eventually corner Victor, who commits suicide. He leaves the field clear for a healing romantic union between antiseptic British lovers played by Derek Farr and Dulcie Grey. Their normative heterosexual coupling finally eliminates any lingering traces of aberrant male trauma from the film. *Wanted for Murder* is a severely compromised film, but elements in the screenplay and Portman's excellent performance suggest factors that censorship could not entirely remove.

Portman's debonair "male psycho" anticipates later real-life British serial killers such as Haig and Heath. Serial killers inhabit the dark underside of British as well as American society. Victor's role symbolizes certain dangerous images of returning veterans who cannot adjust to peacetime. *Wanted for Murder* also anticipates motifs in *Psycho* and *Peeping Tom*. It also employs devices used by Hitchcock in *Strangers on a Train* such as the fairground carousel, record booth, and reoccurring musical *leitmotif* for the killer, which parallels the "Merry Widow Waltz" of *Shadow of a Doubt* (1943) and "The Band Played On" in *Strangers on a Train*. Ackland (1954, 164) borrowed the musical *leitmotif* from Fritz Lang's use of the *Peer Gynt* theme in *M* (1931). Victor's psychopathology originates from family circumstances. However, the finished film suffered censorship restrictions that diluted radical insights in the original screenplay. The play and first-draft screenplay originally condemned capital punishment. In his autobiography, Ackland (162–63) mentioned that the producer envisaged an American release and cut out all scenes offending Hays Code sensibilities. Among these were several viewing Victor's mother as an ancestor of *Psycho*'s Mrs. Bates. However, faint echoes of the original project appear in the final version.

The opening scene features a fairground Punch and Judy show. This popular entertainment presents wife beating, murder, and capital punishment as normal features of the British way of life. Although Victor blames his father for influencing his serial killer assaults on young females, he is also the victim of a possessive mother and expresses resentment of her by seeking surrogate victims. But *Wanted for Murder* could not explicitly associate violent enactment of sexual desire with a psychopathological British family system based on incest. It conveniently ascribes Victor's aberration to individual hereditary causes. British society thus exhibits a sigh of relief. Victor is not "one of us."

The *October Man* directly relates its portrayal of male hysteria to postwar issues of masculine dilemma. Although made a year before the discovery of Haigh's acid-bath crimes, Murphy (1992, 180) correctly notes that the setting evokes those "shabby respectable lodging-houses of West London where Haigh operated." It also depicts the sterility and viciousness of a stagnant postwar class system that provided an appropriate breeding ground for the activities of fifties serial killer John Reginald Christie.

Jim Ackland (John Mills) survives a coach crash and experiences traumatic survivor guilt over the death of a friend's daughter. Plagued with suicidal tendencies like a disturbed wartime hero, he moves to the death-in-life environment of Brockhurst Common Hotel inhabited by dowdy spinster Miss Selby (Catherine Lacey), vicious gossip Mrs. Vinton (Joyce Carey), and retired businessman Peachey (Edward Chapman). Spurned by female guest Molly, who is involved in a frustrating adulterous relationship, Peachey murders her and places the blame on Jim. *The October Man* views the nihilistically repressive postwar British society as more threatening to Jim than his actual mental condition. Despite the love of Jenny (Joan Greenwood), Jim finds himself presumed guilty by her brother (Patrick Holt), spiteful hotel guests, supercilious police inspector, and Molly's cowardly lover. Jim eventually discovers the truth when Peachey reveals everything to him. Peachey earlier treats Jim as "a condemned man" and recognizes the inhibiting masochistic tendencies in his victim, which he manipulates to his own advantage. Peachey mentions sexual jealousy and class hatred as factors motivating his murderous activity. "I killed her. Why do you think I stayed in this middle-class filth?"

Although *The October Man* ends positively with Peachey's arrest and Jim's conquest of his suicidal tendencies, a somber note remains. Jim's salvation is accidental, the result of arbitrarily convenient *deus ex machina* circumstances rather of any change in the minds of his accusers. Jim symbolizes a traumatically affected postwar male attempting to readjust to a different society. But factors beyond his control frustrate any attempts he makes to overcome his trauma and achieve a positive relationship with Jenny. Jim becomes targeted as a convenient scapegoat by various pathological representatives of a society returning to the worst features of prewar repressiveness and viciousness.

Trevor Howard's Clem Morgan of Cavalcanti's *film noir They Made Me a Fugitive* also typifies the dilemma of the hero returning to postwar society. As a former P.O.W. R.A.F. flyer, Clem sublimates his frustrations with peacetime society in alcohol and sex. When he describes himself to vicious spiv Narcy (Griffith Jones) as "bored, bored. If it wasn't for Ellen I'd have done myself a mischief," his middle-class girlfriend Ellen replies, "What he needs is another war." Narcy offers Clem a criminal world of "free enterprise." When Narcy later tires of this "very neurotic" amateur and falsely incriminates him, Clem escapes from prison to seek revenge. Although he loses Ellen to Narcy and strikes up a tentative relationship with Narcy's former girlfriend, Sally (Sally Gray), the film offers no possibility of any permanent healing relationship. Clem is already tarnished by his war experiences. He significantly describes his criminal activities to the frustrated Mrs. Fenshaw, who wishes him to murder her husband. "I went on doing what the country put me in uniform to do after they took it back." When Sally later extracts pellets from his back, Clem traumatically mumbles in a foreign language, recalling his captivity. Clem finds himself used and abused by a society that ignores his dilemma. Narcy initially enrolls Clem in his criminal activities ("We need a bit of class in our specialty") and then frames him. Mrs. Fenshaw later murders her husband and blames Clem for the crime. She sees him as a convenient victim for whom another criminal offense would make no difference. Although Inspector Rockliffe (Ballard Berkely) believes in Clem's innocence— "How'd you come to get mixed up with cheap scum like Narcy? You had an excellent war record"—he uses him as bait and sends Clem back to jail after Narcy lies in his dying confession. Even though Rockliffe knows the truth, he abides by the letter of a repressive legal and social situation.

As Murphy (1992, 154–55) shows, *They Made Me a Fugitive* evoked critical condemnation for images of an ugly postwar society many preferred to ignore. Narcy's cynical asides to the contemporary government's "brave new world" darkly counter official optimism and "the simple sentimentalities of *The Courtneys of Curzon Street*" (Murphy, 155). "Don't be so reactionary. This is the century of the common man." The film also engages in "bad taste" by indirectly suggesting that aged Aggie

FIGURE 13. Inspector Rockcliffe (Ballard Berkely) returns Clem (Trevor Howard) to jail away from Sally (Sally Gray) in *They Made Me a Fugitive*.

(Mary Merrall) enjoys sex with her "boyfriend." Her role parallels Flora Robson's Countess Platen in *Saraband for Dead Lovers* (1948). *They Made Me a Fugitive* offends British sexual taboos by acknowledging that older women are sexually active. It also avoids the typical romantic happy ending of the heroine waiting for the hero's release from prison. When Sally engages in a "soppy" farewell to Clem, pledging, "I won't forget you," her more embittered lover replies, "That's what I was afraid of."

Like *Daybreak*, *Dear Murderer* reveals postwar male impotence motivating masculine violence. Both films star Eric Portman, an actor specializing in roles embodying male insecurity at this time. *Dear Murderer* functions as a critique of a postwar lifestyle of the affluent upper class whose lives revolve around adultery and violence. Lee Warren (Portman) commits the perfect crime by killing his wife's former lover, Richard Fenton (Dennis Price), and making it look like suicide. He then attempts to incriminate her new lover, Jimmy Martin (Maxwell Reed), before Vivien (Greta Gynt) seductively manipulates him into changing the evidence. *Dear Murderer's film noir* overtones present Vivien as a "spider woman" and postwar upper-class British society as little different from its selfish counterpart in *Laura*. Like *They Made Me a Fugitive*, any positive realization of desires is impossible in an environment returning to prewar murderous class values.

As in *Dead of Night*, postwar British society fears of a strong American economic competitor play significant roles in certain films. In *Dear Murderer*, Lee's transfer to a New York office makes possible Vivien's affair with Richard. Edward Dmytryk's *Obsession* (1949) clearly relates Dr. Clive Riordan's (Robert Newton) scheme to rid himself of an American rival with impotent British fears of a strong postwar economic competitor. The film contains two scenes in Riordan's club where its members express worries about America's growing supremacy on the world stage. Storm Riordan (Sally Gray) is as selfish and manipulative as Vivien in *Dear Murderer*, preferring a more masculine and affluent Yank (Phil Brown) to her boring train enthusiast husband.

Further down the social scale, *Daybreak* shows Eric Portman living a double life like his character in *Wanted for Murder*. But this time, Portman's character is in control of both his profession and his murderous impulses. Again affected by censorship factors (Aspinall, Murphy, 86–87), this Sydney Box production features Portman as public hangman Mendoza living an everyday life as kindly barber Eddie Tribe. When he inherits the barge business of his despised father, he falls in love with

FIGURE 14. Riordan (Robert Newton) plans to avenge his humiliation on an American rival in *Obsession.*

dance hall girl Frankie (Ann Todd). Both characters are affected by past traumatic family relationships. They lost their mothers at an early age and hated their fathers. Despite their problematic backgrounds, they marry and attempt to live a hopelessly idealistic family relationship. Since they are victims of past behavioral patterns that return to dominate them, their marital relationship is a fragile edifice built on denial. Although Frankie dismisses a romantic movie to her more romantically inclined older partner as "It doesn't happen. Men don't do that in real life," they begin a fantasy marriage despite their different ages and backgrounds. Eddie is clearly impotent. As Landy (1991, 267) notes, "Their interactions settle into something more akin to father-daughter relations than those of a couple. Childlike, she seeks to please him and succeeds for a short time."

The arrival of handsome Danish seaman Olaf (Maxwell Reed) disrupts this fragile union. Olaf offers a torrid sexual relationship to Frankie, to which she succumbs. It leads to a violent confrontation between Eddie and Olaf on the barge. After Eddie falls overboard, Olaf is convicted for his presumed murder. Stricken with guilt, Frankie commits suicide. Although Eddie finds he cannot execute Olaf in his official capacity as hangman, he later hangs himself in his barber shop. *Daybreak* again depicts the impossibility of any positive form of desire existing in postwar Britain. The flawed personalities of Eddie and Frankie as well as the (Hollywood) un-British "film star" (Landy, 267) nature of Olaf's desiring threat presents a sexual crisis leading to tragedy and masochistic violence.

Terence Young's *Corridor of Mirrors* is another neglected, but fascinating, work dealing with a dangerous world of desire. It also makes unconvincing arguments for the necessity of postwar repression. Set in 1938, with a 1945 prologue and epilogue, the film centers around eccentric artist Paul Mangin (Portman) who believes in reincarnation and desires to live in the past. He hopes to find a love he lost during a previous life in 1486 Italy. Discovering her in Mifanwy Conway (Edana Romney), Paul attempts to "charm" her into his artistic world. His activities parallel Lermontov's dominance of Vicky in *The Red Shoes* (1948), as well as Scottie Ferguson's manipulative activities in Hitchcock's *Vertigo* (1958).

Co-scripted by Romney and Rudolph Cartier (who would later produce fifties BBC television classics such as *1984* and the *Quatermass* series), *Corridor of Mirrors* inserts the viewer into Paul and Mifanwy's oneiric fantasy. Several scenes show them dancing deliriously in a renaissance world of artistic imagination set against Paul's corridor of mirrors. Although tempted to leave her mundane thirties nightclub existence and join Paul forever, Mifanwy loses her nerve and attaches herself to Owen Rees (Hugh Sinclair) in much the same way as Vicky aligns herself with Julian in *The Red Shoes*.

Influenced by *Laura* and echoing postwar reincarnation escapist films such as *Portrait of Jennie* (1949), *Corridor of Mirrors* realizes that seductive wish-fulfillment desires for romance and escapism are now impossible in the postwar era. It foreshadows the ideological message of *So Long at the Fair*. While Mifanwy prefers boring Owen (played by an actor who would later embody typical male British virtues by his very name of "Bob Britain" in the 1961 television sitcom *A Life of Bliss*, whose title character would always be "terribly shy and still a bachelor"), the innocent Paul decides to face the gallows in his own impeccable manner. "I've always had a liking for dramatic effects." As in *The Red Shoes*, an eccentric artist becomes the most fascinating character in the entire film. Paul's seductiveness appeals more than a dull husband who takes Mifanwy into the rural isolation of North Wales for a future domestic life coping with three obnoxious children. Despite its fascination with Paul's artistic world, *Corridor of Mirrors* chooses to privilege a repressed, bourgeois family life rather than follow radical alternatives.

David MacDonald's *Bad Lord Byron* is an interesting postscript to the final cycle of Sydney Box productions. Although not officially associated with Gainsborough, the film has several affinities to the studio's previous works and critiques their melodramatically voyeuristic pleasures. Landy (1991, 87) comments that the "episodic structure of the film, which moves from courtroom to flashback, from inviting the spectator to be a voyeur to inviting him to be a juror, are awkwardly juxtaposed." She views the film as attempting to recover patriarchal values. However, this reading denies the presence of formal and thematic features that provide alternatives to the repressive nature of earlier Gainsborough films. *The Bad Lord Byron* also emphasizes positive directions involving desire and freedom the wartime films never followed.

Rather than aiming to captivate female desires in solipsistic voyeuristic ways to reimpose status quo resolution, *The Bad Lord Byron* deliberately aims to juxtapose, "awkwardly," visual spectacle with rational argument presented in a heavenly courtroom. Employing a quasi-Brechtian discourse, *The Bad Lord Byron* contrasts the deceptively seductive lure of costume spectacle with a sober theatrical courtroom world to compare different values of freedom and sexuality. It concludes by asking viewers to make up their minds and resolve for themselves the question of

Byron's identity. If most of *The Bad Lord Byron's* females differ from earlier Gainsborough counterparts, this is because they reflect the problematic nature of postwar womanhood rather than earlier wicked ladies personified by Margaret Lockwood. The film makes clear that Byron is more sinned against than sinning in an England whose repressiveness clearly echoes its real-life postwar world. It presents Byron as dying in the cause of Greek independence, as an aristocrat infuriating the House of Lords by condemning class oppression, and a figure trapped by narcissistic female desires making him either a passive spectacle for sexual pleasure (Lady Caroline Lamb) or a reluctant partner in a marriage he finds restrictive and oppressive (Augusta Leigh). Eventually, Byron discovers that he can only achieve true sexual and political liberation by leaving England entirely. He finally meets his true partner, Teresa Guiccioli (Mai Zetterling), in Venice and aids the cause of Italian and Greek independence. Unlike *So Long at the Fair, The Bad Lord Byron's* Europe is the only place permitting free expression of personal and political freedom. It is the one territory where Byron can actively intervene against oppressive forces rather than his repressive homeland.

Criticized during its original release and neglected today, *The Bad Lord Byron* is the last forties film suggesting any hopes of positively realizing those personal and political structures of desire British ideology attempts to frustrate. It needs reevaluation as one of several (admittedly limited) cinematic alternatives suggesting liberation of desire as a healthy solution for a repressed British social structure. The film represents emergent rather than resilient values. It clearly finds the British character and its crippling social structure inimical to alternative expression of desires on political and sexual levels. At the climax, the judge's face emerges from the shadows, and Byron challenges the viewer as he looks directly into the camera. It leaves the verdict on Byron's character for the viewer to decide. The same is true about whether British culture may ever realize desire in positive ways. Unfortunately, later works in British cinema reveal an industry and audiences failing to rise to the challenge of Byron's question.

CHAPTER SIX

Postwar Archers

As the previous chapter notes, postwar Britain experienced a partial return to conservative family values and hegemonic dominance of patriarchal values. However, in analyzing the 1945–1950 period, Harper (1992, 217) warns us that women were not "mere passive victims of social policies" and argues that more ambivalent cinematic depictions of male and female roles sometimes occur. Even if a major contemporary female producer such as Betty Box avoided radical sexual politics in her films, "Conversely, male film-makers did not automatically expose the coarse workings of a punitive patriarchy and they produced some films which could be categorized as feminist." (Harper, 218). She cites *Gone to Earth* (1950) as one such example. But most representations depict class and gender interests as "usually displaced, complicated or disguised" (216).

The postwar Archers films display this productive ambivalence. It was the only way such ideas could appear in an industry dominated by censorship restrictions and axioms of "good taste" structuring forties British ideas concerning quality cinema (see Ellis, 1978a). Although critics such as Raymond Durgnat attempt a political reading of the 1946 *A Matter of Life and Death* (U.S. title, *Stairway to Heaven*) in terms of its Tory critique of the Welfare State, the film actually refuses any such easy categorization. This applies to most of the Archers' productions. As Murphy (1992, 117) recognizes, both *A Matter of Life and Death* and *Black Narcissus* (1947) "are love stories but of such a unique nature that they defy classification." A cinematically hybrid mixture of European and Hollywood romantic expressionism dominates the work of Powell and Pressburger. But relevant cultural, historical, and social influences also affect these productions. Despite Powell's tendency to view his films as artistic creations exclusively, they are neither ahistorical nor confined to the realm of "art for art's sake." If The Archers recreate the Himalayas in Pinewood studios, this isolated environment was by no means immune from contemporary British sexual and social tensions as the nuns discover in *Black Narcissus*.

Various characters in *A Matter of Life and Death* (*Stairway to Heaven*), *Black Narcissus*, *The Red Shoes* (1948), *The Small Back Room* (1949), *Gone to Earth* (1950), and *The Tales of Hoffmann* (1951) inhabit artificial environments seemingly unrelated to the historical issues of the day. However, these environments take the form of different cinematic microscopes isolating deadly viruses operating within the national character. Rather than eliminating "unwholesome elements" in the body politic/sexual as certain hegemonic cinematic productions do, these films focus upon harmful, repressive features operating within British society and its national cinema. Instead of submitting to false illusionary discourses of "British cinematic realism," Powell and Pressburger devise their own fantastic worlds of visual *ostranomie* to "make strange" psychic operations of everyday life and thus expose a pathological cultural climate inimical to desire and personal freedom. The various formal devices employed by their postwar works (fantasy, melodrama, ballet, wartime realism, costume drama, and opera) highlight the psychic mechanisms of an oppressive world of British culture and society that opposes the free operation of desire. Characteristically, the Archers conclude their artistic career with *Oh Rosalinda!!* (1955), a romantic opera emphasizing the absurdities inherent within the play of sexual desire, as well as other more deadly absurdities dominating cold war politics. Set in a Vienna divided among American, British, French, and Russian zones, *Oh Rosalinda!!* began its drama in the bedroom and concluded it there after an operatic play of amorous contradictions and misunderstandings. Although the film still awaits critical reappraisal, Powell and Pressburger anticipate a slogan used in a later turbulent period—"Make Love, Not War." The sterile climate of 1955 Britain made such realization impossible.

In different ways, the Archers' films present conflicting worlds of competing male and female desire. They often employ excessive melodramatic devices to depict females struggling to realize their independent desire in hostile male environments. *The Red Shoes* and *Gone to Earth* also reveal the melodramatic existence of insecure male desires influencing various forms of patriarchal dominance. Despite portraying the major obstacles affecting the realization of female desire, the Archers' films often conclude in ways that are neither ideologically recuperative nor punitively negative. As Harper (1992, 227) notes, the Archers' females were "not passive bearers of tradition, but key speakers of it." Many of the films insist that

> elite groups which outlawed desire could not survive, and that sexual repression was as dangerous for females as for males. . . . *The Red Shoes* . . . extended the debate into the constitution of the artistic temperament. It did not argue that women had to choose between marriage and a career but that domesticity was inimical to any creative drive. Both sexes inside the coterie had love affairs. In *The Red Shoes* it was family life, with its suffocatingly mean horizon, which defeated artistic creativity. Its sexual politics were thus bohemian.

Postwar Archers films complement contemporary productions featuring Eric Portman as a psychotic sacrificial victim of a repressive society (*Wanted for Murder, Dear Murderer, Corridor of Mirrors, Daybreak*), as well as those grim moralistic dramas revealing the impossibility of desire in a hypocritical society such as *Good Time Girl. The Small Back Room* also deals with issues of male trauma present in films such as *They Made Me a Fugitive* and *The October Man.*

As Powell (487) states, *A Matter of Life and Death* was a project designed to improve Anglo-American relationships, which the team "decided should be a love story." It complements *Oh Rosalinda!!* in showing how troubled personal and political realms may achieve eventual positive resolution. Powell (536) followed Pressburger's suggestion of filming "Two Worlds, one in color, the other in monochrome," by using technicolor for the "real world" and black and white for the heavenly realm. Although Durgnat (29–30) suggests the latter choice expresses "perennial Tory criticisms of the Socialist Utopia—that is, the Welfare State," John Ellis (1978b, 93) convincingly argues that the film engages in a "series of profound reservations about the realist aesthetic and realist filmmaking" by contrasting two contradictory cinematic discourses of documentary and fictional narrative in its construction. Sexuality represents the main problem in the film. It may resolve desire within a "heavenly" realm organized according to the realist aesthetic. Or it may choose the disruptively technicolor world of a fantastic realm represented by its Hollywood rival intruding into the everyday world of "reality." Ellis believes the film offers two subject positions for viewers torn between conflicting documentary and narrative fictional discourses. However, *A Matter of Life and Death* does attempt to resolve a perennial problem affecting British cinema in showing how the two realms really complement each other. This leads to a positive ending affirming the validity of desire. Powell and Pressburger thus humorously play with two opposing positions dominating the minds of contemporary critics and filmmakers by deliberately undermining their divisive qualities. Technicolor dominates the "real" world, while monochrome characterizes an "other" world usually depicted in fantastically colored devices. *A Matter of Life and Death* concludes by not only synthesizing these opposing formal worlds but also resolving cultural questions over desire and national identity in a democratically pluralist and international manner.

As Ellis (93) notes, *A Matter of Life and Death* begins with a color documentary-style tour of the universe moving toward an increasingly disruptive mode of narration before introducing Peter (David Niven) and June (Kim Hunter). According to classical theories of cinematic narration, the climax must answer problems raised in the beginning. These opening scenes merging monochrome and color foreshadow the climactic resolution between earthly and heavenly realms when representatives of the fantastic descend the staircase and enter a "real" world of technicolor. Divided by space but connected by radio, the doomed airman and helpless American W.A.F. begin a seemingly futile courtship. After losing his parachute, Peter decides to bail out rather than face a fiery death. His miraculous survival and escape from the inventory of the heavenly realm causes a cosmic crisis. Since Peter escapes the attention of Conductor 71 (Marius Goring) due to an English fog, the ordered heavenly realm must attempt to rectify its error and persuade the "one who got away" to face the consequences of "the night my number came up" (to pun the titles of two fifties British films dealing with realistic and fantastic worlds). Since Peter falls in love with June, he regards his circumstances as changed. He begins an appeal leading to a unique meeting of the heavenly court for the purposes of judgment.

Although *A Matter of Life and Death* emphasizes the dilemma affecting the romantic relationship between Peter and June, it also attempts to resolve cinematic contradictions between the two modes of narration it employs in its construction—documentary realism and fiction—by resolving issues of desire in a utopian merger of form and content. Earthly and heavenly realms are formally divided worlds. Heaven's monochromatic structure of order, punctuality, and regulated relationships between the sexes appears antithetical to Durgnat's description of earth's "selfless individualism of romantic love" (1971, 30). Dominated by the icy nanny figure of the chief recorder (Joan Maude) and admired by the prewar civil servant English pilot (Richard Attenborough), the gigantic, bureaucratic heavenly realm appears hostile to the realization of desire as any contemporary realist British movie. Yet, even there Bob's (Robert Coote) unrequited (but seemingly permissible) yearning for Kathleen Byron's angel and the "over sexed" invasion of brash American pilots led by the ubiquitous Bonar Colleano suggest that not everything may run like clockwork in the heavenly realm. The angel actually breaches regulations in allowing Bob to wait for Peter at the heavenly entrance. She also admits that mistakes have happened within heaven's recently past memory of a thousand years. Conductor 71's foppish manner also suggests gay overtones influencing his earthly visitations to Peter and constant invitations to play chess for eternity. However, he is also an accepted member of an inclusive heavenly community comprising the diverse national figures of John Bunyan, Negro servicemen, Sikh soldiers, people from all historical eras, and female nurses and officers. This heavenly realm is not really Durgnat's (1971, 30) "monotonous superficial routinization" typifying a one-dimensional world. It contains contradictions capable of breaching its supposedly monolithic facade. The same is true of the "real" world. It certainly appears a lush, "fantastic" technicolor environment. But England's demiparadise is also under the control of the camera obscura gaze of Dr. Reeves (Roger Livesey). Although more benevolent than Thomas Colpepper, this country secular priest exhibits disturbing reminders of his *Canterbury Tale* predecessor when he spies on a village girl conversing with Yanks in the square. His actions not only evoke the gaze of the Glue Man but also anticipate the murderous gaze of Mark Lewis in *Peeping Tom*. Reeves's accidental death saves him from the deadly temptations experienced by Colpepper and Lewis when he moves from being earthly judge (and potential executioner) to defending counsel in the heavenly realm. As Ellis (1978, 96–98) notes, Reeves has an unrequited passion for June as well as ambiguous desires toward Peter that removal to the heavenly realm resolve.

A Matter of Life and Death argues for a union between British and American culture stylistically mediated by merging two opposing national cinematic styles harmoniously. Reeves describes Peter's condition as involving "highly organized hallucinations comparable to an experience in real life, a combination of vision, hearing, and idea." This dilemma articulates the film's project of resolving postwar conflicts, whether cultural, national, or romantic, into some form of positive unity. Early scenes in the film suggest the importance of merging opposing positions. Peter describes his personal resolution of political contradictions by being "Conservative by nature" but "Labour by experience." Synthesis and unity are important features of *A Matter of Life and Death*. By focusing upon the romantic relationship between Peter and June, the Archers make a unique argument against cinematic and cultural isolation. Ironically, the British cultural climate will soon fall again into these traditional behavioral patterns characterized by isolation and insecurity. Even country dweller Reeves admits that June's presence in his village is worth more than any ambassadors. Peter opens his heart to an unseen American woman in what may be his last moments of life. The dilemma is finally resolved in the heavenly courtroom. Both Reeves and American British xenophobic Abraham Farlan (Raymond Massey) admit to negative aspects of their national cultural worlds (boring cricket commentary and banal crooner). They move toward an eventual rapprochement recognizing that Justice and Love rule over and above the Law of the Universe. Representatives of the heavenly court finally descend the staircase and enter a technicolor world where all sides are equal. Although Farlan eventually recognizes the genuine love Peter has for June, one more obstacle remains.

As Harper (1992, 227) points out, by taking Reeves at his word and mounting the staircase in her lover's place June finally proves her love for Peter to the satisfaction of Farlan and the heavenly realm. Her action symbolizes "her high place in the chivalric order" of the Archers universe of desire "without which social groups must falter." June begins a noble gesture that could lead to her death. But she escapes the fates of Vicky in *The Red Shoes* and Hazel in *Gone to Earth* by performing an act based upon selfless love for her partner rather than one necessitated by the repressive exigencies of a cruel social world. Peter can only watch in impotence as the staircase begins to transport June toward the heavenly realm. But her gesture finally stops the staircase. It confirms Reeves' point that although "nothing is stronger than the Law in the universe, there is nothing stronger than love on earth." Antithetical realms of law and desire converge. Finally, the judge (Abraham Sofaer), who is also Peter's surgeon on earth, sums up his ruling by quoting from Sir Walter Scott's lines, "Love

FIGURE 15. June (Kim Hunter) proves her love for Peter (David Niven) by breaching heavenly and national boundaries opposing desire in *A Matter of Life and Death*.

is Heaven and Heaven is Love," and pronouncing that "the rights of the uncommon man must always be respected." After the monochromatic heaven experiences a technicolor world beloved by Conductor 71, the final sequence reveals Peter awakening from his operation and expressing a utopian victory with male and female as allied partners in the fulfillment of desire. "*We* won, darling" (italics mine). Unfortunately, despite *A Matter of Life and Death*'s optimistic conclusion, other Archers productions reveal powerful obstacles preventing positive resolutions of desire.

As Michael Walker (9) notes, "*Black Narcissus* is a rare creature indeed: a great British movie." Roy Stafford (1986) also sees it as a significant film uniting various genres, such as horror, melodrama, and colonial discourse within a Himalayas constructed in Pinewood Studios. The film also contributes several key insights into the nature of the contemporary British psyche. Although Powell later denied that *Black Narcissus* contained elements of a "critique of British insularity and imperialism" (Tony Williams, 1981a, 13), such features indirectly complement the film's dominant theme of sexual repression.

An Anglican order of nuns, based in Calcutta, sends a group of five to turn the former mountain seraglio of Mopu into a mission offering educational and medical services to the surrounding population. The nuns clearly wish to colonize a former native dominion in the name of Western values aided by the old general (Esmond Knight), a local ruler seeing many advantages from co-operating with the powerful British Empire. *Black Narcissus* is set in the prewar era before the contemporary postwar struggles leading to independence and partition. Unlike movies, such as *They Were Sisters*, that seek return to a supposedly secure thirties world to solve personal and social problems, *Black Narcissus* reveals the impossibility of this peculiarly British "eternal return." With the exception of sturdy Sister Briony (Judith Furse), each sister slowly becomes affected by the sensual atmosphere of an environment their order (and culture) does its utmost to deny. The sisters also have to come to terms with certain respective individual past problems they joined the order to deny. Sister Philippa (Flora Robson) forgets her task of growing a mundane vegetable garden on the slopes of Mopu and finally creates a glorious technicolor version of an English country garden. As Walker (12) comments, affected by the return of past memories, she produces a "*horticultural* return of the repressed." Sister Blanche (Jenny Laird) falls victim to desires for popularity (and sublimated love) from her sisters and native population by trying to help a sick child rather than diplomatically withdrawing from a situation that proves dangerous. As Mr. Dean (David Farrar) warns, the native population blames them for the child's death. Sister Ruth (Kathleen Byron) represents the most extreme case among the colonizing sisters. Despite knowing Ruth's unsuitability for the demands of the order she has joined, Mother Dorothea (Nancy Roberts) suggests that newly appointed Mother Superior Sister Clodagh (Deborah Kerr) take her along and give her responsibility to "make her feel important." Although Dorothea sarcastically suggests that Clodagh spare Ruth some of her "own importance" after Clodagh queries whether it is good for Ruth to feel important, the nature of her remark reveals her as equally arrogant and full of pride as the novice mother superior she criticizes. As Walker notes, Sister Ruth (10) certainly embodies Sister Clodagh's "return of the repressed" feelings concerning her relationship with Mr. Dean. But the social order also bears responsibility for creating the situation the sisters face. Operating on the levels of fantasy and melodrama, *Black Narcissus* contains an embedded cultural subtext suggesting that an emotionally repressive British culture and society are more deserving of condemnation than its victims and scapegoats.

The High Anglican Convent of the Order of the Servants of Mary exists in the Raj city of Calcutta. Although desiring to do good works for the native population, the order is not only culturally inept in terms of understanding the nature of its environment but also psychologically crippled by past events related to their own colonial culture. We never learn what originally motivated Sisters Briony, Philippa, Blanche, and Ruth into convent life. But Sister Clodagh's confession to Mr. Dean contains suggestions indirectly illuminating the other problems affecting the other sisters. In her evening conversation with Mr. Dean before Sister Ruth's final breakdown, Sister Clodagh speaks of the Mopu environment's "overwhelming" effect on them all. As Powell notes, the "*special* environment" of Mopu (Tony Williams, 13) or the fantastic expression of a collective inner landscape, affects them all. She informs Dean, "I couldn't stop the wind from blowing, and the air from being as clear as crystal, and I couldn't hide the mountain." She then tells him about her past relationship in Ireland with a man who eventually jilted her in a small community. "I had shown him that I loved him." Clodagh's sense of sexual humiliation and shame in her national repressive community not only leads to an unsatisfactory celibate life but also her problematic sublimation of desire. All the sisters suffer from different psychologically crippling aspects of British colonial and cultural imperialism.

Like the other nuns, Clodagh discovers that she cannot escape her past. If Mr. Dean reawakens her repressed sexual feelings with Sister Ruth functioning as Clodagh's dualistically monstrous "return of the repressed," secondary characters such as the young general (Sabu) and Kanchi (Jean Simmons) embody another "return of the repressed" formula. They consummate the very desires their colonial masters repress. The young general and Kanchi reenact Clodagh's relationship with her Irish boyfriend, Con (Shaun Noble). Stafford and Walker show that Clodagh's three flashbacks to her past parallel present actions in *Black Narcissus* involving these two colonial "others." Clodagh's flashback to her memories of a hunt introduce the young general, who arrives on horseback. Clodagh's memory of her narcissistic look in the mirror wearing her grandmother's emerald earrings evokes Kanchi's flirtatious gaze at herself in the mirror when she sees the young general. Con left Ireland and deserted Clodagh for a more affluent life in America. The young general wears affluent clothes. Sister Clodagh later remarks, "He reminds me of Con." The young general's costumes symbolize Con's desire for affluence he will never achieve in Ireland. Furthermore, the young general's acquisition of Black Narcissus perfume from a British army store is not merely a humorous reference. It reveals Britain's relationship to a world that colonial discourse attempts to segregate and define as other, whether racially or sexually.

When Ayah (May Hallett) whips Kanchi for stealing, she slyly offers the young general a stick to continue the process. She clearly attempts to encourage a relationship structured on unhealthily unequal power norms involving class, gender, and masochism. He refuses the offer, but he and Kanchi run away together and fulfill their desires. Although he later apologizes to Clodagh for his behavior, he speaks in a diplomatically polite manner rather than expressing spontaneous feelings of atonement and guilt. Their final meeting follows Sister Ruth's death. It reveals the young general's mature acceptance of a relationship that his repressed, civilized colonial masters cannot deal with. He now intends to become a warrior rather than a product of a problematically disturbed colonial system. Although the young general and Kanchi function as symbols of unconscious Western desires in *Black Narcissus*, they do emerge unscathed from their sexual relationship unlike their white masters.

As Clodagh rushes to a darkened exterior toward the end of the third flashback, her parents express hopes that "something will be settled." This remark not only articulates parental concern for Clodagh's future but also reveals that she is really a marketable commodity in their eyes. Her

FIGURE 16. Sister Clodagh (Deborah Kerr) attempts to save the soul of her national and sexual alter ego Kanchi (Jean Simmons) in *Black Narcissus*.

family's remarks darkly parallel the duplicit activities of Ayah, who conspires to initiate a relationship between the young general and Kanchi. The flashback appropriately concludes with Clodagh rushing out into the darkness, foreshadowing Sister Ruth's later sexual pursuit of Mr. Dean in the dark expressionist forest environment.

Although Ruth aggressively pursues Dean, the latter watches her from a concealed place in the forest as if fearing his status as an objectified sexual prey of an active female. When Dean vehemently states he loves nobody, his brutal rejection (traumatically shot in red expressionist lighting from Ruth's point of view) parallels Con's earlier abandonment of Clodagh in Ireland. Dressed in crimson and wearing garishly red lipstick, Ruth resembles a *film noir femme fatale*. Like Clodagh, she violates patriarchal values by actively pursuing the man. Her descent into hysteric madness parallels Clodagh's repressed feelings over her social and sexual humiliation in Ireland.

Dean also represses his sexual feelings toward Clodagh. When he first brings Kanchi to St. Faith's, his question to Clodagh about his former charge—"Are you sure there's no question you're dying to ask me?"—has more than humorous overtones. Yet, despite accommodating his clothing and behavior to his new environment, Dean cannot penetrate the cultural barriers separating him from Clodagh. Walker (12) points out that Dean and Clodagh finally move toward a "conscious sublimation" of feelings after their repressed feelings result in Sister Ruth's traumatic death. Recognizing Ruth as a symbolic scapegoat for their culturally conditioned feelings, Clodagh asks Dean to do "one last thing—look after the grave." Before they part she offers him her hand. But he holds her hand rather than shakes it. As Walker comments, "The gesture is as eloquent as in Jane Austen." The two characters arrive at some form of realization. Tragically, they cannot move toward the reciprocal desire of Peter and June in *A Matter of Life and Death*. But they do eventually recognize those dangerous, culturally prohibitive structures of desire dominating them as individuals and social subjects. It is a limited victory. *Black Narcissus* at least recognizes that repression and colonialism are dangerous for the British character.

Although Powell (653) mentions historical reasons for the postwar appeal of The *Red Shoes* "for women who were girls at the time, and who were growing up in countries that had been racked by war," he brusquely dismisses any suggestive cultural and material readings for "the real reason" of the film's success. Ironically, Powell's preferred reading—"We had all been told for ten years to go out and die for freedom and democracy . . . and now that the war was over, *The Red Shoes* told us to go and die for art"—is as revealing as the other reactions he dismisses. *The Red Shoes* is certainly a great artistic achievement illustrating the Archers' championship of fantastic romantic expressionism rather than traditional British cinematic realism. However, fantasy and realism are really different ways of dealing with the same social problems. Although the world of *The Red Shoes* appears to exist in an artistic vacuum, it examines an issue peculiar to late forties cinema: the problem of the independent woman. The Archers approach the issue by using fantastic devices to expose the excessive nature of repressive constraints in British society. They never resort to any artificial ideological resolution.

Despite her class background, Vicky Page (Moira Shearer) desires to dedicate her life to an independent existence as a ballerina. However, as Cynthia Young shows, the mythic elements and fairy tale components of *The Red Shoes* accompany a text clearly conscious of patriarchal dominance. Vicky temporarily achieves her desire before falling victim to another form of romantic illusion. She cannot achieve her initial ambition without submitting to the authoritative control of Boris Lermontov (Anton Walbrook) who, like Doctor Coppelius, creates a living puppet. *The Red Shoes* never presents Vicky as entirely submissive. As Young (115) notes, Vicky enters the narrative as a woman wishing to engage in a quest for self-fulfillment and self-definition, not as a sexually threatening *femme fatale*. She is quite willing to undergo downward mobility in the ballet company to achieve her ambition. In her early scenes with the domineering Lermontov, she holds her ground with him in conversation and returns his male gaze. At her aunt's party, the shot-reverse shot sequence shows her parrying Lermontov's verbal and visual domineering manner. When she performs in a charity ballet, one shot shows her confidently maintaining her performance as she stares back at Lermontov's obsessive gaze in the audience. On Irina's final night with the company, she listens in silence and coolly assesses Lermontov's polemic against romantic love. Up to this point, Vicky is in control of her destiny. However, when Lermontov offers her the prime role in the ballet version of Hans Christian Anderson's *Red Shoes*, Vicky achieves her artistic ambitions. But she becomes torn between submission to two patriarchal authorities: Lermontov and young composer Julian Craster (Marius Goring), with whom she falls in love. As Young (116) shows, both Lermontov and Craster aim to insert Vicky "into the text" of their various creative projects and subordinate her in different ways.

Like *A Matter of Life and Death*, *The Ballet of the Red Shoes* combines realist and fantastic discourses to express Vicky's desiring dilemma. She becomes an object in the text dancing madly in the red shoes given her by the demonic shoemaker (Leonid Massine) and separated from her mundane lover (Robert Helpmann). The ballet begins on the realistic domains of an actual stage. It then employs various cinematic devices to depict the dominant role of the fantastic as a structuring force conditioning Vicky's dilemma. During the ballet the shoemaker's shadowy figure changes to superimposed images of Lermontov and Julian, their arms "raised in a gesture of entrapment, of condemnation mixed with desire" (Young, 117). They parallel Helpmann's later gestures in the ballet as a priest torn between condemnation and desire. His crucified posture also evokes images of those earlier gestures by betrayed lovers such as Hardt in *The Spy in Black* and Van Leyden in *The Silver Fleet*. The reverse close-up of Vicky's gaze during this scene foreshadows the shot of her maddened gaze prior to her suicide in the final sequence of *The Red Shoes*, which merges realist and fantasy discourses in the same manner as the actual ballet.

After her success, Vicky falls in love with Julian, who narrates his own controlling "fairy tale" as they travel romantically in a carriage by night. Speaking of a future day when he will tell a young girl of his former love for the great Vicky Page, he hints that Vicky "will *lose* him as a *result* of her ambitions, therefore she must give up her career" (Young, 118). Julian removes her from Lermontov's control, but he silences her creativity so that she becomes relegated to a muse influencing his turgid opera, *Cupid and Psyche*. This work contains neither the vitality of his earlier "Hearts of Fire" composition nor his rewritten *Red Shoes* musical score. However, the two musical scores complement each other. As Young (116) notes, like *The Red Shoes Ballet*, the Cupid and Psyche myth "dramatizes female transgression and its punishment."

The Red Shoes deals with female and male crisis situations, the latter complementing postwar British cinematic masculine hysteria discourses involving anxiety over the "problem" of the female subject. Although privileged males in postwar society, Lermontov and Julian display deep-rooted insecurities motivating their respective desires to control the female body. Although a revered father figure dominating his ballet "family," Lermontov frequently hides in offices or darkly lit apartments. He often wears dark glasses, concealing his vulnerability from the outside world. Eager to play the part of romantic lover, Lermontov becomes disturbed when he learns about Vicky's affair with Julian. He not only contradicts his own rules over romantic involvement but also astonishes his colleagues by making emotionally irrational comments about Vicky's performance after discovering their affair. Lermontov violates the strict rules of his chosen "religion" by ignoring conductor Livvy's (Esmond Knight) opinions about Julian's new musical score. He abuses his artistic authority by unjustly humiliating the young composer. When he learns of Vicky and Julian's marriage, he masochistically smashes his fist into his image in a darkened apartment mirror. His violent gesture also anticipates those tormented gestures of Sammy in *The Small Back Room* (who smashes the empty glass frame that formerly contained Sue's photo) and Hoffmann in *Tales of Hoffmann.* Before Dmitri (Eric Berry) informs him of Vicky's return to Monte Carlo, he is about to write her what may be a romantic letter as an equal rather than the seductively controlled authoritarian figure he reverts to on meeting her again. As Scott Salwolke (157) notes, Pressburger incorporated many of his negative character traits into the impresario during screenplay revisions so Lermontov becomes a compendium of Serge Diaghlev, Alexander Korda, and Michael Powell. Julian's behavior also harms Vicky. Like Lermontov, he is really wedded to his own career and ignores Vicky's creative frustrations during their marriage. The drama reaches its crisis when two controlling males verbally battle for Vicky's body and soul in her dressing room.

Vicky's dressing room mirror reflects the clashing images of Julian and Lermontov as she prepares for her return performance in *The Red Shoes Ballet.* Despite his insecure demeanor, Julian wears a black leather overcoat, which gives him a sinister appearance. Dangerous and ambivalent figures such as Captain Hardt in *The Spy in Black* and Dr. Reeves in *A Matter of Life and Death* wear similar apparel. Julian's dark costume complements the color of his ballet surrogate's sober priestly demeanor as he condemns a transgressive heroine before his moralistic congregation. Julian's black overcoat also complements the color of Lermontov's evening attire. Their costumes signify both males as destructive authoritarian mirror images. As Powell (1987, 658) succinctly notes, Vicky turns "blindly from one man to another like a broken doll between them," her face collapsing into a hysteric mask resembling her role in *The Red Shoes Ballet* as she faces two controlling males demonically represented by the shoemaker. Her appearance also foreshadows her facial reactions when the red shoes appear to control her suicidal tendencies. Although Julian weeps in her lap like a little boy seeking comfort from his mother, his maniputively hysterical performance is as destructive to Vicky's mental condition as Lermontov's authoritative, sneering sarcasm. Life, art, reality, and fantastic realms of unconscious forces move toward the destructive climax. Unable to resolve these irresolvable contradictions of desire, Vicky merges her life with art. She sees suicide as the only way to escape patriarchal oppression. Her death represents a dark version of the Archers' "reconciliation of opposites," which occur on a more positive level in *A Matter of Life and Death*.

For Young (119), Vicky's absurd death both unveils the vicious nature of masculine desire and emphasizes the tragically devastating climax affecting all characters. Unlike the average realist British forties movie, *The Red Shoes* does not conveniently attempt to suppress its contradictions by an ideologically imposed evasive ending. If the woman dies, the male realm suffers psychological devastation. Both Lermontov and Julian end the film as "broken" as Vicky's body on the railway tracks. Young concludes, "Just as patriarchal logic seduces Vicky into its own text, it denies the author an alternative text—a fairy tale—through which he might 'revise' himself fully. Like Lermontov, a text's author is also imprisoned, made 'spectacle,' by the limitations of narrative reproduction." *The Red Shoes* artistically and symbolically depicts those psychological obstacles that hinder and cripple any positive realization of desire in the postwar era.

As Powell (1992, 11, 15–16) notes, *The Small Back Room* is really a love story filmed in a more realistic manner, emphasizing the intelligence and strength of Sue (Kathleen Byron). It is one of the best adaptations of a Nigel Balchin novel, articulating Balchin's mordant psychology and bleak dramatic overtones antithetical to contemporary audiences wishing to forget the war and move toward Ealing comedy's comforting securities. Set in the bleak period of spring 1943, *The Small Back Room* focuses on the male crisis suffered by civilian scientist Sammy Rice (David Farrar). Despite Sue's various attempts to alleviate his insecurities, Sammy masochistically drowns in self-pity, using his tin leg as an excuse for his dilemma. He avoids Sue's frequent sympathetic overtures to come to terms with his condition. "Why don't you take that thing off? You know it hurts. You take it off when I'm not here." For most of the film, Sammy masochistically indulges in misery to avoid resolving his male crisis. He and Sue exist in an unhealthy *fort-da* masochistic relationship. "I take things from you with both hands. I always have. I keep kicking this foot of mine. When I have a bad patch on I like someone to flutter around, so that I can be a perfect swine to them. And you still seem to like it." Sue's reply is also revealing. "Wouldn't it be silly to break up something we both like, only because you don't think I like it?" She also perceives Sammy's character flaws, which hinder his job effectiveness and may lead to the authorities closing down his unit. "You'll hang around hating it and expecting everybody else to be sorry for you."

The film opens with Lieutenant Stuart (Michael Gough) attempting to find Sammy's research unit in a building populated by uniformed servicemen of all nationalities. He wishes Sammy's help in dealing with a new deadly explosive device invented by the enemy. It is evident that, despite his legitimate civilian status, Sammy feels an outsider in a uniformed wartime community. His lethargy also conditions his role in the civilian community. Although Sammy is really the brains of his research outfit, he subordinates himself to the lesser talents of Professor Mair (Milton Rosmer) and his ingratiating advertising-minded boss R. B. Waring (Jack Hawkins) who lives by the motto The sales side has to impress people. Trapped in a claustrophobic wartime blackout world signified by cellars and acoustically intrusive road drills penetrating committee meetings, Sammy prefers to dwell in passivity and self-pity rather than resolve his personal problems.

The Small Back Room visually depicts Sammy's male dilemma by juxtaposing Sue's photo in his apartment with the tempting symbol of a whisky bottle. Although Sammy tells Stuart that the bottle is really meant for Victory Day, it also functions as an object of wish-fulfillment temptation that he unconsciously hopes will achieve realization. During their frequent brief encounters after work, Sammy and Sue engage in a ritual game in which she tempts him with the offer of a drink he usually refuses. However, *The Small Back Room* emphasizes that Sammy is a victim of masochistic male anxieties that he must overcome to win Sue and achieve victory over self-destructive feelings inhibiting his participation in the war effort. Sammy's contact with people often leads to self-induced feelings of inadequacy and blame. Although he shows integrity by revealing flaws in his research unit's project to the military during a committee meeting, he allows the devious Waring to humiliate him afterward. Despite showing sympathy to the marital problems of Corporal Taylor (Cyril Cusack), Sammy indulges himself by passively listening to his subordinate's confession of male impotence rather than actively resolving his own personal problems. Sammy uses Taylor's feelings to fuel his masochistic suspicions over Sue's fidelity. He unconsciously and deliberately forgets the exact day of their weekly tryst in the Hickory Club and blames her when she arrives late. But, as the first hickory tree scene astutely reveals, Sammy is a prisoner of self-induced impotent desires. He appears framed through a grille watching other couples dance and feeds like a masochistic vampire on his thwarted desires. When he returns home and waits for Sue, he believes her absence places him in the same position as Taylor. He then undergoes an expressionistic nightmare involving a giant whisky bottle and clocks. Sammy thrives on punitively morbid feelings concerning Sue's absence. In one scene, he appears in a crucified position against multiple clocks, evoking images of Gustav Frolich's underground torment in Fritz Lang's *Metropolis* (1926). He also masochistically desires punishment. He later drunkenly attempts to provoke former boxer and sympathetic barman Knucksie (Sidney James) into a fight he will obviously lose. Eventually, Sue tires of Sammy's self-abuse and removes all signs of her presence, including her photograph. Like Lermontov, another abusive male in the Archers' gallery, he sees his reflection in the glass and smashes it a few minutes later with a poker. Sammy then opens another whisky bottle and falls into drunken oblivion.

However, redemption soon arrives. Stuart phones the drunken scientist with news of the discovery of two bombs in Chesil Bank. When Sammy eventually arrives, he learns of Stuart's death. An ATS Corporal (Renée Asherson) reads Stuart's last words to Sammy prior to his unsuccessful dismantling of the bomb. This poignant scene (which does not occur in the original novel) resembles the opening of *A Matter of Life and Death* but with less positive overtones. Unlike Peter, Stuart's "voice" now really echoes from the grave. Sammy decides to dismantle the other bomb device. He becomes stimulated by Stuart's heroic action, as well as the touching nature of the sublimated relationship between Stuart and the corporal, which will now never achieve realization. By dismantling the bomb, he takes Stuart's place as an actively heroic surrogate lover. Sammy's attitude now contrasts with his earlier negative feelings generated by Taylor's domestic problems and his masochistically symbiotic identification with him. This identification suggested that Sammy desired to put himself in Taylor's place and lose an important relationship. Forgetting his disability and wearing soldier attire, Sammy proves himself by dismantling the device. By choosing to overcome his destructive desires, he is now ready to enter an equal relationship with Sue, acquire leadership of his research unit in a military context, and exercise responsibility for others, such as Taylor. Choosing leadership over masochistic self-pity, he helps Taylor deal with his domestic problems by canceling his transfer to another unit. The film ends with Sammy's reunification with Sue. She makes an opening gambit in a game she now knows he will always win, "Have a drink, Sammy." Both are now entering a world of positive and equal desire.

Despite its minor position in the Archers' canon, *The Small Back Room* insightfully examines a particular form of sexual relationship. Like the lovers in *I Know Where I'm Going*, both Sammy and Sue realize that any true union involves equality. The male hero acquires respect and love by sacrificing an inhibiting form of behavior. Torquil violates his family taboo by entering the castle. Sammy rejects negative dependence on alcohol and self-pity and decides to take responsibility for himself and others. Unlike the novel, where Sammy returns to find R. B. Waring as deputy director in a scenario that is virtually unchanged, the film version emphasizes the hero's victory by having him take responsibility for both himself and his unit. In the film, Sammy also gains Sue's acknowledged respect for his victory. But the future success of their relationship remains open. However, they do begin again on the right path.

Although *Gone to Earth* superficially resembles another British cinematic costume literary adaptation, the Archers engage in a serious critique of social life on artistic and cultural levels. Heroine Hazel Woodus (Jennifer Jones) is an 1897 Shropshire child of nature resembling Margaret Lockwood's Jassy. Both heroines have gypsy mothers and suffer social alienation from a repressive society. Hazel rebuts criticisms by her puritanical Aunt Prowde (Beatrice Varley) by affirming her female independence and pride in being "born in a caravan." But, like certain Gainsborough melodramas, everyday social forces conspire to destroy Hazel's "other" identity. As in *The Red Shoes*, the Archers employ excessive romantic, expressionistic technicolor techniques, making *Gone to Earth* more than a mere literary adaptation. The chosen stylistic treatment reveals intuitive insights into relevant social forces that even Powell himself admits in *Million Dollar Movie*. When he refers to Squire Reddin's mansion, Undern, as "a lovely, old moldering pile" (44), Powell mentions that 1949 "was a nostalgic time to be making the film" (45). He compares the dislocating conditions following the Second World War with previous postwar periods, such as those following World War I. The film follows the book by Mary Webb. Pam Cook (1986, 354) also notes that "a profound pessimism pervades the book, written toward the end of the First World War and suffused with violent, painful imagery as life and hope are trampled underfoot in a merciless drive toward death." Similar feelings influence the film version, which emphasizes the dangerous effects of a dominating and deadly masculine gaze on the woman's body.

As portrayed by Jennifer Jones, Hazel Woodus is an independent female who lives outside society. Like Vicky Page, her involvement in a male-dominated world leads to eventual destruction. But, unlike Vicky, Hazel does not develop any intuitive creative powers, and her options are limited. Her position resembles the eroding status of postwar women doomed to subordinate roles within British society. *Gone to Earth* emphasizes that the options available for Peter and June in *A Matter of Life and Death* and Sammy and Susan in *The Small Back Room* are no longer possible.

Like *The Red Shoes*, *Gone to Earth* depicts a heroine torn between equally suffocating forms of control by two males, neither of which offers her any constructive alternatives. Ignoring her deceased mother's wise advice about the dangers of romantic involvement ("Tears and torment was married life. You're not made for marriage like me. Eat in company but sleep alone.") Hazel falls victim to the brutal, masculine sexual dominance of Squire Jack Reddin (David Farrar) and an impossible claustrophobic platonic marital life offered her by Baptist minister Edward Marston (Cyril Cusack). Both men offer sacrifices to gain her body. Reddin belatedly offers her marriage after Marston's proposal. Like Lermontov in *The Red Shoes*, Reddin moves from a position of dominance toward romantic dependence but, unlike his predecessor, finally reveals his vulnerability to Hazel. She later comments that he broke down in tears following their first night of love. Marston engages in a disastrous celibate union with a passionate female who will never be content in a relationship her husband defines as asexual and familial. Before he proposes, he prays, "What I want is not for myself. I want to protect her, to change her, in my house, like a flower. And this I promise. I shall ask nothing of her, nothing until she wants to be a wife to me." However, Hazel merely thinks of him as a parental figure: "You're my father and mother both." She may later affirm Marston as her "soul" before Reddin, but this is clearly no substitute for the equal warm-blooded relationship she actually desires. Although Marston proves himself superior to Reddin in suffering social humiliation by taking Hazel back, any mature marital relationship for them is impossible. Although he resigns himself to leaving the ministry after he heroically defies his congregation and takes blame for driving Hazel into Reddin's arms, it is too late. The film moves toward its log-

FIGURE 17. Hazel (Jennifer Jones) faces victimization by postwar British patriarchy in *Gone to Earth.*

ical conclusion, with Hazel leaping down a mineshaft with her beloved pet, Foxy. Like Vicky in *The Red Shoes*, this is the only way she can resolve her personal dilemma caused by a repressive society. *Gone to Earth* concludes with a huntsman repeating the traditional cry when the fox escapes, a cry heard in the very beginning of the film: "Gone to Earth!"

As Thierry Kuntzel points out in "The Film Work 2," the end echoes the beginning in several narrative films. This certainly applies to *Gone to Earth*. It reinforces the predetermined nature of the heroine's end in a world where hostile social forces dominate her. *Gone to Earth* visually emphasizes Hazel's entrapment throughout the film. After Hazel rescues Foxy in the opening scenes, she returns to her father's home. When she opens the door, she appears framed in a coffin her father, Abel Woodus (Esmond Knight), makes. As Pam Cook (1986, 354) points out, *Gone to Earth* follows the novel in seeing evil not as an abstract entity "but as materially present in social institutions, in people's minds and hearts . . . and through a network of male looks." Hazel's future entrapment by two opposing masculine gazes first appears when she visits Much Wenlock during celebrations for Queen Victoria's 1897 Diamond Jubilee. As she walks through the streets wearing a new green dress, a dandy appears, briefly looking at Hazel. Powell frames him within an entrance similar to Hazel's earlier framing within the door of her home. The dandy looks at Hazel, whose image is reflected on the windows of the shop he is leaving. Despite Hazel's innocence about a sexually dangerous male gaze, which later proves murderous, social forces choose to blame the victim. Aunt Prowde refuses to let her stay the night, thus preventing her meek son, Albert (George Cole), from taking Hazel to the "magic lantern show tonight." She throws Hazel out of the house, leading to her entrapment by Reddin later that night, and condemns her innocent sexuality. "It's a disgrace the way you look. You look like an actress. You quite draw men's eyes." Reddin later frames her by comparing Hazel to a glamorous female portrait in Undern Manor. "Do you like the picture, or is it the dress you like?" He later spies on her through a window frame as she tries on the dress, which resembles an Elizabeth Haffenden Gainsborough costume. Hazel removes her green dress to try on a red dress, the color symbolizing both passion and violence, as well as the red coats of the fox hunters who will eventually harass her to death. When Hazel later meets Reddin in the country, he tramples the red roses she has brought under his feet.

By contrast, Marston gazes at Hazel as she sings in a demure white dress, framing her according to his own male construction of her identity.

Although Edward rebuts his mother's class concerns in a manner echoing Stewart Granger's Harry in *Fanny by Gaslight* ("She is not of your class, Edward." "What does class matter?"), social factors disastrously affect his future relationship with Hazel. Ironically, when he congratulates Hazel on her singing, a villager unconsciously articulates the community's repressive attitudes toward her with the sentence, "Have a tart (let), Minister." (Obviously, the play on a vulgar British term for loose woman is deliberate here.) Although Edward attempts a nonsexual marriage with Hazel, his good intentions are equally as destructive as Reddin's. On her wedding night, Hazel looks out of her window and sees Reddin gazing at her as he leans on a tombstone. Throughout the film shadow imagery expresses Reddin's power over Hazel until the climactic scene of his eventual sexual victory over her. His shadow slowly covers Hazel's near the ironically named God's Little Mountain. Hazel eventually realizes the poignant overtones of her earlier words—"It seems all this world's a big spring trap, and us in it"—as she eventually moves toward her fate. The final foxhunting scene represents the deadly culmination of various symbols of male violence threatening her throughout the film whether repressive mechanisms of social control, a male-orientated death drive, or hopeless idealistic spiritual values inappropriate for Hazel's real personality.

Gone to Earth pessimistically concludes the Archers' work of the forties. Brief utopian hopes represented by *I Know Where I'm Going, A Matter of Life and Death*, and *The Small Back Room* are no longer viable in the fifties. *The Tales of Hoffmann* takes this pessimism to its logical development by further emphasizing the chaos and impotence behind a male creative drive involving disastrous consequences for females.

The Archers and most critics perceived little relationship to the contemporary historical background. For Monk Gibbon (10), *The Tales of Hoffmann* "probes no social problem. It probes only the imagination of man. It lightens rather than enlightens the care of our mortal existence. It belongs to the domain of art and music rather than to that of psychology or sociology." However, it is difficult to isolate this film entirely from issues of authorship and social context.

Kevin MacDonald (324) sees significant parallels to *The Life and Death of Colonel Blimp, I Know Where I'm Going*, and *The Red Shoes*. Like *Blimp*, the story is told in flashback from the perspective of a narrator, who like Blimp sees only what he wants to see and suffers from self-induced deception throughout the course of the film. After a prologue introducing Hoffmann's deadly alter ego, Councillor Lindorff (Robert

Helpmann) and the performance of the *Dragonfly Ballet* by Stella (Moira Shearer), the film moves into the narrator's three tales. They involve views of the female as artist (Antonia), tender maiden (Olympia), and courtesan (Giulietta), "three souls united in one." Hoffmann sees his new love, Stella, as the ideal synthesis of the woman for whom he has been searching. However, the film reveals that Hoffmann's supposedly pure artistic visions are flawed in many ways. His various female muses are selfish constructions of the masculine ego and male gaze. Although he seeks to attract each woman under the deceptive lure of romantic love, his desires are really as deadly as those influencing Mark Lewis of *Peeping Tom*. They result not only in the destruction of the female (Olympia, Antonia) but also in the victory of a deadly hegemonic form of masculine supremacy.

In the "Tale of Olympia," Hoffmann becomes deceived into viewing the mechanical doll, Olympia (Moira Shearer), as a living being by the aid of magic glasses given him by Coppelius (Robert Helpmann). Both Coppelius and Spalanzini (Leonid Massine) play upon Hoffmann's sexual controlling desires until the poet finally discovers the deadly reality hidden beneath a deceptive male gaze. Olympia finally suffers Vicky's fate of dismemberment in *The Red Shoes*. As in other Archers' films, *The Tales of Hoffmann* emphasizes significant features of male vulnerability and destructiveness affecting the achievement of desire. The prologue introduces ominous overtones dominating the entire film. When Lindorff views the theatrical poster advertising Stella's performance, his shadow covers not only her name but also her miniature ballerina figure. He enters the theater and spies on her from behind the scenery in images evoking Reddin's equally dangerous activities in *Gone to Earth*. The opening ballet specially created for the film initiates a pattern occurring throughout *The Tales of Hoffmann*. It shows Cancer (Edmond Audran) eyeing Stella with a controlling male gaze. However, his liaison with female dragonfly Stella results in his destruction reinforcing parallels with other negative controlling forces of romance, creativity, and destruction present in other Archers productions. When the action moves to the tavern, Lindorff appears at the top of the stairs. The camera tilts down to reveal Hoffmann's faithful companion, Niklaus (Pamela Brown), at the bottom. Lindorff and Niklaus represent opposing elements in the film battling for Hoffmann's soul.

Helpmann appears three other times in the film, playing characters whom MacDonald (321) correctly recognizes as representing an "evil emanation" of Hoffmann's own psyche that prevents him gaining the female

FIGURE 18. Hoffmann (Robert Rounseville) pursues Olympia (Moira Shearer) in *The Tales of Hoffmann.*

object of his desires whether Olympia, Giulietta (Ludmilla Tcherina), or Antonia (Ann Ayars). In "The Tale of Giulietta," Helpmann appears as the demonic Dr. Dapertutto. He plays on Hoffmann's initial condescending attitude toward courtesan Giulietta and uses her to trap Hoffmann. Both Hoffmann and Dapertutto exhibit manipulative attitudes toward Giulietta. While Dapertutto controls her like a puppet similar to Lermontov's dominance of Vicky in *The Red Shoes*, Hoffmann falls prey to romantic desires that eventually leave him as impotent as Julian Craster. Hoffmann temporarily loses his own soul to Giulietta but finally regains it. "The Tale of Giulietta" ends with a close-up of Hoffmann's restored image fragmented in the mirror within which he originally lost it. As well as echoing scenes in *The Red Shoes* and *The Small Back Room* when Lermontov and Sammy smash their reflections, the cracked glass also parallels the splintered frames of Hoffmann's magic glasses in "The Tale of Olympia." Although the male achieves some realization of his fallibility, the destructive nature of his dominant controlling passion indelibly scars his psyche. "The Tale of Antonia" involves Hoffmann's doomed love for consumptive singer Antonia. Although forbidden to sing, the arrival of Hoffmann and Dr. Mirakle (Helpmann) equally evokes deadly creative passions in Antonia, paralleling those destroying her predecessor, Vicky, in *The Red Shoes*. The solicitous Hoffmann wishes to save her by preventing her from singing again. However, his demonic counterpart, Mirakle, sows doubt into her mind by suggesting Hoffmann's jealousy over her artistic abilities and his probable future abandonment of her. "The time will come when his passion will expire." Eventually, Mirakle achieves his deadly ambition by evoking the voice of Antonia's dead mother and stimulating the daughter to accompany mother in a song of death. The murderous nature of male creative control again counterpoints images in *The Red Shoes*. Mirakle resembles Lermontov and Massine's demonic shoemaker from the earlier film with his controlling gestures. Hoffmann's position parallels the weaker (but equally controlling) figure of Julian Craster. One overhead shot reveals performers, audience, and conductor all participating in the doomed romantic frenzy of the concluding scenes. Antonia's formerly solicitous father, Crespel (Mogens Wieth), also appears trapped within a deadly creative frenzy, conducting his daughter in the final bars of her deadly consumptive operatic song. He may also have conducted Antonia's mother in the same way.

"The Tale of Antonia" concludes in the unmasking of Hoffmann's three opponents as incarnations of Lindorff. Images then reveal the three female victims (Olympia, Giulietta, and Antonia) merging into Stella, who performs the concluding romantic ballet with Cancer. In the epilogue, Stella rushes to the tavern to find Hoffmann in a drunken stupor. Hoffmann is his own worst enemy since he again acts in a self-destructive manner designed to frustrate his own desires. Stella then leaves him for his rival, Lindorff, in a pessimistic conclusion resembling those of *The Red Shoes* and *Gone to Earth*.

However, *The Tales of Hoffmann* suggests that things could have been different. Throughout the entire film, Niklaus appears as frequently as both Hoffmann and Lindorff and often vainly attempts to prevent his friend from pursuing the path to self-destruction. As portrayed by Pamela Brown, Niklaus represents Hoffmann's creatively aware, sensitive qualities that never overcome the destructive powers of male irrationality. The Archers originally envisaged a more positive ending that unfortunately ended on the cutting room floor. In the original opera, Hoffmann's muse finally appears to him in a halo of light, pointing out positive directions for his frustrated energies. She suggests he devote his talents exclusively to poetry. Hoffmann replies, "Thy glances mild and sweet. My pain and grief destroy." Powell originally intended to film this ending and reveal the real reason for Niklaus's presence throughout the film. She was Hoffmann's golden muse who accompanied him throughout all his adventures in the opera. In opera, a female soprano sang the role of Niklaus. Influenced by Pamela Brown's androgynous qualities, Powell (1992, 95–96) attempted to shoot a climax in which another creative path awaited Hoffmann as an alternative to the destructive nature of male creativity frustrating positive achievement of desire. Unfortunately, Brown's half-naked golden muse never reached the screen. The attempt was a lost opportunity for British cinema in a era where frustration and repression soon became dominant motifs affecting the realization of positive forms of desire as the world of Ealing Studios significantly shows.

CHAPTER SEVEN

Ealing and Beyond

Before critical reevaluation of the Archers and Gainsborough melodrama, Ealing Studios' world of cosy comedy was the dominant image of forties and fifties British cinema. While J. Arthur Rank failed to capture the American market, a small studio producing films on a limited budget perversely succeeded in "projecting Britain and the British character." These films proved popular among American audiences and became in George Perry's (173) words, "the quintessence of the British cinema." Ealing comedies remain entrenched in public consciousness. Voices even emerged in the stagnant post-Thatcherite nineties decade identifying Britain with the studio's cultural world. (Siedentop, 4) If Rank's big-budget opulence failed to capture American hearts and minds, low-budget character eccentricity succeeded. The causes of this success are many. Dickensian literary character eccentricity and ideologically dominant narrative trajectories were certainly present. S. M. Eisenstein (194) astutely analyzed the political overtones of Dickens's attraction for both D. W. Griffith and American cinema. Barr (6) and Stead (1989, 26–28, 131, 162) notice this presence in its various manifestations. But it was one inhibiting the achievement of personal and political freedom in capitalist society. This literary discourse highlighting the arbitrary intervention of benevolent good intentions acts as a dominant hegemonic force repressing socially liberating forces. As Laurence Kardish (59) notes, wartime and postwar films such as *The Foreman Went to France* (1942) and *Whisky Galore* (1949) do reflect progressive feelings, but the studio also firmly repressed them.

Despite Ealing's success in achieving world-wide popularity, the comedies represent retrograde factors in a national cinema that sometimes attempted positive representations of human desire and fulfillment. Inevitably, the frustrating presence of class and sexually repressive factors contaminates the final product. Charles Barr's classic work on Ealing Studios succinctly analyzes several factors contributing to its significance in wartime and postwar eras. He (8–12) sees Ealing as a cosy, middle-class institution engaged in a "mild revolution" antithetical to working-class values and the fulfillment of desire. It eventually succumbs to stagnation and decay by the fifties. Ealing suffers from a *poverty of desire*—a term aptly coined by Ernest Bevin—affecting various representations that regard desire as a dangerous force needing repression. This occurs not only in Hamer's "Mirror" contribution to *Dead of Night* (1945) but also the last major work of the studio, *The Ladykillers* (1955), which aptly illustrates George Orwell's 1942 definition of a crippling national psyche in his essay "The Lion and the Unicorn." "England . . . is a family in which the young are generally thwarted and most of the power is in the hands of irresponsible uncles and bedridden aunts. Still, it is a family. It has its private language and its common memories, and at the approach of the enemy it closes its ranks" (Barr, 14).

The analogy is not unique to Ealing. It is a recurrent feature of the British psyche. In *Forever England*, Alison Light draws attention to certain thirties literary traditions that influence the British character. Analyzing the novels of Ivy Compton-Burnett, Light (1991, 53) notes their appeal to English writers and intellectuals seeking to retreat from the class unity of the new Labour government. Her fictional families represent psychic prison camps determining collective human relationships in the wider world to deny "connections between self and modes of historical and social belonging" (46). They also contribute to a "scandalous deformation of spirit" (58). Although differences exist between the worlds of Compton-Burnett and Ealing, they both exhibit a common cultural malaise inhibiting realization of individual freedom and desire. "Instead of an idealised lost England of pastoral retirement and superior sensibility we confront a confined and inward-looking family, divided from the rest of the world by their private loves which act to keep them apart from society like the low wall and railings at the front of the house" (37). As Light (230, n.63) notes, these features resemble Freud's definition of a "family romance" described in his "Three Essays on Sexuality." They also operate on the levels of class and national culture.

Ealing Studios viewed itself as "a family business, set on the village green of the queen of the London suburbs" (Barr, 6), an institution combining the headmasterly rule of Michael Balcon with the country air of a repressive British tradition. It was a tradition astutely recognized by the one maverick director in Mr. Balcon's academy for young gentleman who fought in vain against a suffocation eventually leading to the quaint Brigadoonlike world of *The Titfield Thunderbolt* (1952). "To Hamer the family is a noxious response to sexuality: it constrains. Its sole virtue is its ability to confer privilege, and this has nothing to do with togetherness, and everything to do with inheritance." (Laurence Kardish, 61)

This is certainly so when inheritance involves crippling psychic features of a national tradition. During early wartime, Graham Greene wrote two interesting literary articles recognizing dangerous ideological tendencies within the English character. "The Don in Mexico" (1940) condemns the provincial insularity of a Cambridge professor who ignores direct evidence of political persecution in favor of tourist triviality. Greene's condemnation operates on more than one level. "It would be funny—the whimsicality, the self-importance, the ignorance—if it were not so heartless" (Greene, 338). In his 1941 essay "Eric Gill," Greene bemoans a particular national characteristic blocking the realization of Gill's radical nature. "That overpowering tradition of eccentricity simply absorbed him until even his most outrageous anti-clerical utterances caused only a knowing smile on the face of the faithful" (Greene, 350).

Ealing films embody this ideological insularity as productions such as Hamer's *Pink String and Sealing Wax* (1945); *It Always Rains on Sunday, The Loves of Joanna Godden* (both 1947); *Against the Wind, Saraband for Dead Lovers* (both 1948); the Ealing comedies of *Hue and Cry* (1947), *Passport to Pimlico, Whisky Galore, Kind Hearts and Coronets* (all 1949); *The Lavender Hill Mob* (1951); *The Ladykillers* (1955) show. Non-Ealing productions such as *Esther Waters* (1947) and the critically neglected Neagle-Wilcox productions of *The Courtneys of Curzon Street* (1947), *Spring in Park Lane* (1948), and *Maytime in Mayfair* (1949) also reveal relevant points of comparison. The Neagle-Wilcox films were contemporary box-office successes that reveal a changing audience mood wearying of the early years of the age of austerity and demanding conservative forms of consumer gratification.

Pink String and Sealing Wax and *It Always Rains on Sunday* are Ealing's melodramatic response to the chaotic feelings of instability unleashed by *Dead of Night* (1945). While architect Walter Craig attempts in vain to seek narrative closure in *Dead of Night*, succeeding Ealing films impose ideologically induced repressive closures on forces they see as dangerous to British society. These forces involve different forms of desire. Desire becomes a potentially emergent element in certain films of Robert Hamer, one of the most interesting and frustrated talents in forties British cinema. As Gerry Turvey (18) shows, Hamer was familiar not only with key movements of British cinema in the thirties and forties but also with French and German cinema. Unlike Hitchcock, Hamer became drastically constrained by British cinema's institutionally restrictive traditions inherent in documentary and realist approaches.

It is a mistake to separate so-called creative Ealing directors such as Hamer and MacKendrick from others such as Cornelius, Crichton, and Dearden. A common cultural context influences their different responses. Like the Archers and Hitchcock, Hamer exhibited a less parochial cultural sensibility. His work often attempts to reveal warning notes of damaging tensions structuring the British psyche before the eventual studio-imposed repression. Philip Kemp (71) aptly describes these tensions as "evoking a dark, dangerous, perversely attractive world of violence and sexuality" clearly upsetting to figures such as the "straitlaced Balcon."

Pink String and Sealing Wax attempts a return to the supposedly secure past as opposed to those recently disruptive historical visions exhibited in the "Christmas Party" and "The Haunted Mirror" episodes of *Dead of Night*. The figure of Mervyn Johns links the films. But, unlike his predecessor Craig, he is now a repressive Victorian father fully in control of his world. Although *Pink String* is adapted from a play by Roland Pertwee, Hamer's collaboration to the screenplay undermines whatever secure returns to Victorian values Balcon may have seen in the project. Unlike *Dead of Night*, the film operates according to a rigid narrative cinematic form of the end answering the beginning. It opens and closes in a Brighton newspaper office with the editor (Charles Carson) dictating a narrative to his compliant female secretary. The scene resembles those Ealing conferences where Balcon was often the dominant figure. Hamer depicts repressive father Edward Sutton (Mervyn Johns) relishing his role in sending a female poisoner to the gallows. His sadistic feelings counterpoint the more genteel, yet equally authoritarian, manner in which he rules his household, making the lives of everyone an absolute misery. As Barr (67) recognizes, after humiliating his son's romantic feelings, Sutton pushes him into a dangerous lower-class underworld, "as if it were a mirror world, of drink, lust, at the centre of which is the landlord's wife,

Pearl" (Googie Withers). Like Sutton's daughter, Victoria (Jean Ireland), Pearl's potentials are trapped in a frustrating patriarchal relationship. She is married to the abusive Joe Bond (Garry Marsh). Sutton condemns Victoria's desires to train as an opera singer. Pearl's plans to escape Joe's control represent a dark mirror image of the strategy Victoria uses to achieve her desired career. Like *It Always Rains on Sunday, Pink String and Sealing Wax* uses secondary characters to parallel the roles of the leading protagonists. Genteel prostitute Miss Porter (Catherine Lacey) also embodies Edward's repressed wish-fulfillment desires concerning the dark world Victoria may fall into if she disobeys her father's orders.

Edward discovers that Pearl has implicated his son, David (Gordon Jackson), in poisoning her husband. He calls her bluff and indirectly causes Pearl to commit suicide by virtue of his stern, Victorian, patriarchal code of honor. However Pearl is the emotional center of the film. Her "fallen woman" plight results from social constraints. After Edward's condemnation Hamer's camera follows her in empathy as she realizes the full enormity of her situation as a victim of Victorian values. The camera tracks back as she walks to the railings before plunging to her death. As she pauses, a child appears at her side, ironically evoking her ideologically proscribed "proper" destiny of wife and mother, which her independent desires refuse. The film ends with a photograph of the Sutton family attending the wedding of David, which Edward adamantly opposed. It unsuccessfully attempts an abrupt narrative closure that can never eliminate the dark picture of patriarchal oppression and human destruction evoked by a director completely opposed to Balcon's Ealing philosophy.

It Always Rains on Sunday also deals with the problem of a woman trapped within a "poverty-of-desire" situation. The film is a composite work employing disparate elements of British documentary realism and German expressionist-derived *film noir*, as well as "transplanting Prevert-Carne poetic realism into an English context" (Kemp, 71). Like *Pink String*, it uses the role of secondary characters to foreground melodramatically "working-class socialisation and female sexual repression" to subvert Balcon's realist mode of production (Whitaker, 21).

The central issue of *It Always Rains* involves Rose Sandigate's (Googie Withers) awakening of desire when her former lover Tommy Swann (John McCallum), now an escaped prisoner, returns to her drab environment. As Whitaker shows, the film uses mirror imagery to contrast Rose's entrapment in a repressive family structure with her desires for freedom. However, unlike Gainsborough melodrama, Hamer shows desire compromised by a hopeless romanticism inaccurately idealizing the handsome male as supposed liberator. Rose's desires also conflict with the repressive social mechanisms of her community. Both Rose and stepdaughter Vi (Susan Shaw) desire males whose masculinity is a mere masquerade. Rose's other stepdaughter, Doris (Patricia Plunkett), embodies Rose's repressed side. Like Rose, Doris receives a proposition from a dubious male. But businessman Lou Hyams (John Slater) later retreats from manipulating his victim, unlike Tommy. Deciding to maintain a benevolent community profile, Lou deceives Doris's stodgy fiancee, Ted (Nigel Stock), about his real intentions. Ted's character mirrors that of Rose's husband, George (Edward Chapman). His attitude to Lou also foreshadows George's final benevolent decision in not wishing to know the real facts about Rose's involvement with Tommy. George repressively forgives Rose in order to return her to sexual imprisonment within the local community. Unlike Lou, Tommy's dreams of criminal affluence land him in Dartmoor and subject him to the pursuit of Detective Sergeant Fothergill (Jack Warner). Morrie Hyams (Sydney Tafler) uses his glamorous position as bandleader to pursue Vi, who knows nothing about his real everyday life as a repressed husband and father. Although Fothergill represents an upright figure of the law, his ruthless harassment of three spivs contributes indirectly to the murder of a criminal fence by one of them (Whitey). George's authoritarian attitude toward Vi drives her away from home into a future in which she may repeat Rose's past mistakes. He only feels at ease with his young son, Alfie, whom George teaches to play a mouth organ Alfie acquired after blackmailing Morrie about his involvement with Vi. Like father, like son, George will obviously use his silence over Rose's affair with Tommy to blackmail her into future domestic submission. Whitey (James Hanley) and Tommy encounter each other at the climax. Their mirror-image relationship suggests two wayward sons pursued by the same punitive Oedipal patriarch. The film may use Ealing documentary-realist techniques to depict a contemporary East End community, but Hamer's opposing cinematic techniques emphasize the repression and violence necessary for normal community existence echoing similar forces operating in "The Mirror" and *Pink String*. Although Hamer reproduces Balcon's attitudes toward desire as a disruptive force (particularly in demonizing Tommy, Vi, and Whitey), he depicts his producer's mandate in such an excessive manner as if conscious of its ideologically arbitrary nature. Hamer appears to be one Ealing director conscious of the studio's repressive ideology. He also attempts to subvert it whenever possible.

Although Charles Frend is credited as director of *The Loves of Joanna Godden*, Hamer's influence may occur in the film. As with *San Demetrio London* (1943), Hamer temporarily took over directing when Frend became ill. Since Hamer was the only Ealing director who intuitively encouraged strong female performances as well as understanding contemporary ideological prohibitions against feminist expression, the film forms an interesting comparison to Googie Withers's other collaborations with Hamer. Shot before *It Always Rains on Sunday*, *The Loves of Joanna Godden* is an interesting companion piece to *The Root of All Evil*, showing Ealing's awareness of dominant ideological trends during the late forties.

Like Jackie Farnish, Joanna Godden (Googie Withers) symbolizes the dangerous postwar independent female whose desires for autonomy bring disaster on herself, her immediate family, and the surrounding community. As Landy (1991, 232) notes, the film "exemplifies what Charles Barr has called Ealing's typical 'constraint on energy, meaning sexuality, and violence.' Joanna's prodigious energy is curtailed. Step by step, the narrative forecloses on Joanna's desires, disciplining and humbling her, and finally fulfilling her father's desire, prescribed in his will to marry Arthur." Arthur is played by John McCallum, who embodies the same image of oppressive male control as in *The Root of All Evil*. Set in the Romney Marsh area of 1905, *The Loves of Joanna Godden* traces its heroine's progress and fall from the time she inherits her father's farm to her eventual confession of the errors of her stubborn ways. Rebuffing Arthur's proposal in favor of marrying the farm, Joanna decimates her father's pedigree flock by following bad advice, spoils her younger sister Ellen (Jean Kent) by sending her to a posh boarding school, attempts to act like a repressive Victorian father by expelling a pregnant farm girl from under her roof, and dominates her upper-class fiancé Martin (Derek Bond), as well as Arthur. Joanna's egotism results in a disastrous marriage between Arthur and Ellen. Martin drowns while Joanna sleeps on a beach. Although Joanna is not directly responsible for Martin's death, the montage sequence leading to his demise indirectly suggests that female sexual desire is deadly for the male. As Joanna dozes, her sleep becomes more disturbed as the sea claims her betrothed. The editing associates Joanna with the cruel sea. Before she awakens and calls for Martin, an overhead close-up reveals her caught within a nightmare of desire as she murmurs, "Martin. Kiss Me." This sequence metaphorically expresses Ealing's attitude toward independent female desire. Although Googie Withers's performance suggests an alternative female independence reacting against a repressive text, the climax retrogressively confirms the earlier comments of a village yokel: "She's a filly that's never been broken, and she needs a strong man to do it." Cut to Arthur! The film affirms Ealing's typical reactionary patriarchal closure with Joanna's submission to Arthur. But this ending opposes the radical climax of Sheila Kaye-Smith's 1922 original novel *Joanna Godden*, which sees its heroine finally realizing that all males are weak. Joanna decides to bear an illegitimate child and become a single mother in an even more reactionary culture than Balcon's Ealing Studios.

Ealing comedies should not be isolated from their failed box-office predecessors such as *Against the Wind* and *Saraband for Dead Lovers*. The later comedies never explicitly articulate the repressive features contained in these films. But they rely heavily on such forces for their success. As Barr comments concerning *Frieda* (1947):

> there is a *suppression* of a dark world: a reluctance . . . to go behind the bland exterior of the hero and his community and actually investigate their passions and their conflicts. It makes us ask seriously what kind of adult hero, or heroine, Ealing can encompass and whether there is any dynamic in this community that can reach onwards and forwards.

Both *Against the Wind* and *Saraband* contain dark forces that seriously inhibit any independent expressions of desire. They also suggest that negative undercurrents structure Ealing's vision of benevolent communities both in earlier films, such as *Johnny Frenchman* (1945), and in later comedies.

Like *The Loves of Joanna Godden*, *Against the Wind* contains revealing parallels to another contemporary film—*The Small Back Room*. Both films failed at the box office since they evoked bleak images of wartime experiences audiences preferred to forget. Like *The Small Back Room*, *Against the Wind* presents a dark picture of wartime relationships. The eventual "happy ending" involving Michele (Simone Signoret) and Johnny Duncan (Gordon Jackson) appears more unrealistic than Sammy and Sue's final union in the Archers' film. As George Orwell noted in *1984*, totalitarian-inclined repressive forces dominated the world in which he wrote his supposedly futuristic novel, a fact acknowledged in Michael Radford's later 1984 film version. Radford's film not only related Orwell's vision to the austere world of its literary creation but also cast as

Winston's betrayer an actor well known for his repressive roles in two key films of this era (*Esther Waters, Gone to Earth*), Cyril Cusack.

As Barr notes (198) *Against the Wind* is a "neglected but efficient film" retaining a certain "wartime toughness" that gained a lukewarm box-office response. It resulted in both director (Charles Crichton) and scenarist (T. E. B. Clarke) eventually following Ealing's path toward cosy, undemanding comedy. The film also echoes pre-Ealing comedy films such as *Frieda, Johnny Frenchman,* and *The Captive Heart* that Barr (64) sees as suggesting potentials that they retreat from exploring. *Against the Wind* depicts the bleak world of wartime Britain. But the mood evoked belongs to the present as well as the recent past. The film deals with a sabotage group that operates in occupied Belgium. Masterminded by the Michael Balcon figure of Ackerman (James Robertson Justice), the group's major aim is to achieve success by molding its disparate figures into a cohesive wartime community. Ackerman regards individual desires as disruptive. This foreshadows later comedy attempts at evoking a repressive wartime community spirit to counter disruptive tensions in British society. *Against the Wind* emphasizes subordination of individual desire into public goals no matter how ruthless the latter are. In his first encounter with Ackerman, Father Phillip (Robert Beatty) enters a world in which his previous moral codes no longer function. He meets Julie (Gisele Prevert). Julie's convenient death before their mission begins saves Phillip from the danger of consummating his romantic feelings toward her. Michelle mourns over betrayal by her collaborationist lover and regrets Ackerman's insistence that another woman agent carry out a suicidal revenge mission against him. Jacques (Paul Dupuis) denies his former lover in Belgium, who condemns him as a traitor. Only after his death by suicide does she learn the truth. Before Michelle inducts Johnny Duncan into the group, she learns about his role in various "dirty tricks" operations. One involves parachuting sexy underwear outside German brothels so that the Gestapo will accuse these "unfortunate women" of spying for the British! The brutal fate these sexually active women face does not matter to Ackerman or Balcon. *Against the Wind*'s world regards desire as equally dangerous as the enemy. Although the film ends with a successful mission completed by the three survivors—Phillip, Michele, and Johnny—the final image ironically rejects any attempt at neat Ealing closure. Safe from Julie's temptations, Phillip shuts a farm gate after Michelle and Johnny depart. However, after he leaves, the gate stubbornly swings open again as if rejecting Balcon's ideological vision.

Saraband for Dead Lovers is usually dismissed as one of Rank's disastrous attempts to force Ealing into the international market. But it is an unjustly neglected film and has more in common with the studio vision than is generally supposed. Directed by Basil Dearden, it utilizes several Ealing talents, such as co-scenarist Alexander Mackendrick, Joan Greenwood, and Francoise Rosay, as well as a figure associated with Gainsborough melodramas—Stewart Granger. *Saraband* may be viewed as Balcon's answer to a rival studio whose sexuality he found distasteful. It is an elaborate technicolor production filmed in predominantly somber hues of blue, purple, and red, which succinctly evoke dark, repressed feelings as the restored version reveals. However, as William K. Everson (343) notes, *Saraband* has legitimate claims to be regarded as a British *film noir*, especially when its American black and white television release gave it "even more of a noirish stance" with doom-laden sets "becoming even more menacing and claustrophobic when drained of their rich color."

Saraband deals with the doomed relationship between Sophie Dorothea (Joan Greenwood), wife of the future British King George I and mother of George II, and Swedish mercenary Count Koenigsmark (played with typical debonair flamboyance by Granger). Unlike *The Man in Grey* and *Fanny by Gaslight*, the heroine never fulfills her romantic desires. Instead, she suffers solitary confinement in a German castle for the rest of her life. Like Joan Greenwood's later status in *The Man in the White Suit* (1951), Sophie's identity becomes reduced to an object of bodily exchange in a corrupt patriarchal economy.

Narrated in *film noir* flashback imagery, *Saraband* opens with Hanoverian officials allowing the unseen, dying Sophie Dorothea to write a letter. An envoy (Guy Rolfe) speaks of the necessity of official approval in a manner resembling Balcon's attitude during script conferences—"We will read the letter and inform our own judgment." *Saraband* then reveals a past world of Hanoverian politics dominated by political and sexual repression. It leads toward a conclusion unthinkable for most contemporary British cinematic representations—the death of dashing hero Stewart Granger in an unhappy ending. For Ealing the "unthinkable" was certainly logical in a narrative governed by historical accuracy as well as a studio hostility toward another studio indulging in the realization of individual desires. *Saraband* significantly expresses features that later Ealing comedies conceal, deny, and depend on—a community world of sexual and social repression. Barr (66) astutely recognizes the significance of a line where Koenigsmark tells Sophie of his visit to a mad England popu-

FIGURE 19. Doomed lovers Sophie (Joan Greenwood) and Koenigsmark (Stewart Granger) in Ealing's *Saraband for Dead Lovers*.

lated by "the sanest lunatics in the world." It is a country he describes as denying freedom but dominated by triviality. "Do you know what has really changed England's history in the last fifty years? The Civil War? The Bill of Rights? Habeus Corpus? Not a bit of it. It was Nell Gwynn, the first cup of tea, and the wart on Oliver Cromwell's nose." Koenigsmark's dialogue unconsciously parallels Graham Greene's reservations concerning the dangerous aspects of eccentricity in British culture. *Saraband* then moves toward its repressive conclusion, showing the sneaky murder of Koenigsmark, the incarceration of Sophie, the impending execution of Countess Platen (Flora Robson)—an act "justified" as much for her undignified expression of middle-aged sexuality as treason—and the world-weary resignation of the Electress (Francoise Rosay). "The hour drags to the end of the day like a great stone that you roll uphill. I know what I speak. We have no right to love than the town clock has to the irregularity of time."

After *Saraband*, Ealing turned to light relief by producing its celebrated series of comedies following the unexpected success of *Hue and Cry*. *Hue and Cry* deals with a group of schoolboys mobilizing against a criminal gang with a climactic battle on the bomb sites of London. Although lighter in tone than *Passport to Pimlico* (both scripted by T. E. B. Clarke), the film cannot entirely deny dark tensions in the postwar community. In *Hue and Cry*, children discover that a criminal gang uses a comic strip serial to convey coded messages. When young Joe (Harry Fowler) and his friends track down pulp comic author Felix H. Wilkinson (Alastair Sim), they ascend a Gothic staircase anticipating the world of Hammer horror and listen to the threatening tones of a male voice. They soon discover that the voice does not come from an Eric Portman debonair psycho but an eccentric writer who chooses to sublimate his impotent masculinity into the world of children's comic strip fiction. The sequence featuring Wilkinson begins and ends with an ominous overheard staircase shot, suggesting that darker worlds exist beneath Ealing's cosy appropriation of wartime community ideals. After mother's scornful put-down of Joe's fantasies ("You've got a bit of sausage on your chin."), the next scene shows a young boy playing outside a bombed landscape. He loudly imitates sounds of explosions and machine guns he probably heard some years before. The scene opposes family attempts to deny fantasy by showing its undeniable presence outside in a world affected by wartime trauma. Joe's escape into comic strip fantasies also suggests his sublimation of destructive memories caused by wartime conditions. *Hue and Cry* reveals that reality and fantasy are complementary. The boys achieve real-life enactment of comic strip fantasies by mobilizing against a postwar criminal underworld represented by Nightingale (Jack Warner) and his *femme fatale* accomplice Rhona (Valerie White). But, like most Ealing films, *Hue and Cry* cannot logically explore the nature of certain dark narrative features. Both Nightingale and Wilkinson represent dark father figures the narrative wishes to reject. In the climactic scenes, Joe chases Nightingale into a bombed building. Before the two engage in their last physical conflict, Joe hears Nightingale's off-screen laughter mocking his pursuit. It is accompanied by a high-angle shot similar to the earlier scene introducing Wilkinson's voice. *Hue and Cry* equates Nightingale's spiv black marketeering activities with a world of comic book fantasy it regards as unhealthy. Unlike Gainsborough and Archers productions, the film makes its version of the fantastic real so that it can finally eliminate it from the narrative. By revealing Nightingale's use of the fantastic for real-life criminal purposes and depicting a vehicle for childish escapism as the product of a dotty old writer, *Hue and Cry* ideologically moves toward rendering any alternative tendencies within the fantastic as hopelessly compromised and tarnished. Furthermore, the kids are a younger version of Ealing's collective male grouping. As the one token female in their entourage, Clarry (Joan Dowling) is generally ignored and sometimes scorned. Despite the exuberant nature of the final battle, the youngsters merely represent another Ealing community mobilizing against those darker elements in postwar society who threaten "our mild revolution." *Hue and Cry* chooses to conclude in a whimsically repressive scene. As Barr (95) notes, the fantasy liberation of youthful energies becomes safely contained, with the boys back once more "in the choir, singing under the watchful eyes of parents and vicar."

Passport to Pimlico represented Ealing Studio's definitive breakthrough into comedy. The film has received so much critical attention that further commentary appears superfluous. It was the first studio exploration of national eccentricity that emerged during one of the harshest periods of the postwar Labour government's "age of austerity" and offered light relief from the drab world of rationing. *Passport to Pimlico* appeared in a period that also saw the beginning of the end of the Labour government's utopian aspirations (see Williams, 1994, 99–100). Inhabitants of a London borough find a charter granting them freedom from wartime rationing and restrictions. But, rather than consciously search for new desires and personal freedom, they move toward conservative isolationism. At the climax, they return to the fold, deciding to accept repression after refusing to explore the implications of their new freedom. As Barr notes, their return to England represents a regressive recreation of a wartime unity now irrelevant to the different conditions of postwar society. This forms an ironic contrast to a period when colonies began seeking independence from the British Empire. As the 1984 *National Fictions* anthology shows, this World War Two–related ideological British national identity later became an important oppressive "structure of feeling" deliberately evoked by Thatcher during the Falkland/Malvinas escapade. Despite its temporary independent status, Burgundy is always a little England mobilizing its energies to maintain repressive identities and repulse any invaders.

The Bugundians' desire for freedom from control does not extend to sexual and consumer liberation. During the siege conference, Pemberton (Stanley Holloway) curtly rejects his daughter Shirley's (Barbara Murray) advice, while his wife (Betty Warren) warns her about her modest sunbathing attire, "You don't go to the door like that!" Mrs. Pemberton also deflates her husband's salacious Riviera holiday dreams by caustically remarking that the Serpentine makes him seasick! Although Shirley falls for the charming European duke of Burgundy (Paul Dupuis), three British prohibitive signifiers of noisy backyard cats, gargling male, and father calling his daughter indoors prevent even the most discreet kiss. Like daydreaming artist Gulliver (Robert Beatty) in *Another Shore* (1948), fishmonger Frank Huggins (John Slater) settles for second best (Jane Hylton's Molly) when Shirley eludes him. Appalled by the invasion of a nightmarish consumerist society, the Bugundians begin a forties version of a Moral Majority "Clean Up Burgundy" campaign. Their community returns to the fold, accepting repressive constraints in much the same manner as Graham Greene's fictional British characters resign themselves to the revealingly stagnant national mileau known as "Greeneland." The climax parallels Rose Sandigate's return to the bleak world of *It Always Rains on Sunday* represented by haddock on Sunday. In *Passport to Pimlico* the community accepts its former rationing books, and falling rain affects its outdoor celebration.

Barr believes that Mackendrick and Hamer's Ealing films are far superior to those of Clarke and Crichton. But *Whisky Galore* and *Kind Hearts and Coronets* are really different expressions of Ealing's common ideological problems and are not as radical as they appear. Barr (118) commends the "ancestral Celtic shrewdness and toughness" celebrated by

Whisky Galore that allows the islanders their climactic victory over the pompous rulebook-oriented Captain Waggett (Basil Radford). However, although *Whisky Galore* disavows T .E. B. Clarke's gentle wish-fulfillment comedic mechanisms, coercive features are still present. As Andrew Britton (1978, 48) noted, the Darwinian nature of the "survival of the fittest" concept of *Whisky Galore* is by no means as positive as Barr believes.

Although audiences may cheer the ingenuity of the islanders in achieving their whisky, it is at the loss of recognizing negative coercive methods used toward fulfillment of this goal. Like General Candy, Captain Waggett adheres to outmoded rules of conduct that cause his downfall. As the Home Guard lay barbed wire on the Isle of Todday, he comments, "We play for the sake of the game. The Germans play for the sake of winning." However, unlike *The Life and Death of Colonel Blimp*, the film never allows any sympathetic (but critical) space for his position nor makes any attempt to convert him by rational argument. Waggett eventually becomes a comedic straw dummy. He becomes symbolically castrated by the mocking laughter of his wife (Catherine Lacey) after the islander's victory. However, Waggett (a figure for whom the director had some sympathy) does at least attempt to operate according to the agreed laws of wartime with which the islanders comply until the arrival of the whisky ship. Although Waggett's behavior is stuffy and obstructive, this does not necessarily mean that islander methods are totally acceptable.

Unlike *I Know Where I'm Going*, where the eventual union between Celt and English occurs on a level of equality and surrender of inhibiting character traits, *Whisky Galore's* community operates on the level of allowing access only on total submission to its rules. This is the dark side of an Ealing tradition elsewhere represented as benevolent and eccentrically harmless. The subplot involving Sergeant Fred Odd (Bruce Seton) and Peggy Macroon (Joan Greenwood) illustrates this. Peggy insists that Fred propose to her in Gaelic. He fulfills this demand. However, the community demands his illegal compliance in retrieving the whisky. Although Barr (115) applauds the manner in which Fred undergoes an initiation into the "locals' codes of perception and value" by being "brought progressively to a fuller and more ruthless commitment," it parallels the authoritarian dominance Mrs. Campbell (Jean Cadell) exercises over her submissive son, George (Gordon Jackson). As Fred remarks to the passive-aggressive comments of Macroon (Wylie Watson) concerning his proposed wedding, "You can't have a wedding without a *reitlach* and you can't have a *reitlach* without whisky"—"This is blackmail!" He is absolutely correct in his judgment. Although Fred leaves an anachronistic community represented by Waggett for Macroon's cunning island enclave, his new world is dominated by oppressive rules governing his access toward personal desire. *Whisky Galore* may present an alternative world to T. E. B. Clarke's survival of the unfittest, but it is still a world resembling the unquestioned submission of *The Brothers*, whatever "natural justice" arguments Barr (112) makes for not allowing the whisky to go to the bottom of the sea. The eccentric depictions of the islanders should not blind us into not recognizing the ruthless methods they employ toward fulfilling their goals.

Kind Hearts and Coronets is a major achievement of Ealing Studios that emerged in spite of Michael Balcon's disapproval (see Barr, 119). As well as illustrating Hamer's diagnostic examination of the repressive mechanisms of British culture, *Kind Hearts* employs a playful, ironic interplay with audience sensibility. Like *The Bad Lord Byron*, it concludes by leaving audiences to judge the narrative for themselves and consider whether the film engages in ideological complicity or evaluative critique. Britton (1978, 48) regards the use of first-person narrative in *Kind Hearts* as leading to the seduction of the audience into a problematic and indulgent identificatory position with a dubious hero engaging in the same type of oppressive activities that originally caused his social subordination. But, although *Kind Hearts* does not explicitly present "a sense of the total reciprocal exploitativeness and oppressiveness of Darwinian capitalism" (Britton) as does *It Always Rains on Sunday*, it employs a particular version of an ideologically dominant class fantasy whereby the socially oppressed fictionally identify with their more affluent oppressors despite real life barriers separating them. This ideological mechanism dominates British culture in past and present as the popularity of *Upstairs Downstairs* and contemporary *Masterpiece Theatre* heritage productions show. Although the film invites us to identify with its *Room at the Top* predecessor, the joke is really on us and Louis (Dennis Price) as the climax shows. *Kind Hearts* undermines the cynical nature of Louis's social climbing visually and verbally.

> Think back over Hamer's films from *Dead of Night* on, and you find a gallery of individuals, across the range of classes, whose sexual and emotional drives are strongly repressed and as strongly burst out, only to be dampened down in an adjustment to the prevailing Ealing/British dispensation which, in a consolidation of the spirit of wartime, accepts restraint on sex drive and ambition and class resentment. (Barr, 120)

FIGURE 20. Alec Guinness embodies George Orwell's "stuffy Victorian family" of "England, Your England" in *Kind Hearts and Coronets*.

Kind Hearts dramatizes this in the story of Louis Mazzini. He is both a dynamic *actant* following the path of class mobility and a figure whose controlled narration represents cold emotional national sterility necessary for success. Like the two protagonists in Hamer's *Spider and the Fly* (1948), he is an emotionally crippled product of his society. Although Hamer invests his hero with a deceptively attractively dynamic aura (similar to the political masks of Margaret Thatcher and Tony Blair), he teases his audience to discover dark features in a supposedly pleasing persona. Like Richard III, Louis invites viewers into his confident strategy toward social mobility. But he is still "a villain" like his Shakespearean predecessor. As Barr (126–27) comments, *Kind Hearts* is capable of an Oedipal reading, depicting Louis as a child wishing not only to achieve the father's position but also to acquire the mother represented by glacial aristocratic Edith (Valerie Hobson), whose repressive behavior drives her husband to drink. Although Sibella (Joan Greenwood) represents the seductive alternative to Edith, Louis's commitment to upward mobility results in self-induced repression and murder. Devoid of any alternative political and sexual channels for his energy, Louis devotes his energies toward achieving his desired birthright. Hamer's seductive use of narration deliberately implicates the audience into his hero's deadly fantasy, which Barr equates with cinema's affinity to the dream process. *Kind Hearts* may invite its audience to see Louis in Barr's sense as "an agent for quite radical class resentments" (128). But it also seeks to entrap them into unconscious compliance with ideologically repressed mechanisms governing its particular structure of desire. Although Louis eventually succeeds in his goal, he willingly and violently uses socially repressive devices in his murderous campaign. Like Joe Lampton, he achieves his room at the top at great emotional cost. *Kind Hearts* is a superior product of a studio usually ideologically complicit with oppressive social forces. But Hamer's treatment lays bare the negatively manipulative behavioral patterns Louis uses in his rise to power. Barr (129) notes that "Louis *has* hardened himself to carry out his resolution: he doesn't marry for love himself but goes after rank, money, and land. He has defeated the enemy by their own weapons and their own ruthlessness. And once he becomes Duke, he grows even more into his mask, becomes impregnable, supercool—except sometimes when he looks back, in his memoir."

Hamer leaves the ending open. After his release from prison, Louis remembers he has left his incriminating memoirs behind. He is now trapped in more ways than one. Awaiting him are two mother figures in carriages—the repressed Edith and her sensual counterpart Sibella. He will offend one by leaving with the other. Louis now has to murder one controlling mother figure after the end of the narrative. Ironically, Louis's actual birth in the film leads to the death of his own father (also played by Dennis Price). He is caught in a dark Oedipal revenge fantasy structured by socially repressive class, familial, and sexual behavioral patterns victimizing everyone. Louis may nonchalantly return to claim his memoirs, but he still faces a castrating Oedipal dilemma of which carriage he will enter if he returns. He will have to submit to a dominating mother figure in any case. The governor may read his manuscript and arrest him. Whatever options Louis has, negative structures of desire still imprison him physically and psychically.

Both *The Lavender Hill Mob* and *The Ladykillers* are ideological footnotes to the studio's poverty-of-desire philosophy. Both films treat the well-worn theme of the robbery that goes wrong. Scripted by T .E. B. Clarke and directed by Charles Crichton, *The Ladykillers* is little better than a middle-aged cosy dream subverting social values in the light-hearted manner of a *Boy's Own* schoolboy joke before returning to conformity in the manner of *Hue and Cry*. *The Lavender Hill Mob*'s opening scene features the dynamically attractive Audrey Hepburn in a brief role before consigning her into oblivion—a classic example of Balcon's fear of sexuality! Scripted by William Rose and directed by Mackendrick, *The Ladykillers* represents the last great Ealing comedy whose ideological message has been aptly analyzed by Barr as an allegorical postwar fantasy. The gang represents the Labour government, whose alternative directions are soon quashed by the stifling nature of British conservative Victorian values represented by Mrs. Wilberforce (Katie Johnson). Mrs. Wilberforce is named after a politician remembered for abolishing slavery. But his role as one of the most antidemocratic representatives of his era is usually forgotten (except by figures such as Herman Melville and E. P. Thompson). As Barr (171) notes, the gang's "success is undermined by two factors, interacting: their own internecine quarrels, and the startling, paralysing charisma of the 'natural' governing class, which effortlessly takes over from them again in time to exploit their gains." It is an image applicable both to the frustrating circumstances of Thatcher's 1979 electoral success, which resulted from the ideological losses of the Callahan Labour government, and Blair's 1997 New Labour victory, which opportunistically profited from the gains of Thatcherism before extending them into directions unthought of by their originator. The "outsider" status of Rose and

MacKendrick (both born in America) contributes to the film's artistic richness and ideological message. While *The Lavender Hill Mob* grudgingly allows for the brief presence of an attractive female before expelling her from Mr. Balcon's Academy for Young Gentlemen, *The Ladykillers* is distinguished by the absence of such a figure. As noted by Barr (170), "Everything is redolent of age and tradition, specifically of English tradition, and of Ealing's celebration of that tradition."

Opening scenes reinforce this verdict. As if recognizing the threat, a baby cries and rocks its carriage when Mrs. Wilberforce looks at it. When Mrs. Wilberforce leaves the police station after reporting an imaginary crime to the superintendent (future *Dixon of Dock Green* Jack Warner), a hearse passes her in the street. Repeating the climax of *Passport to Pimlico*, rain falls as a gusty wind knocks over a street artist's portrait of Churchill as wartime leader, an action signifying Ealing's recognition of the death of its motivating wartime consensus. Mrs. Wilberforce returns to a home situated in the dead end of a street still standing after structural damage during the Blitz as an indestructible signifier of repressive Victorian values. The film superbly allegorizes British sterility in the early fifties and beyond.

However, the ideology structuring Ealing Studios is not confined to Balcon's academy. It operates in other contemporary films. Although *Esther Waters, The Courtneys of Curzon Street* (1947), *Spring in Park Lane* (1948), and *Maytime in Mayfair* (1949) appear arbitrary by comparison, they illustrate similar patterns of ideologically motivated hegemonic recuperation of individual desires operating in other films.

Like *The Loves of Joanna Godden, Esther Waters* is a revealing contemporary cinematic literary adaptation. It resembles *Fanny by Gaslight* in depicting the rise, fall, and rise again of its heroine. Its structure is relevant to the postwar era as *Fanny* was to wartime. Esther (Kathleen Ryan) enters employment in a country manor, becomes seduced and abandoned by handsome groom William (Dirk Bogarde), suffers various personal disasters before finding and marrying William (thus legitimizing their son), and then returns to her former life of servitude with understanding mistress Mrs. Barfield. Unlike *Fanny*, where hero and heroine eventually reunite and leave a repressive British world behind them, *Esther Waters* accepts that world at face value and sees no alternative to it. Filmed in a British cinematic naturalist style, *Esther Waters* artistically and thematically espouses the deterministic aspects of that tradition and never seeks avenues beyond it. Despite their various personal misfortunes, mistress and faithful servant reunite at the climax to express joy at Esther's son embarking on a career of faithful naval servitude. Unlike Phyllis Calvert's Fanny, who has an independent existence of her own, Kathleen Ryan's Esther is a woman who never questions a social system resulting in her oppression. She finally decides to relinquish any form of liberating desire and live entirely through a son who will soon become a mainstay of a coercive British Empire. The concluding scene is ironic. When Mrs. Barfield tells Esther, "You must be very proud of him," the camera cuts and tracks into the latter's ecstatic face, "I am very proud of him, very proud indeed."

Apart from that of Sarah Street (124–34), the Anna Neagle-Herbert Wilcox films have received little critical attention. However, they represent Durgnat's concept of a mirror for England as much as any other films of this period. Three Neagle films exhibit hegemonic illustrations of a changing postwar mood. After 1947, Neagle replaced Margaret Lockwood as top box-office British female star. Her contemporary star significance in this era is thus revealing. *The Courtneys of Curzon Street, Spring in Park Lane*, and *Maytime in Mayfair* represent the beginning of a process in British cinema when the mood changes from People's War communal aspirations toward individualistic, consumer-orientated fantasies dependent upon the restoration of thirties class values.

Although Anna Neagle is generally associated with aristocratic roles as in *Victoria the Great* (1937), she was also capable of playing different class roles. During her career she played various women transformed into heroines by extraordinary circumstances in past and present, whether the setting be the Restoration (*Nell Gwynn* [1934], the pre-Regency era *Peg of Old Drury* [1935], or the contemporary circus (*The Three Maxims* [1936]). But, as Street (134) notes, despite "the pleasures offered to female audiences of seeing such women on screen as major protagonists, the potential feminist appeal of her films was qualified by their association with specific historical circumstances, by Wilcox's over-riding concern for nationalist rhetoric and by Neagle's image as the middle-class 'lady' who was hard-working and courageous but never radical." Neagle's popularity waned during the fifties, but in her heyday her star persona embodied reassuring aspects of solid middle-class traditional values enduring during periods of social change.

The Courtneys of Curzon Street represents the Neagle-Wilcox equivalent to Balcon's concept of "our mild revolution." It is a film of accommodation recognizing residual forces present within British culture but incorporating them into the mainstream to ensure continuance of dominant ideological tendencies. The film opens in the Courtney residence on New Year's Eve, 1899. Classes mix during a servant's ball. Lady Courtney follows the tradition of dancing with her butler, a tradition permissible as long as it does not destroy the hierarchical system structuring class values. But the New Year sees Edward Courtney (Michael Wilding) proposing to Irish maid Kate (Anna Neagle), an act causing temporary rupture of the social order. Although they marry, rigid class codes personified by bitchy ex-lover Valerie (Coral Browne), an initially hostile Lady Courtney, and a boorish guardsman drive them apart. However, Edward and Kate reunite in a period of national crisis during World War I where she performs on a concert stage to an egalitarian group of soldiers. This scene ideologically expresses the Neagle-Wilcox concept of entertainment uniting all classes as long as traditional barriers remain. Mobility is permissible as long as the system remains intact. In Kate's place, mobility accommodates working-class figures as long as they adhere to dominant class values. Once found suitable, they may replace weaker members of the ruling class in a socially Darwinist manner that allows the system to gain new blood and continue. Valerie offends Edward by her sexual promiscuity. A snobbish Victorian lady disdainful of Kate later reappears briefly as a flapper in the twenties. The films of Neagle and Wilcox often demonize the socially unstable twenties in a manner similar to conservative Reagan-Thatcher condemnations of the sixties. Kate and Edward's daughter-in-law is a self-absorbed twenties product who dies in childbirth. As Kate comments, "She wasn't strong enough, Edward. She wouldn't fight." Their son dies on the northwest frontier as if in punishment for his earlier snobbish attitudes to Kate's music hall performance before a mixed class audience after the announcement of the Armistice. As Landy (1991, 313–14) notes, the film operates according to concepts akin to the transatlantically popular *Upstairs, Downstairs* television series.

> Through the portrayal of Cathy, the film reveals that family stability is built on the efforts of the working class to save the family. . . . The film bows to social change in its acknowledgement of the possibility of marrying out of one's class, but it also reveals, in spite of its optimism, that entry into the upper class mileau entails a commitment to traditional social values.

Spring in Park Lane represents the Neagle-Wilcox equivalent of *My Man Godfrey* (1936) with Michael Wilding playing the William Powell role. However, serious concerns dominate this silly fantasy of an impoverished aristocrat impersonating a butler who eventually wins the hand of the upper-middle-class secretary and niece (Neagle) of a rich uncle (Tom Walls). Street (133) pertinently sees both this film and *Maytime in Mayfair* as embodying "contextual social factors of postwar austerity and the attraction of bright fantasies set in the wealthiest parts of London all without a hint of class conflict." It is a vision opposed to Ealing. But *Spring in Park Lane* embraces the seductive aspects of popular consumerist desires, demonized in figures such as Garland in *Passport to Pimlico* who oppose Ealing communal standards of austerity, and reworks them in particular hegemonic ways. As *The Courtneys of Curzon Street* demonstrates, the aristocracy may be better dressed and speak impeccably but its better elements (excepting retrograde figures embodied by Coral Browne, Peter Graves, and Nicholas Phipps) are really "like us after all." Audiences thus may take pleasure in gaining visual gratification from a world of their betters in which they will never participate. However, unlike *The Courtneys of Curzon Street*, *Spring in Park Lane* sees the gradual elimination of working-class figures into minor roles embodied by stereotypical Irish housekeeper and silly maid (Lana Morris), who seemed to have shamelessly emerged from a thirties film. *Spring in Park Lane* is less important for its trivial plot and more for its cultural associations. Its popularity expressed public disenchantment with the continuance of World War II communal austerity and a developing fascination with a world dominated by fantasy images of benevolent class structures, glamour, and sexually appealing costumes.

Maytime in Mayfair is the weakest of the postwar London films, but it fully embodies the fantasy consumerism of this era. It is the one film of the Neagle-Wilding series where working-class characters are conspicuous by their very absence. Although Anna Neagle portrays independent middle-class businesswoman Eileen in a film dominated by self-reflexive playfulness—"She runs the business and does a bit of designing on the side. She reminds me of Anna Neagle"—she eventually becomes embodied on a pedestal in a male fantasy strongly resembling a British version of Laura Mulvey's arguments in "Visual Pleasure and Narrative Cinema." Like Doris Day in her sixties comedies, Eileen skillfully outmanoeuvres her male rivals. But the highlight of *Maytime in Mayfair* is Wilding's dream fantasy of Eileen as a fashion model being undressed and then costumed in the latest New Look fashion. As in Hollywood films of the depression, *Maytime in Mayfair* disavows troubling historical issues to present fantasy consumerist spectacles unavailable to the majority of audiences still suffering from wartime rationing restrictions. Desire becomes commodified within traditional male-female relationships.

As Street (133) notes, "For all their frothy ebullience, the 'London series' nevertheless reflected fear of change and anxiety about the postwar world during the awkward transition period when the optimism of the 1940s evaporated into a cautious conservatism in the 1950s." They also highlight a growing sterility that will infect British cinema up to the mid-fifties when dominant modes of consensus again become key factors—but not without some elements of residual resistance.

CHAPTER EIGHT

Conclusion

The first part of the 1950s reveals a depressing world of British cinema where dominant ideological tendencies hinder any radical expression of emergent forces. Indeed, the whole history of British cinema generally involves suppression or dissipation of any alternative oppositional tendencies reaching any form of coherent radical opposition. This explains the general dismissal of British cinema by figures such as Francois Truffaut and journals such as *Movie*. Before 1956, the picture is certainly grim. After that year, the Suez crisis, the appearance of *Look Back in Anger* and its effect on British cinema, Hammer horror, and "kitchen sink" cinema results in a different scenario—but one not entirely satisfactory in definitively challenging the status quo.

Barr notes that the first part of the decade appears to be characterized by conformist males, bloodless heroines (awaiting the emergence of Christopher Lee's Count Dracula), rural eccentricity, and victorious little old ladies in a world where the wartime community spirit has long vanished. However, as several critics such as Britton and Calder show, wartime spirit was compromised even in its heyday. Films such as *The Gentle Sex* (1943) accepted the presence of women in the services as long as they were subject to the condescending voice-over narration and male gaze represented by Leslie Howard. In a promising but neglected article, Andrew Britton (1989, 38) highlighted problems of certain wartime documentary representations exemplifying "some extremely depressing things about British culture in general, and the relationship to it of British social democracy in particular." He critiqued conservative ideological elements in the work of Humphrey Jennings which also characterized postwar culture, namely, "the drastic ideological limitations of Labourism, and in particular of its historical failure to disengage itself from, or provide a coherent and intelligible alternative to, the assumptions and discourses of the dominant class culture" (44). This feature also appears in certain films of the immediate postwar era. *The Blue Lamp* (1950), *Holiday Camp* (1947), *Madeleine* (1950), *Pool of London* (1951), *Dance Hall* (1950), *The Cruel Sea* (1953), *The Dam Busters*, and *The Ship That Died of Shame* (both 1955) are all problematic films. But they also contain revealing representations of frustrated desires struggling against dominant conformist constraints.

Although Barr defines *The Blue Lamp* (1950) as an ideological example of a tired "daydream" involving an unrealistic community ideal, its vision is not just confined to Ealing Studios. *The Blue Lamp* became the basis for a long-running television series featuring Jack Warner in *Dixon of Dock Green*, a character who dies in the original film. Like Count Dracula, he rose from the dead in a different way to become a cosy enunciator of British moralistic working-class values. *The Blue Lamp* contrasts an idyllic national community comprised of police and criminals sharing a common code of values with a dangerous emerging youth culture characterized by Riley (Dirk Bogarde), Spud (Patric Doonan), and Diana (Peggy Lewis). They represent a "new breed who lack the order and self-discipline of the professional thief" and are "all the more dangerous because of their immaturity," as well as being a nightmare alternative version of the youngsters in *Hue and Cry*. While redeemable "good-time girl" Diana is the product of "a childhood broken and demoralized by war, Riley and Spud have avoided arrest by "natural cunning and propensity for violence." Like Gwen Rawlings, Diana's world is dominated by the flashy glamour of Hollywood movie magazines making her masochistically vulnerable to Riley's sadistic charms. She has also run away from a dysfunctional family like her predecessor in *Good Time Girl*. As in *Cosh Boy* (1952), which contains no explicit reference to wartime disruption, youth subculture represents the dark underside of a wartime experience that may (Diana) or may not (Riley, Spud) be recuperated by a postwar conformist society following appropriate forms of parental discipline.

George Dixon represents the moralistic head of a community opposed to this threatening underworld. He has lost his son, Bert, during

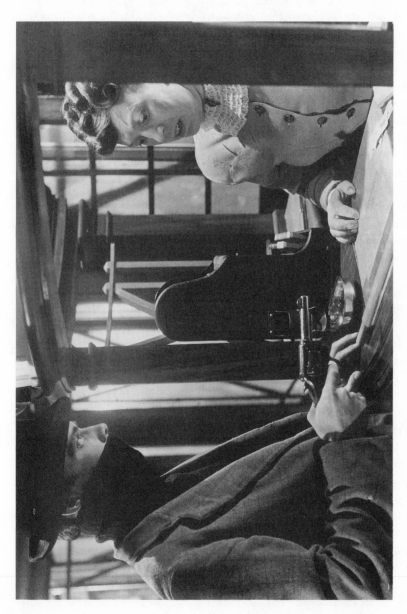

FIGURE 21. Riley (Dirk Bogarde), as postwar British demonic son, threatens Ealing values in *The Blue Lamp*.

some wartime naval expedition. Although Dixon dies in the course of the film, his place is soon filled by surrogate son Andy Mitchell (Jimmy Hanley), who has, presumably, seen wartime service. He leads a consensual community comprised of police and responsible underworld forces against demonic unrecuperable "son" Riley in the climax of the film. Andy takes the place of his surrogate father, George Dixon, in the concluding shot repeating the opening scene of the film.

Although Barr's analysis of Ealing's cosy *Blue Lamp* world is accurate, it is also important to note that its values were shared by other studios. Muriel Box's female policewomen film *Street Corner* (1952) and the Gainsborough production *Holiday Camp* (1947) accept this conservative consensus. *Street Corner* presents its policewomen as staunch upholders of community values whose attitudes toward law and order differ little from those held by their male counterparts. It is less interesting than *The Blue Lamp* but still continues the earlier film's dominant ideology of a community world depending on the necessary repression of energies that cannot be openly acknowledged in postwar society. Although made by a studio generally regarded as Ealing's stylistic and ideological opposite, *Holiday Camp* and *The Blue Lamp* also contain common themes. They both feature working-class communities as well as Jack Warner and Jimmy Hanley in leading roles. The two films also reveal the impoverished nature of working-class representation in an era characterized by the ideological and economic bankruptcy of a Labour government that never challenged the dominant conservative attitudes stifling British society.

Kenneth Annakin's *Holiday Camp* is lightweight at best, but it provides revealing images of contemporary cultural attitudes. It features Jack Warner as working-class patriarch Joe Huggett, a role the actor preferred to his familiar Dixon of Dock Green persona. Based on a popular radio series of the time, Joe Huggett represented a transitional role for Warner when he moved away from villainous roles as in *Hue and Cry* (1947), *Against the Wind,* and *My Brother's Keeper* (1948) toward the authority police figures of *It Always Rains on Sunday* (1947), *The Ladykillers,* and *The Quatermass Experiment* (both 1955). *Holiday Camp* also contains additional dialogue by Ted Willis, who would later play an instrumental role in the creation of George Dixon.

Joe Huggett takes his family to a Butlins-style holiday camp two years after the cessation of hostilities. His family comprises his wife (Kathleen Harrison); wimpish son Harry (Peter Hammond), and daughter Joan (Hazel Court), whose husband died in the war. Joan is now bringing up their baby as a single mother. The Huggetts hope she will find a suitable mate at the holiday camp, a role sailor Jimmy Hanley fulfills. *Holiday Camp* contains a gallery of diversely intersecting characters. Joe Huggett proves his patriarchal prowess by beating a gang of card sharp spivs at their own game and refusing the sexual advances of a good-time girl. He regains the money his spineless son lost in a card game. Although Joe proves his prowess, the victory represents the continuing dominance of oppressive patriarchal power in the community. In *Easy Money* (1948), Warner gives another son (Jack Watling) an undeserved and humiliating tongue lashing, embarrassing him in front of his friend. George Dixon later becomes a kinder and gentler working-class version of Joe Huggett.

Another Ealing theme also occurs in *Holiday Camp*. Joe and his wife nostalgically muse about their honeymoon near a waterworks. They think about returning but resign themselves to never visiting the site. "We'll go there one day." The scene foreshadows Barr's poverty of desire theme structuring Ealing representations where haddock on Sunday in *It Always Rains on Sunday* and the flowers of *The Blue Lamp* express Orwell's definition of the English lack of "aesthetic feeling." *Holiday Camp*'s waterworks complement Barr's definition of *The Blue Lamp*'s flowers, which both "act as a 'sanctification' of a lifestyle that has no aesthetic or imaginative dimensions, of its very qualities of prose, duty, restraint, acceptance" (94).

Other characters in *Holiday Camp* perform significant narrative functions anticipating ideas in *The Blue Lamp* and fifties cinema. Like Diana, Angela (Yvonne Owen) is saved from *Kind Hearts and Coronets'* "fate worse than death" when serial killer Binky Hardwicke (Dennis Price) turns his attention elsewhere. Angela is a former WAF. Her role now illustrates dangers facing the independent woman in postwar society. Unlike Riley, Hardwicke is a more mature (but nonetheless dangerous) character in the postwar community. Like killer Neville Heath, he cashes in on his glamourous cultural capital wartime role as Squadron Leader Hardwicke for a week of license in the holiday camp before police arrest him as the mannequin murderer. Hardwicke's final victim is the pathetic, romantically inclined Elsie (Esma Cannon), whom he murders outside the camp in a scene characterized by *film noir* lighting. Spinster Miss Harmon (Flora Robson) lost her sweetheart during World War I and eventually comes to terms with her situation. She compensates by adopting a young couple, aspiring pianist Michael (Emrys Jones) and pregnant girlfriend

Valerie (Jeanette Tregarth). But conservative matriarchal attitudes condition her generosity when she forces Michael to choose between his creative aspirations and domesticity. Although Miss Harmon wishes Michael to think about the future in a responsible manner, creativity and family life are incompatible elements in her ideological vision. The film cannot envisage any alternative way to combine these two opposing desires. This narrative blockage foreshadows Mrs. Pemberton's put-down of her husband's escapist musings as "seasick on the Serpentine" in *Passport to Pimlico* as well as the drab repressive conclusion facing aspiring South Sea artist Gulliver (Robert Beatty) in *Another Shore*, whose creativity falls victim to a conventional marriage.

Holiday Camp contains elements that become dominant features of early 1950s cinema involving the triumph of repressive forces and demonization (and eventual elimination) of socially undesirable elements (especially sexually active and violent behavior). As Landy (1991, 317) comments:

> The film is addressed primarily to the question of postwar readjustment as it evokes memories of loss due to the war, images of dislocation, the disaffections of youth, the existence of violence and criminality, and poses the recuperated family and the community as the arbitrators of existing social conflicts. The holiday camp is a metaphor for social unity based on mutual recognition of sexual, economic, and domestic problems.

The problem of the independent woman also occurs in David Lean's *Madeleine* (1950). Although set in the past and based on fact, the film also speaks to the concerns of 1950 in terms of expressing fear of female sexuality. *Madeleine* is a little-known work by a director who soon came to epitomize the hollow formalism of narrative epic cinema. But, as Anderegg (69) notes, it is "one of the most intriguing of Lean's lesser-known films." Based upon a celebrated Scottish murder trial of 1857 that led to a "not proven" verdict by a jury, *Madeleine* cinematically presents its audience with a deliberately ambiguous study of female sexuality frustrating "an audience's normal desire and expectation to be let in on the secret that history has failed to reveal."

Madeleine is a significant film that deserves wider viewing. It occupies a transitional stage in David Lean's career when he moved between different studios at a time when turbulent historical circumstances affected British politics and film studios. It is tempting to examine *Madeleine* exclusively in terms of Lean's directorial vision. However, other factors structure the film, the most important of which is the role of Ann Todd as its star. Like Anna Neagle, Ann Todd's significance as a national star commodity during the mid- to late forties has received little critical examination. Lean married Todd soon after directing her in *The Passionate Friends* (1949) and divorced her following the completion of *The Sound Barrier* (1952). After gaining stardom in *The Seventh Veil*, Todd appeared in a number of major films of the decade, such as *Daybreak*, Hitchcock's *The Paradine Case*, and the Anglo-American *film noir* co-production *So Evil My Love* (both 1948), as well as her films with Lean. After the fifties, her screen career rapidly declined. However, despite Todd's glacial, unemotional acting style, the roles she played in the forties were variations on the role of an independent woman trapped within patriarchal structures of desire. Although *The Seventh Veil, Daybreak, The Passionate Friends*, and *So Evil My Love* never satisfactorily deal with the role of the independent woman, *Madeleine* offers more positive directions for Todd's performance. Lean later regretted that he ever made the film. It appears that the main initiative came from his former wife, whom he regarded with hostility during the remainder of his life. As he later stated, "Ann was terribly stuck on this idea. . . . But it wasn't really my cup of tea" (Silverman, 87). Significantly, her final film with Lean cast her in Anderegg's words as "the woman who cannot fathom what it is that men do until, in the end, she is brought around to accept, to acquiesce, not because she truly understands but because, finally, that is all a woman *can* do" (78).

Madeleine completely rejects such imagery. The screenplay by Stanley Haynes and Nicholas Phipps celebrates the power of independent female desire. Although closely following the ambiguous facts of the original case, the film contains several scenes contrasting the rigid, repressive family structures dominating Madeleine's life with her desire for escape. When she first visits her future home, she is attracted to the dark basement area where she later meets her lover, Emile (Ivan Desny), at night. Forestalling her authoritarian father's plans to force her to marry dull suitor Minnoch (Norman Woolard), Madeleine earnestly waits for bedtime when she can extinguish the lights and dance in expectation of Emile's visits. Lean's frequent use of the moving camera highlights the ecstasy of a desire that can only express itself in the dark confines of a *film noir* basement area. The film visually emphasizes the repressive nature of her patriarchal entrapment. Mr. Smith sadistically forces his daughter to comply masochistically both with his authoritarian demands and with the removal of his boots. Madeleine soon discovers that Emile is little better than a social climber who merely seeks to use her to regain his lost class position. Emile drops the role of adoring lover and blackmails Madeleine into a dead-end situation in which she will merely pass from one form of patriarchal oppression to another.

Throughout the film Madeleine is constantly under an oppressive male gaze, whether by father, lover, courtroom artist, or jury. The film often engages in contrasts between the patriarchal gaze and Madeleine's own independent point of view. Many scenes balance and contrast male and female looks. The film also contradicts Laura Mulvey's arguments in "Visual Pleasure and Narrative Cinema." Many scenes express the heroine's vivacity, independence, and free spirit, which significantly counterpoint the glacial conformist mask she wears in everyday society. During a secret meeting on a Scottish island, Madeleine stimulates her reluctant lover into dancing a Highland reel at the same time as a working-class village community engages in unrepressed joyful dancing below. Prior to the sexual climax of both dances, Madeleine seizes Emile's cane and throws it away. The sexual connotations of this act need no emphasis. Two other scenes in the film reveal Emile dropping his cane during moments of vulnerability and signifying Madeleine's powerful desires foreshadowing his eventual destruction. When Madeleine is on her way to trial in a carriage, Lean cuts to a close-up of a truncheon in the hands of a policeman, symbolizing the Law of the Father bringing her to trial. But, ironically, it is obviously ineffectual to deal with the mob outside. Whatever the audience's eventual attitude to Madeleine, the scene where Emile brusquely rejects her love and offer to run away with him empathizes with her betrayal, particularly after he remarks, "If we marry, we marry into your life, not mine." He clearly deserves whatever will happen to him.

Madeleine moves toward its eventual conclusion. The predominantly male jury cannot decide on her guilt or innocence. They deliver the Scottish judicial "not proven" verdict. Madeleine rides away in her carriage as the opening male narration by James McKechnie again attempts to interrogate the female under the camera eye. However, the film ends with a close-up of Madeleine, who will never answer male questions of her presumed guilt. Todd exhibits an ambiguous expression, denoting that only Madeleine knows the actual secret. As Anderegg (69) notes, "*Madeleine* is thus both an ambiguous film and a film about ambi-

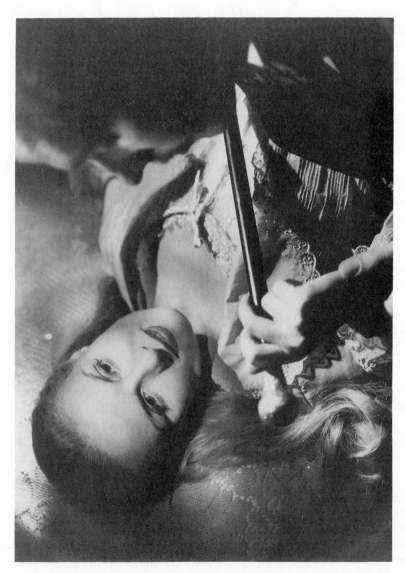

FIGURE 22. Madeleine (Ann Todd) holds her lover's "cane" in *Madeleine*.

guity." It is a remarkable cinematic achievement for a decade characterized by disappointing female representations.

Barr (202) sees Basil Dearden's *Pool of London* as an example of "a
densely packed compendium of Ealing life." It certainly contains key
examples of the studio's use of documentary realism (as in the opening
scenes), excellent use of locations, and tight narrative style. But *Pool of
London* is more than a typical Ealing film. It contains several un-Ealing
features of homosexuality and miscegenation characteristic of Dearden's
later films *Sapphire* and *Victim,* as well a lighting style defining it as yet
another example of British *film noir.* Like *The Lavender Hill Mob* and *The
Ladykillers, Pool of London's* main narrative deals with a failed robbery. But
the treatment is much harsher and more realistic in terms of anticipating
features that would erupt in British society during the 1950s—the Not-
ting Hill racial riots and the Wolfenden Report on homosexuality.
Although George Orwell's sense of "decency" returns at the climax when
seaman Dan (Bonar Colleano) gives himself up to the police and saves his
mate, Johnny (Earl Cameron), from implication in his criminal activities,
the conclusion leaves several elements in abeyance. *Pool of London* does
not contain an ideologically satisfying harmonious resolution like previous Ealing narratives.

Dan's freewheeling activities in breaching British customs and
rationing regulations lead him into dangerous involvement in a criminal
underworld that parallels his supposedly harmless everyday activities.
Although Dan's friendship with Johnny appears legitimate on the surface,
it contains elements of subversive homoerotic bonding that the film visually expresses. Several scenes show Dan and Johnny looking at either other
either barechested or wearing singlets in subconscious gay imagery. When
Vernon (played with unmistakable gay overtones by Max Adrian) propo-
sitions Dan into his criminal scheme, his gaze displays an overtly sexual
version of the one shared between Dan and Johnny. As Vernon's accomplice suggestively mentions, "Someone wants to meet a nice obliging
sailor."

As played according to Bonar Colleano's swaggering Yank performance style, Dan appears self-assured, but he later confesses to Sally
(Renée Asherson) that his masculinity is merely a sham. "I get a girl each
time I give her a pair of nylons. No I don't kid myself." Dan's regular girlfriend is the repulsive Maisie (Moira Lister) who merely tolerates his presence because of black market gifts. She later influences him into using
Johnny as an unwitting accomplice to smuggle stolen items on board

ship. As she persuades Dan, "With a colored boy, its even better. Think what you could do for him." Earlier, when she learns about Customs' confiscation of desired nylons Dan attempted to give her, she racially harangues Johnny's friend Pat (Susan Shaw): "You must be hard off to go with him to get them!" *Pool of London's film noir* style visually emphasizes some very un-Ealing themes of race and sexuality.

Dearden presents the relationship between Pat and Johnny sympathetically and realistically. But despite the attraction both feel to each other, the studio cannot approve of their union. Johnny thus falls further into a *film noir* world denoted by shadowy lighting and canted angles before he is thrown out of a drinking den to the dismissive remark, "They're all the same." This parallels the theater attendant's earlier comment to Johnny when he throws him outside. "Some of our customers who pay for their seats are a bit particular." The term particular appears before in the conversation between Dan and Vernon over how particular Dan is about the way he makes money. It signifies connections between the dark worlds of racism and homosexuality, which further disrupt wartime consensus ideology and rigid heterosexual boundaries.

Although Sally eventually acts as Dan's super-ego in a voice-over sequence influencing his decision to avoid Johnny's implication in the crime, any happy-ever-after relationship between them appears problematic. As a cast-off girlfriend of sailor Harry (Leslie Phillips), mousy Sally gives in to a drunken impulse to sleep with Dan in a second-best situation, a decision she regrets the morning after. Although Ealing gives its seal of approval to their eventual union, it is doomed to failure. Dan will face deportation after his sentence even if he attempts to continue a relationship based on no solid foundations. *Pool of London* is less remarkable as a typical Ealing Studios film but more as a work expressing tensions that will emerge later in British society. *Film noir* and Ealing studio documentary realism oppose each other, the former style emerging as more powerful. Finally, as Higson (1997, 170) has noted, *Pool of London* also contains a strong melodramatic discourse making it a "fascinatingly complex hybrid film" that "presents an image of an equally fluid, insecure and hybrid nation."

Charles Crichton's *Dance Hall* (1950) is unusual for its foregrounding of female characters. But it expresses the studio's decline into fifties stagnation as well as continuing to emphasize its subordination of female sensibility. After the credits, the film begins with a tracking shot in Ealing's documentary realistic mode, showing the main characters at work in a factory. The situation, however, is far removed from *Millions like Us*. Although the women now "naturally" work in the previous male domain of the factory, their desires are strongly regulated toward patriarchal goals of marriage and family.

Dance Hall operates on two settings: the factory and the dance hall. The latter area provides a fantasy trap for romantic escapism eventually leading to marriage. At the climax, all remaining unmarried female characters (with the exception of Jane Hylton's Mary) enter the New Year with engagement rings, even an obviously too-young Georgie (Petula Clark) engaged to equally too-young boyfriend Peter (Douglas Barr). When Eve (Natasha Parry) marries Phil (Donald Houston), she immediately gives up her job to become a housewife. The film initially aligns itself with Eve's frustration over her housewife existence and her desire to join former workmates at the local Palais. But it never engages in a critique of the suffocating nature of fifties married life. This is absolutely impossible within Ealing Studio ideology. Carole's (Diana Dors) relationship to silent, dominating Neanderthal Mike (James Carney) acts as a comic counterpoint to Eve and Phil's marriage. Despite the unsuitable pairing of both partners, the male rules the roost. Eventually, Eve and Phil reunite in a very un-Ealing sexually suggestive shot. They embrace outside beside a broken pipe gushing water! Obviously Balcon allowed this Freudian metaphor, assuming it suggests pregnancy healing a problematic marriage.

As in *Good Time Girl*, Bonar Colleano returns in his stereotyped role of demonic, affluent Yank corrupting British society with natty suits, Benny Goodman records, and abrasive sexuality. One scene associates Colleano's Alec with *film noir* lighting. He attempts in vain to entice Eve up to his apartment in a dark, rain-swept street to listen to his jazz records. However, Alec does get to sleep with Eve. She attempts to confess this to Phil, but he does not want to know as he is obviously aware of his responsibility for driving a nice English girl into the arms of an oversexed Yank. Alec eventually gets his come-uppance in a fight with the equally unsavory Phil near the end of a film concluding with virtually all female characters moving toward the secure domains of patriarchal marriage.

Medhurst (35) notes that the 1950s British war film genre has received very little critical exploration. They are often characterized as "at best worthily dull, at worst the absolute epitome of the cinema of tight-lipped middle-class repression soon to be rightfully swept away by the social realist impetus of the late 1950s." But several examples of the genre reveal instances of questioning a repressive masculinity endemic to both actual wartime conditions and cinematic representations. Textual disruptions are undeniably scarce. But, as Medhurst (38) notes, if we read them as "films about repression, rather than as hopelessly repressed films, then their interest becomes clear." They are important cultural documents testifying to the questionable nature of rigidly dominant arbitrary constraints on desire. British war films of the 1950s no longer display the egalitarian principles of the People's War ideology. Neither do they exhibit the sterile, unemotional dimensions of the now-unwatchable *In Which We Serve* (1942). In diverse, yet intersecting, ways, *The Cruel Sea, The Dam Busters,* and *The Ship That Died of Shame* reveal male submission to norms of duty and the emotional costs of such submission.

Based upon Nicholas Monsarrat's 1951 best-selling novel, Ealing's *Cruel Sea* reproduces most of the studio's familiar tenets: serious subject matter, documentary realism, understated performances, and sober style. However, although following the original novel, the film also intermittently "begins to question imposed forms of masculinity" (Medhurst, 37). The opening narration by Ericson (Jack Hawkins) speaks about men as the heroes, ships as the heroines, and the only enemy being "the cruel sea that war has made more and more cruel." Like most wartime representations, it upholds standards of duty, masculinity, and the survival of the fittest. But the film's definition of fit and unfit involve surprising directions. Ericson and subordinate officer Lockhart (Donald Sinden) survive to the end of the war. They work together in a film that clearly recognizes the nonsexual, yet obvious, love between them enabling both to endure the hardships of wartime service. *The Cruel Sea* cannot consciously acknowledge the logical directions this relationship could take. Instead, it disavows the homoerotic implications onto the scapegoat figure of "unmanly" Sublieutenant Baker (John Warner), whom the cruel sea later claims when a torpedo hits the *Compass Rose*. Baker's figure parallels that of the effeminate R.A.F officer played by Arthur Howard (an actor associated with nonmasculine roles in British film and television) in a brief scene in *The Dam Busters*, in which Howard is clearly not "man enough" to go on the heroic raid. As Medhurst significantly notes, the scenes between men and women are "deeply unsatisfactory" since the film's main implicit emotional weight lies upon an unacknowledged, repressed "love between men that is a major force propelling that project" (Medhurst, 37).

Ironically, Ericson and Lockhart represent the "fit" who will survive, while the "unfit" represent various figures whom the text expels because they contradict the film's ideological definition of fifties masculinity. Unfitness involves factors of class as well as sexuality. The *Compass Rose* officers are all gentlemen with the exception of First Lieutenant Bennett (Stanley Baker), formerly a used-car salesman in civilian life. Medhurst (38) notes that his "proletarian aggression (and significantly, vigorous heterosexuality) simply cannot be contained by the text, and so he is ousted by a highly unconvincing narrative device." However, this device is not as "unconvincing" as it may appear. Gentlemen officers represented by Lockhart and Morell (Denholm Elliot) use their knowledge of Bennett's hidden insecurities to remove him from the *Compass Rose* by playing on psychosomatic fears of a duodenal ulcer. Lockhart and Morell remove not only a disturbing remnant of the People's War class mobility from the text but also a figure whose repressed insecurities echo their own. Bennett must ideologically depart from the film because of disturbing connotations of class and sexuality. He is an upwardly mobile upstart "wicked gentleman" paralleling Margaret Lockwood's "wicked lady" of 1945. Furthermore, the original novel stated that Bennett's nationality was Australian. The film changes this to a lower-class form of British nationality. Also, the novel's Bennett is more sexually aggressive by having frequent, unashamed liaisons with prostitutes during his shore leave than his cinematic counterpart. Ealing obviously altered the character for several reasons involving censorship, the desire not to offend an Australian market where they also made films on locations, and affirming a conservative fifties hegemony of putting uppity People's War working class characters firmly in their place, as seen with Richard Attenborough's character in *The Ship That Died of Shame.*

Other characters leave the text for various reasons. During the sinking of the *Compass Rose*, Morell, Petty Officer Tallow (Bruce Seton), and engineer Watts (Liam Redmond) die at sea. Morell dies because he cannot control his wife's sexual desires (presented in typical Ealing terms as disgustingly aberrant) at home. The working-class figures of Tallow and Watts are ideologically "kinder and gentler" versions of the upstart, upwardly mobile proletarian figure represented by Bennett. But, like the novel, *The Cruel Sea* cannot approve their desires for a peaceful domestic life in wartime. Emotionally weak Sublieutenant Ferraby (John Stratton) survives. But he collapses into unmanly nervous breakdown by revealing dependence on his wife (June Thorburn) rather than the masculine world of the *Compass Rose.*

The film explores Ericson's character and his negotiation of male insecurity. As several critics note, Ericson emotionally breaks down after he decides to attack a U-boat supposedly using the bodies of sailors awaiting rescue as a decoy. The depth charges kill the sailors, while the U-boat disappears. A sailor condemns Ericson as a "bloody murderer," an incident absent from the novel. Despite comfort offered by other rescued seamen, Ericson drowns his grief in drink and later reveals his tear-stained, emotionally distressed face to Lockhart, who sympathizes with his senior officer and puts him to bed. When Ericson gains another ship, he engages in an obsessive pursuit of U-boats to sublimate his feelings of guilt. The latter part of *The Cruel Sea* depicts Ericson as a British version of Ethan Edwards in *The Searchers*. He violently denies the friendship and solidarity offered by Lockhart until he has finally sunk two U-boats. But the film takes no pleasure in this victory. It clearly regards it as a barren and unsatisfactory substitute for dangerous emotional feelings Ericson chooses to repress. This motif does not feature in the actual book, which depicts Ericson sinking a U-boat in retaliation for his decision to drop the depth charges. It also occurs prior to the sinking of the *Compass Rose*. The screenplay highlights Ericson's guilty feelings by moving incidents from the original book to another point in the film. It suggestively underscores the hysterical male obsessiveness motivating its leading character.

The Cruel Sea approves a heterosexual relationship between Lockhart and Second Officer Julie Hallam (Virginia McKenna). But like most contemporary depictions, it appears bloodless and unemotional. The original novel also depicts Lockhart learning of Julie's death at sea. It removes the pregnant female from the text to concentrate on the somber nature of the male relationship between Ericson and Lockhart. In their last scene together in the film, Julie realizes that Lockhart is particularly fond of Ericson and regards the male wartime relationship as "the only possible relationship war allows you." Julie comments significantly that "women don't have that kind of relationship." The scene ends when Lockhart confesses that he emotionally broke down like Ericson during a National Gallery concert after thinking of the "*Compass Rose* and some of the men who died." The next sequence reveals the dangerous nature of Lockhart's assignment, as well as Ericson's developing aggressive nature. Although Ericson eventually tracks down his version of Melville's *Moby Dick*, he ends the film a victim of desires he has suppressed and sublimated in the line of duty.

As Medhurst (38) notes, *The Dam Busters* is a film that both faithfully reconstructs the events leading to a successful raid and scrupulously seeks "to efface sexuality from itself." Like other wartime representations, it stresses duty and sacrifice. But the cost of this is ominous. Unlike *The Cruel Sea*, which did at least make some token acknowledgement of females, *The Dam Busters* totally eliminates them from the text with the exception of Mrs. Barnes Wallis. The film contrasts a sacrificially repressed male group with the regressive domestic confines of the Wallis household. Although, for Medford, *The Dam Busters* admittedly establishes "an eccentric intellectual as the true centre of a text which would otherwise be a flag-waving exercise in nationalistic machismo," it also depicts private emotional life as regressive and infantile. When we first see Wallis (Michael Redgrave), he appears as a child among children conducting his experiments in the back garden and mothered by his adoring wife (Ursula Jeans). When Wallis despairs about official interest in his bouncing bomb, he speaks in language reminiscent of Ealing's "poverty-of-desire" philosophy. While not desiring haddock on Sundays, he thinks of his garden. "If it doesn't snow, I'll put in some broad beans." However, mother knows best. Mrs. Wallis suggests he contact one last official who approves the project. Afterward, she vanishes entirely from the text so Wallis can devote himself to his scientific duty.

As Medhurst (38) recognizes, the other textual hero, Guy Gibson (Richard Todd), "is even further removed from emotional and familial structures than the scientist." This is true of the human but not of the animal world. Gibson's real affinity is with his dog, Nigger. When we first see Gibson returning from a raid, he is overjoyed to see his four-legged friend and speaks excitedly about his forthcoming holiday hunting "rabbits in Cornwall." However, like *The Cruel Sea*, *The Dam Busters* explicitly affirms a call of duty involving denial of personal relationships. If Mrs. Wallis disappears from the text, so does Nigger. While Gibson briefs his men about the forthcoming raid, Nigger is excluded from the private session. The dog searches in vain for his master and is eventually killed by a hit-and-run driver. Ironically, the raid on the dam does have an emotional resonance since Gibson decides to use his dog's name as a code word in his briefing. More than coincidentally, this decision immediately leads to the unhappy animal's demise. After receiving the news of his dog's death in a traditionally British, unemotional manner, Gibson arranges for it to be buried outside his office. He orders the burial to synchronize with the exact time the planes conduct their deadly raid. Despite the unfortunate name, Nigger represents Gibson's only emotional attachment.

Earlier in the film, Gibson and a friend decide to have a night in London. They attend a chorus girl show. But Gibson's attentions are less

FIGURE 23. The housemaster figure of Guy Gibson (Richard Todd) instructs his boys in *The Dam Busters*.

attracted toward the leading lady than to her function in providing him with a clue about low-level flying. Unlike her dangerous female spy counterpart in *Next of Kin* (1942), the woman occupies a functional role in the text. She does not signify a sexual desire deadly to a uniformed male but occupies a subordinate role involving the solution of a scientific problem. In *Next of Kin*, women are dangerous to the war effort whether they be Nazi spies or blackmailed refugees. *The Dam Busters* firmly relegates them to marginally subordinate and unthreatening figures.

While other flyers write their last letters before the final raid, Gibson gazes lovingly at Nigger's lead, looks at the paw scratches on his door, and then abruptly drops the lead into his wastepaper basket. Similarly, as Medhurst (37) recognizes, the one moment the squadron members release themselves from the restraint of duty involves Gibson's assent to a "moment of physicality . . . when one squadron joyously debags another." Almost immediately afterward, orders for the mission interrupt the homosexual overtones of the horseplay. Gibson again becomes a housemaster ordering his boys to bed rather than allowing them to fall into buggery! These instances appear minor in relation to the entire text, but they articulate deep emotional overtones involving repressing any form of desire that may hinder the wartime effort.

Basil Dearden's *The Ship That Died of Shame* is an appropriate film to conclude this study. Based on a short story by the author of *The Cruel Sea*, this Ealing production signifies both the studio's grudging recognition of the end of the wartime consensus and the presence of disruptive factors that will finally dominate postwar society. Scripted by John Whiting, Michael Relph, and Dearden, the film begins with an opening narration similar to that of *The Cruel Sea*, in which main character Bill Randall (George Baker) looks back on the past: "The beginning, like everything about me, went back to the war." However, while *The Cruel Sea* ends on a tone of tired achievement that does not threaten the dominant order, *The Ship That Died of Shame* concludes with a recognition that the old order with its masculine codes is no longer relevant to a changed society.

Many parallels exist between *The Cruel Sea* and *The Ship That Died of Shame*, suggesting that Basil Dearden directed the latter film as a darker, subversive version of the former. The film also counters the ideological vision of *In Which We Serve* acutely diagnosed by Calder (1991, 230). "Class is sublimated in 'service' to a common cause, which is all very Myth-of-the-Blitz-like. The ship transcends the men, the Royal Navy transcends the individual ship—England transcends all." But *The Ship That Died of Shame* operates as an ironic counterpoint to wartime myths concerning community and sexuality.

Like Julie Hallam in *The Cruel Sea*, Randall recognizes that ships "are not like women at all." However, the ship *1087* acts in the film in a manner akin to Sally's influence on Dan in *Pool of London* by expressing the voice of conscience on the aberrant male. The opening narration identifies the ship in female terms, anticipating its future role both as moral conscience of the wartime community and as containing repressed feminine desires within the male psyche. As Bill states, "I know about ships. They are made of wood and metal and nothing else. They don't have souls, they don't have wills of their own; they don't talk back." But the film gradually undermines Bill's judgment. It becomes evident that *1087* reacts against abusive male machinations in the postwar period.

Bill's voice-over narration continues, "The beginning like everything about me, went back to the war." During the opening sequence, Dearden introduces audiences to the three major protagonists: Bill, First Lieutenant George Hoskins (Richard Attenborough), and Coxswain Birdie (Bill Owen). Despite differences in class and rank, Bill and Birdie take pleasure in describing *1087* in female terms, "She's a honey, old *1087*." This bonding is not shared by George, whose role parallels Bennett's in *The Cruel Sea*. Like Bennett he has obtained officer rank despite his lower middle-class origins. George's attempted manipulative calculations of *1087*'s combat track record link him to Garland of *Passport to Pimlico*. *The Ship That Died of Shame* thus shares Ealing's anti-acquisitive wartime philosophy. But this time the negative elements are not easily denied or expelled from the community. Unlike Garland, Jackie Farnish, and Bennett, George represents a major problem for the film. When Bill meets him later at a naval reunion, he finds that George has succeeded in building an affluent existence for himself in postwar society. George immediately seduces Bill into joining him to renovate *1087* for black market activities. The boat will bring "a few things to lighten up the postwar darkness" in the Labour government's age of austerity. When Bill later discovers the decommissioned derelict *1087*, his face lights up like a man rediscovering his lost love. George gives Bill the deed of ownership, clearly cognizant of his romantic attraction. "She's always been yours anyway. Our aim in life is to make people happy." With Birdie pleading to join them, the key wartime crew members of *1087* reunite in a "moral crusade" revolt against the restrictive conditions of Labour austerity. George earlier stated to Bill, "I can't scrape a living these days with all these ruddy restrictions." They engage in black market trips across the Channel until they find themselves plunging further in a dark world of criminality unconceivable during their wartime days.

As in *The Cruel Sea*, males have a stronger relationship with a boat symbolizing the female principle than they do with actual women. However, *The Ship That Died of Shame* shows the dark perversity of this relationship more explicitly than the earlier film. Like Ericson and Lockhart, Bill has a heterosexual relationship, but it immediately falls victim to the film's repressed desires. As played by Virginia McKenna, Helen Randall parallels Julie Hallam in *The Cruel Sea*. However, she immediately dies some minutes after her introduction in a manner suggesting repressed masculine impatience and violence against the female principle. She is first seen in the film through Bill's binoculars as if she, like the Germans, represents the enemy. Although scenes between her and Bill appear irrelevant, vapid, and overtly sentimental, they are crucial toward understanding the emotional structure of *The Ship That Died of Shame*. Bill's real desires are really centered on *1087* and his unacknowledged homoerotic bonding with Birdie. The *1087* represents a symbolic displacement of a love that cannot be openly expressed. During their scenes together, Helen mentions the unsatisfactory nature of their marital relationship, which obviously had nothing to do with the "awful hotel" of their honeymoon. Bill has now rented a country cottage for a week from an officer "messed up in Dunkirk." Despite the supposedly idyllic honeymoon surroundings they now occupy, Helen expresses doubt over Bill's marital commitment: "Why did you marry me, Bill?" He replies in terms similar to Gibson's view of women in *The Dam Busters*, suggesting she merely provides a convenient function for him. Helen offers Bill "a purpose in things . . . even in this damn war." Recognizing who her real rival is, she warns Bill, "Don't ever do anything silly with that ship of yours." Soon afterward she dies in a bombing raid. Bill's voice-over comments, "After that there was only the ship. Through her I could hit back. There seemed nothing in life—only the ship."

The Ship That Died of Shame reveals male insecurity existing beneath the ideal of total devotion to duty. Like *The Cruel Sea*, it significantly deals with postwar masculine crisis. After the war, Bill cannot settle down to the new society. He drifts from job to job and ends up in a nostalgic Coastal Forces Club Reunion where singer Bubbles Bentley performs Vera Lynn's wartime song, "We'll Meet Again." Bill will soon "meet again" the real object of his desire, a factor a club guest (David Langton) immediately discerns—"I used to envy you that boat. Funny how each of them are different."

Eventually Bill, George, and Birdie end up in a criminal association with retired officer Major Fordyce (Roland Culver), who also resents the egalitarian nature of postwar society. Fordyce comments that "things had changed when I got out of the army. I got tired of working for the plebs after fighting for them." When George comments, "Perhaps you were fighting for the wrong side," Fordyce replies, "That's not so far from the truth." He expresses a very rare Ealing disillusionment with Balcon's concept of "our mild revolution," an idea that is certainly Dearden's. The *1087* eventually revolts against her new criminal role. Her engines frequently stall when she engages in activities more typical of her former enemy than her original wartime mission. When *1087* transports forged British currency, George comments, "Jerry printed them during the war. They would have destroyed the economy." The final humiliation occurs when the group unknowingly offers refuge to child molester and murderer Raines, who hides in an abandoned wartime pillbox. As played by John Chandos (an actor known for his portrayal of criminals and Nazis in British cinema), it is not surprising when *1087* reacts to his presence on board by stalling her engine.

The Ship That Died of Shame reveals the bankruptcy and decline of wartime ideals. George takes to the bottle and unconvincingly denies his knowledge of Raines's identity. He eventually blackmails Bill into helping Fordyce escape by threatening to involve Birdie. When George expresses something Bill denies—"He's attached to you"—the following shot of Bill's face reveals shocked acceptance as he now explicitly recognizes the nature of his real desire.

The film ends with *1087*'s death from shame after taking revenge on George by slicing his body in her propellers like a vengeful, betrayed female castrating her seducer. Despite Birdie's attempts at coaxing her, "Come on, old darling. You can do it. Birdie loves you," both he and Bill realize the ship's final refusal expresses a conscience they denied up to now. "She can't do it. Not after what we've made her do. She's got her pride like all of us. She can't do it. You can't blame her at all." The survivors watch the ship finally go down. Dearden closes the film with a lap dissolve from Bill's head to a nostalgic final image of *1087* in her wartime glory. It is a final tribute to a past era now recognized as redundant and irrelevant to the new decade. George and Fordyce die on the final voyage.

Bill and Birdie remain, but they are casualties from a world of masculine desire gone astray. Repression now becomes impossible for the changing world of a new decade that ends with a ship "representing the nation and the embodiment of approved moral codes and virtues" (O'Sullivan, 179) finally sinking.

A year after *The Ship That Died of Shame*, British society faced turbulent social and historical conditions that received different forms of artistic and cinematic representations. It is beyond the scope of this work to examine the Suez crisis, the appearance of *Look Back in Anger*, Hammer horror's return of the repressed, and late fifties social realism. Both British culture and cinematic representations exist in a dominantly conservative structure of desire. These patterns continue to prevent oppositionally residual elements indirectly expressing social and cultural tensions within cinematic texts becoming radically emergent elements leading to new structures of feeling. Despite challenges to the status quo by female costume melodrama, Powell and Pressburger, and other voices, the picture remains the same. Powerful hegemonic controls allow controlled residual expressions of alternative forces mediated within traditional modes of representation. They prevent them from taking revolutionary emergent forms that may threaten the status quo. British cinema has never been revolutionary, either artistically or politically. It has never really matched the artistic achievements of other national cinemas. However, films such as *They Came to a City, I Know Where I'm Going, Perfect Strangers, A Matter of Life and Death, The Small Back Room, The Bad Lord Byron*, and *Madeleine* present images of alternatives that may influence future emergent structures of desire. These are just a handful of films, *pre-emergent* in nature (see Williams, 1977, 126), but they are important for their very presence. They provide different signals competing against monolithically dominant ideological operations maintaining the status quo in politics and desire. Any form of liberation from dominant hegemonic patterns involves positive unifying modes of desire and politics. As Gramsci recognized, popular culture, especially in certain forms of national cinematic representations, is important. Artists and audiences may learn from the past and construct better representations for the future. Positive structures of desire, feelings, and meanings may result in strategic victories within hegemonic contexts.

BIBLIOGRAPHY

Ackland, Rodney, and Elspeth Grant. *The Celluloid Mistress.* London: Allan Wingate, 1954.

Aldgate, Anthony, and Jeffrey Richards. *Britain Can Take It: The British Cinema in the Second World War.* London: Basil Blackwell, 1986.

Anderegg, Michael A. *David Lean.* New York: Twayne, 1984.

Appignanesi, Lisa, ed. *Desire.* London: Institute of Contemporary Arts, 1984.

Aspinall, Sue, and Robert Murphy, eds. *BFI Dossier No 18: Gainsborough Melodrama.* London: BFI Publishing, 1983.

Balchin, Nigel. *The Small Back Room.* Boston: Houghton Mifflin Company, 1945.

Barr, Charles. *Ealing Studios.* Second Edition. London: Studio Vista, 1993.

Bocock, Robert. *Hegemony.* London: Tavistock Publications, 1986.

Boggs, Carl. *The Two Revolutions: Gramsci and the Dilemmas of Western Marxism.* Boston: South End Press, 1984.

Brittain, Vera. *Lady into Woman: A History of Women from Victoria to Elizabeth II.* New York: Macmillan, 1953.

Britton, Andrew. *"Ealing Studios." Framework* 7/8 (1978): 47–48.

———. "Their Finest Hour: Humphrey Jennings and the British Imperial Myth of World War II." *cineACTION* 18 (1989): 37–44.

Brown, Geoff. *Launder and Gilliat.* London: BFI Publishing, 1977.

Brown, Geoff, and Tony Aldgate. *The Common Touch: The Films of John Baxter.* London: The National Film Theatre, 1989.

Buttigieg, Joseph, ed. "A Special Issue: The Legacy of Antonio Gramsci." *Boundary 2*, 14.3 (1986).

Byars, Jackie. *All That Hollywood Allows: Re-Reading Gender in 1950s Cinema.* Chapel Hill: University of North Carolina Press, 1991.

Calder, Angus. *The People's War.* London: Jonathan Cape, 1969.

———. *The Myth of the Blitz.* London: Jonathan Cape, 1991.

Christie, Ian. *Arrows of Desire.* London: Faber & Faber, 1994.

———. *Powell and Pressburger: The Life and Death of Colonel Blimp.* London: Faber & Faber, 1994.

Cocks, Joan. *The Oppositional Imagination.* London: Routledge, 1989.

Connolly, Cyril. "Comment." *Horizon* 12.69 (1945): 149–53.

Cook, Pam. "Good Time Girl." *Monthly Film Bulletin.* 52.620 (1985): 289–90.

———. "Melodrama and the Women's Picture." *Gainsborough Melodrama.* BFI Dossier 18, 1983, 14–27.

———. "Gone to Earth." *Monthly Film Bulletin* 53.634 (1986): 353–54.

———. *Fashioning the Nation: Costume and Identity in British Cinema.* London: BFI Publishing, 1996.

Corner, John, and Sylvia Harvey, eds. *Enterprise and Heritage: Crosscurrents of National Culture.* London: Routledge, 1991.

Coultass, Clive. *Images for Battle: British Films and the Second World War.* London: Associated University Presses, 1989.

Danischewsky, Monja. *White Russian—Red Face.* London: Victor Gollancz Ltd., 1966.

Dixon, Wheeler Winston, ed. *Re-Viewing British Cinema, 1900–1992: Essays and Interviews.* New York: State University of New York Press, 1994.

———. "*The Halfway House.*" *Liberal Directions: Basil Dearden and Postwar British Film Culture.* Ed. Alan Burton, Tim O'Sullivan, and Paul Wells. Wiltshire, England: Flicks Books, 1997, 108–15.

Dombroski, Robert S. *Antonio Gramsci.* Boston: G. K. Hall, 1989.

Doyle, Arthur Conan. *The Complete Sherlock Holmes.* Vol. I. New York: Doubleday, 1930.

Draper, Ellen. "'Untrammeled by Historical Fact': *That Hamilton Woman.*" *Wide Angle* 14.1 (1992): 56–63.

Durgnat, Raymond. *A Mirror for England: British Movies from Austerity to Affluence.* New York: Praeger, 1971.

————. "Gainsborough: The Times of Its Time." *Monthly Film Bulletin* 52.619 (1985): 259–61.

Eisenstein, Sergei. *Film Form.* Ed. and Trans. by Jay Leyda. New York: Harvest Brace Jovanovich, 1949.

Ellis, John. "Art, Culture and Quality: Terms for a Cinema in the Forties and Seventies." *Screen* 19.3 (1978): 9–49.

————. "Watching Death at Work: An Analysis of *A Matter of Life and Death.*" *Powell, Pressburger and Others.* Ed., Ian Christie. London: BFI Publishing, 1978, 79–104.

Everson, William K. "British Film Noir." *Films in Review* 38.5 (1987): 285–89.

Fluegel, Jane, ed. *Michael Balcon: The Pursuit of British Cinema.* New York: The Museum of Modern Art, 1984.

Gibbon, Monk. *The Red Shoes Ballet and The Tales of Hoffmann.* New York: Garland Publishing, 1977.

Gledhill, Christine, and Gillian Swanson. *Nationalising Femininity: Culture, Sexuality, and British Cinema in the Second World War.* Manchester: Manchester University Press, 1996.

Gramsci, Antonio. *Selections From the Prison Notebooks.* Ed. and Trans. by Quintin Hoare and Geoffrey Nowell-Smith. New York: International Publishers, 1971.

————. *Selections from Cultural Writings.* Eds. David Forgacs and Geoffrey Nowell-Smith. Trans. William Boelhower. London: Lawrence and Wishart, 1985.

Greene, Graham. *Collected Essays.* London: Bodley Head, 1969.

Greenwood, Walter. *Love on the Dole.* London: Jonathan Cape, 1933.

Harper, Sue. "The Boundaries of Hegemony: Scriptwriting at Gainsborough Studios during World War II." *The Politics of Theory.* Ed. Francis Barker et al. Colchester: University of Essex, 1983, 167–78.

———. "Historical Pleasures: Gainsborough Melodrama." *Home Is Where the Heart Is: Studies in Melodrama and the Woman's Film.* Ed. Christine Gledhill. London: BFI Publishing, 1987, 167–96.

———. "The Representation of Women in British Feature Films, 1945–1950, *Historical Journal of Film, Radio and Television.* 12.3 (1992): 217–30.

———. *Picturing the Past: The Rise and Fall of the British Costume Film.* London: BFI Publishing, 1994.

Higson, Andrew. *Waving the Flag: Constructing a National Identity in Britain.* Oxford: Clarendon Press, 1995.

———. "*Pool of London*." *Liberal Directions: Basil Dearden and Postwar, British Film Culture.* Ed. Alan Burton, Tim O'Sullivan, and Paul Wells. Wiltshire, England: Flicks Books, 1997, 162–71.

Holub, Renate. *Antonio Gramsci: Beyond Marxism and Postmodernism.* London: Routledge, 1992.

Hurd, Geoff, ed. *National Fictions: World War Two in British Film and Television.* London: BFI Publishing, 1984.

Hutchings, Peter. *Hammer and Beyond: The British Horror Film.* New York: Manchester University Press, 1993.

Kardish, Laurence. "Michael Balcon and the Idea of a National Cinema." *Michael Balcon: The Pursuit of British Cinema.* Ed. Jane Fluegel. New York: The Museum of Modern Art, 1984, 43–74.

Kaye-Smith, Sheila. *Joanna Godden.* New York: E. P. Dutton & Company, 1922.

Kemp, Philip. "The Long Shadow: Robert Hamer After Ealing." *Film Comment* 31.3 (May–June, 1995): 71–78.

King-Hall, Magdalen. *Life and Death of the Wicked Lady Skelton.* New York: Rinehart & Company, Inc., 1946.

Kuntzel, Thierry. "The Film Work 2." *Camera Obscura* 5 (1980): 7–69.

Laclau, Ernesto, and Chantal Mouffe. *Hegemony and Socialist Strategy: Toward a Radical Democratic Politics.* London: Verso, 1985.

Landy, Marcia. *British Film Genres: Cinema and Society, 1930–1960.* Princeton, NJ: Princeton University Press, 1991.

———. *Film, Politics and Gramsci.* Minneapolis: University of Minnesota Press, 1994.

Lant, Antonia. *Blackout: Reinventing Women for Wartime British Cinema.* Princeton, NJ: Princeton University Press, 1991.

Lawrence, Margery. *The Madonna of Seven Moons.* Indianapolis: The Bobbs-Merrill Company, 1933.

Light, Alison. *Forever England: Femininity, Literature and Conservatism between the Wars.* London: Routledge, 1991.

MacDonald, Kevin. *Emeric Pressburger: The Life and Death of a Screenwriter.* London: Faber and Faber, 1994.

Medhurst, Andy. "1950s War Films." *National Fictions.* Ed. Geoff Hurd. London: British Film Institute, 1984.

Minns, Raynes. *Bombers and Mash: The Domestic Front, 1939–1945.* London: Virago, 1980.

Monsarrat, Nicholas. *The Cruel Sea.* New York: Alfred A. Knopf, 1951.

———. *The Ship That Died of Shame and Other Stories.* London: Pan, 1959.

Mulvey, Laura. "Visual Pleasure and Narrative Cinema." *Screen* 16.3 (1975): 6–18.

———. "Notes on Sirk and Melodrama." *Movie* 25 (1977/78): 53–56.

Murphy, Robert. "The British Film Industry: Audiences and Producers." *Britain and the Cinema in the Second World War.* New York: St. Martin's Press, 1988, 31–41.

———. *Realism and Tinsel: Cinema and Society in Britain: 1939– 1949.* London: Routledge, 1992.

———, ed. *The British Cinema Book.* London: BFI Publishing, 1997.

Orwell, George. *Collected Essays, Journalism and Letters* IV. London: Penguin, 1971.

O'Sullivan, Tim. "Not Quite Fit for Heroes: Cautionary Tales of Men at Work—*The Ship That Died of Shame* and *The League of Gentlemen." Liberal Directions* (1997): 172–93.

Perry, George. *Forever Ealing: A Celebration of a Great British Film Studio.* London: Pavilion Books, 1981.

Pirie, David. *A Heritage of Horror.* London: Gordon Fraser, 1973.

Powell, Michael. *A Life in Movies.* New York: Alfred A. Knopf, 1987.

————. *Million-Dollar Movie*. London: Heinemann, 1992.

Priestley, J. B. *Four Plays*. New York: Harper & Brothers, 1944.

Richards, Jeffrey. "The Brothers." *Monthly Film Bulletin* 52.620 (1985): 288–89.

————. "Wartime British Cinema Audiences and the Class System: The Case of '*Ships with Wings.*'" *Historical Journal of Film, Radio, and Television* 7.2 (1987): 129–41.

Richards, Jeffrey, and Anthony Aldgate. *British Cinema and Society 1930–1970.* Totowa, New Jersey: Barnes and Noble Books, 1983.

————. *The Age of the Dream Palace: Cinema and Society in Britain 1930–1939.* London: Routledge, 1984.

Richards, Jeffrey, and Dorothy Sheridan. *Mass Observation at the Movies.* London: Routledge and Kegan Paul, 1987.

Rowan, Caroline. "For the Duration Only: Motherhood and Nation in the First World War." *Formations of Nation and People.* London: Routledge and Kegan Paul, 1984, 152–70.

Sadleir, Michael. *Fanny by Gaslight.* New York: D. Appleton-Century Company, 1940.

Salwolke, Scott. *The Films of Michael Powell and the Archers.* Lanham, MD: The Scarecrow Press, 1997.

Schwarz, Bill. "The Language of Constitutionalism: Baldwinite Conservatism." *Formations of Nation and People.* London: Routledge and Kegan Paul, 1984, 1–18.

Sellar, Maurice. *Best of British: A Celebration of Rank Film Classics.* London: Sphere Books, 1987.

Shafer, Stephen C. *British Popular Films 1929–1939: The Cinema of Reassurance.* London: Routledge, 1997.

Short, K. R. M. "*That Hamilton Woman* (1941): Propaganda, Feminism and the Production Code." *Historical Journal of Film, Radio and Television* 11.1 (1991): 3–19.

Siedentop, Larry. "The New Right Is Wrong for Britain Today." *The Guardian* (UK) (December 20, 1993): 4.

Silverman, Stephen M. *David Lean.* New York: Harry N. Abrams, 1992.

Smith, Harold, L., ed. *War and Social Change: British Society in the Second World War.* England: Manchester University Press, 1986.

Smith, Lady Eleanor. *The Man in Grey.* New York: Doubleday, Doran and Company, Inc., 1942.

Stafford, Roy. "Study Notes for the Slide Set from *Black Narcissus.*" London: BFI Education, 1986.

Stead, Peter. "The People as Stars: Feature Films as National Expression." *Britain and the Cinema in the Second World War.* New York: St. Martin's Press, 1988, 62–83.

———. *Film and the Working Class: The Feature Film in British and American Society.* London: Routledge, 1989.

Street, Sarah. *British National Cinema.* London: Routledge, 1997.

Summerfield, Penny. *Women Workers in the Second World War.* London: 1984.

Sussex, Elizabeth. "Cavalcanti in England." *Sight and Sound* 44.4 (1975): 205–11.

Taylor, Phillip M., ed. *Britain and the Cinema in the Second World War.* Basingstoke, England: MacMillan, 1988.

Thompson, E. P. *The Making of the English Working Class.* London: Victor Gollancz Ltd., 1964.

Turvey, Gerry. "The Moment of *It Always Rains on Sunday.*" *Framework* 9 (1978/79): 13–21.

Walker, Michael. "*Black Narcissus.*" *Framework* 9 (1978/79): 9–13.

Whipple, Dorothy. *They Were Sisters.* New York: Macmillan, 1944.

Whitaker, Sheila. "*It Always Rains on Sunday*, Part (II)." *Framework* 9 (1978/79): 21–26.

Williams, Raymond. *Marxism and Literature.* New York: Oxford University Press, 1977.

———. *Politics and Letters: Interviews with New Left Review.* London: Verso, 1979.

———. *Problems in Materialism and Culture.* London: Verso, 1980.

———. *Resources of Hope: Culture, Democracy, Socialism.* London: Verso, 1989.

Williams, Tony. "Michael Powell." *Films and Filming* 326 (1981): 10–16.

———. "The Repressed Fantastic in *Passport to Pimlico.*" *Re-Viewing British Cinema, 1900–1992.* Ed. Wheeler Winston Dixon. New York: State University of New York Press, 1994, 95–106.

Wright, Patrick. "A Blue Plaque for the Labour Movement? Some Political Meanings of the National Past." *Formations of Nation and People.* London: Routledge and Kegan Paul, 1984.

Young, Cynthia. "Revision to Reproduction: Myth and Its Author in *The Red Shoes.*" *Reviewing British Cinema, 1900–1992.* Ed. Wheeler Winston Dixon. New York, 1994, 107–20.

Zavarzadeh, Mas'ud. *Seeing Films Politically.* New York: State University of New York Press, 1991.

Zavarzadeh, Mas'ud, and Donald Morton. *Theory, (Post)Modernity, Opposition.* Washington, D.C.: Maisonneuve Press, 1991.

INDEX